FLOOD
of
CONFLICT

The New Orleans Free School Story

by Robert M. Ferris

Published by the
Alternative Education Resource Organization | AERO

Flood of Conflict: The New Orleans Free School Story

Published by

Altenative Education Resource Organization
417 Roslyn Road
Roslyn Heights, NY 11577
educationrevolution.org

Design: Josh Cook
hetalkedofplacesineverheardof.com

Printed in the United States.
ISBN: 097452526X

Acknowledgements

I wish to express my deepest gratitude to my dear friend Kelly Frisch who was my initial typist and editor. Without her generous labor of typing and editing the first two-thirds of this book, this document would never have reached print. I also wish to thank my other dear friends who took the time to correct many mistakes and to make many suggested changes to the manuscript. Thank you, Lee Mullikin, Kiersta Kurtz-Burke, and Mary Garton. I would like to thank my closest friend, Jeanette St. Etienne, and my daughter, Iyana Connors, for their suggested structural changes. Also, I would like to thank Julianne Couch, my copy editor, for her many changes, corrections, and suggestions.

Contents

Unless we destroy ourselves utterly, the future belongs to those societies that, while not ignoring the reptilian and mammalian parts of our being, enable the characteristically human components of our nature to flourish: to those societies that encourage diversity rather than conformity: to those societies willing to invest resources in a variety of social, political, economic and cultural experiments, and prepared to sacrifice short-term advantage for long-term benefit; to those societies that treat new ideas as delicate, fragile and immensely valuable pathways to the future.

Carl Sagan, *The Dragons of Eden*

Introduction

David slew Goliath with a single stone! *The Little Engine That Could,* did! The New Orleans Free School's thirty-two year struggle with the bureaucracy of the Orleans Parish School Board ended in a draw—a double drowning! Go figure. On January 6, 1971, The New Orleans Free School opened its doors to twenty-nine students. Back then, when I met my wife-to-be, Sue, I told her that I was going to write a book about education and the Free School. Now, forty-one years later and almost seven years after Hurricane Katrina, here is that book—a tall tale but a true story.

This story is four stories in one. One is autobiographical. This saga would be somewhat shallow without an explanation of who I am and the circumstances of my life leading up to the Free School. In reality, the Free School became my life and we were inseparable. This book is a continuation of that tale, this life. The second story is about educational theory and practices. I cannot tell the tale without revealing the actual happenings and philosophies of the Free School. The third story is a history book, but it is not the history of a perfect school—the Free School was wrought with many mistakes, conflicts, internal strife, and mishaps. Rather, it is a history of struggle, of one small school daring to be different, engulfed in the flood waters of bureaucracy, drowning one person, then one practice, then another person, then another practice, then another, then another. It is in this third section of the book that I will often use fictitious names when telling the story. My purpose in writing this book is to denigrate no one but to tell the story in an accurate and truthful way as possible. Thus, when I change the name of someone, I will briefly identify the name as fictitious and not the person's real name. Finally, this book ends with the fourth story: an imperative to study our ever increasing numbers of charter schools, a plea to end high-stakes testing presently flooding our public school systems, a demand to fairly and equitably finance public education in the United States, a cry to achieve quality education for all, including our poor and minorities, a call to provide quality public education to our impoverished three- and four-year-olds, and a charge to once and for all put an end to centralized public educational schooling—not an end to public schooling, but an end to bureaucratic miseducation.

Before I begin this tale, let me briefly discuss The New Orleans Free School. Information about the Free School is dispersed throughout this book, particularly in the many primary documents. Reading all of this material will give you a good picture of what the Free School was all about. However, all of this information never succinctly or in one place answers the question, "Why over all these years did so many people support this one little school against such overwhelming odds?" The long answer to this question, of course, is this book. The abbreviated answer is the following. In its first twelve years, the Free School operated as an integrated hippie school with a deep commitment to the power and beauty of each individual. By "hippie," I mean in defiance of tradition and with a strong desire to change culture: we had a passion for learning, creating and being responsive to one another that was infectious. We had students engaged in projects, plays, sleepovers, science experiences, camping trips, and play, lots of play. Kids loved it; parents became friends and all of us became a family.

During the next twenty-two years we became an urbanized public school serving primarily the poor. However, we were able to show that students could learn and learn better and be happier in a more family-enriched and activity-based environment. This approach was not easy and certainly was not without its flaws. But we were able to demonstrate a concern for our students while enabling them to excel in a variety of ways. Most students seemed to love the school and do extremely well. If they came from another school, they almost always significantly improved academically and socially. Almost all of the parents were appreciative and supportive. Whenever new parents enrolled their children in the Free School, I always required that they meet with me first so that I could explain our program to them and begin them on a very personal and more family-like educational experience. In this initial session I would always ask them how they heard or what they heard about the Free School. Almost to a person they answered, "I heard that it was a good school." The New Orleans Free School truly proved to be the little school that could, and did.

I would also interview the prospective students. With the older students, ages 8 and above, I would ask them if they were Saints fans. If they said, "yes," the interview would continue and at the end of the interview I would again greet the parents always praising the students because they were Saints fans. Whenever students would say that they were not Saints fans, I would stop the interview and immediately go to the parents and tell them that I was sorry but we could not accept their children. The parents, of course, were puzzled, disappointed and ask, "Why?" I would shrug my shoulders and say, "Your children told me that they were not Saints fans. I can not let non Saints fans into the Free School." After the parents' perplexed look turned to smiles and laughter, the students and I returned to my office to continue our conversation. The point of this is that we desperately wanted to create an educational experience that enabled the school to be more like a family and less like an institution. We started this educational journey from the first day people walked through our doors.

1

My Years Before the Free School

I grew up in Shreveport, Louisiana, and went to kindergarten, grade school, high school and college in Catholic schools. My most memorable experience in kindergarten was when a classmate failed to show up for school one morning. I organized a group of about six students, including my cousins Woody and Robert, to go to Tommy R's house and bring him to school. He had not showed up for school that day and we wanted to be with our friend. I claimed to know where he lived, but managed to get us somewhat lost. My father found us about three blocks from school and I caught the whipping of my life from my aunt, Louise, who was Robert's mother. He caught the same whipping. I knew why I got the whipping, but I thought it was unfair because we were not skipping school—we were just looking for a friend to bring him to school. I still got the whipping. That was a telling start to a lifetime of trying to do the right thing and catching hell for it.

In spite of that experience, I had a number of "parents" who all treated me lovingly and provided me a great Catholic upbringing. I was raised and lived in the same house (initially above a neighborhood grocery store) with my father, Joe, his brother, Neckley, and three sisters, Rose, Amelia, and Louise. Early in my life Aunt Louise married Hollis (Hotch) and they had three sons, Hollis, Bob, and Pat. Right after Pat was born when I was five years old (around the time of the kindergarten incident) they moved into their own house. I never remember being hit or spanked by any of the adults in my family, except for this one incident.

The three brothers and I grew up almost like we were four brothers. Hollis was a year older than I was. Bob was my age and Pat was a couple of years younger. Almost every night of our lives, we ate at their house or they ate at our house. We four boys went to the same grade school and the same high school. While we were very close, my cousins would occasionally get mad at me and tease me saying that I was adopted. The only reply I ever received from any adult member of my family about their teasing was that the other boys were mad at me and just trying to get me upset. My father was elderly and very sick the entire time I knew him. While I always thought that it was odd that he never, and I mean never, talked about my mother, I never pursued the issue (at least as far as my memory serves me). It was not like I thought about this all the time; it was more like every now and then a thorn stuck in my side.

I was raised so lovingly particularly by my aunts and especially by Aunt Mimi (Amelia) that I never had a burning desire to find out who my mother was. This situation quickly changed toward the end of my senior year of college at Spring Hill College in Mobile, Alabama, when my girl-friend, Marilyn, died. We had recently separated, due to our quarreling over whether marriage would be in our future. I became distraught over her death and consulted with a priest friend and former high school English teacher, Father Michael Kammer, who still lived in Shreveport. He told me he thought that I had a deep fear of commitment that was somehow related to my birth and early childhood.

Now, looking back, I feel that he may have been told the circumstances of my birth by my parents, who were also very close to him. After our conversation, I felt compelled to demand that my parents tell me the truth about my birth. I told them that if they didn't, I would wreak havoc on our entire extended family with non-stop questions until I learned the truth. They huddled for a few minutes and then Uncle Neckley called me to his bedroom. As he slowly began to tell me the story of my birth, Aunt Mimi, Aunt Rose, and my father entered the room. Very quickly we were all in tears, but I learned the truth. Aunt Mimi got pregnant during World War II by a soldier traveling through Shreveport. She went to Buffalo, New York, where she stayed until my birth. Then, my Uncle Joe (the person I thought was my father), who had been away from Shreveport for a long time, brought me home as his son. I cannot judge whether my parents should have told me the circumstances of my birth earlier. I only knew that at the time of my friend's death, I had demons to release. For me, certainly at that moment in my life, truth was necessary.

My mother, Aunt Mimi, was a good Catholic girl who could not face the "shame" of having and raising a child out of wedlock. Thus, she and her brothers and sisters amazingly and lovingly conspired to tell a story about my birth, and that story was believed for many years. I think she only reached the third grade; however, she was a strong, intelligent woman who did well in social and economic life. She ran her own very successful children's and women's clothing store in Shreveport. I was caught off guard by the women's movement because the women in my family were such strong business people. Aunt Rose, the other aunt in our house, owned and ran her own grocery store. I never realized that the women in my family were an anomaly. Aunt Mimi was not just Aunt Mimi to me; she was Aunt Mimi to everyone. While everyone knew that I was special to her, very few knew that she was my mother. I proudly proclaimed as I led the chant at her funeral, "My Aunt Mimi, your Aunt Mimi, our Aunt Mimi."

I never revealed Aunt Mimi's secret to anyone except my wife and two children. I wanted my children to know that she was their grandmother. After this confrontation I distanced myself from my parents for almost two years. To this day I do not know if I did this to punish them or if it was more due to my life's philosophical and political changes prompted by the Vietnam War and the civil rights struggle. I am grateful that, after my two year absence from home, Aunt Mimi and I made peace. One day while working as a VISTA volunteer in Gary, Indiana, I had a craving for Lebanese food. I picked up the phone and called Aunt Mimi. She joyfully gave me the recipes and we were never distanced again. This was truly my ET moment. Many years after this rapprochement she chose to live in New Orleans to be close to me, Sue and to her grandchildren, Mika and Iyana. Aunt Mimi and I were able, many times, to express our love for one another. In fact, the last words we each spoke to one another, "I love you" were on the night she died. How many people are fortunate enough to have that experience with their mother? I may have had a strange birthing experience causing much anguish in our lives, but she was able to have the perfect ending. I can now lovingly remember that moment forever. In 2003 she passed thirty days before her one-hundredth birthday. I still refer to her as Aunt Mimi.

My family went ahead with her already-planned one-hundredth birthday party. Her century birthday, March 3, fell on Thoth Sunday that year, which falls two days before Mardi Gras. Aunt Mimi loved Mardi Gras. Thoth's colorful Mardi Gras parade comes down Magazine Street around noon, only two blocks from our house. Each year I plan a big event for the corner of Bordeaux and Magazine streets followed by a huge Mardi Gras party at our house, sometimes with a live band. The event at this corner usually involves me riding a unicycle dressed in a costume. One year I was the Shadow and three years ago, as I just turned sixty-five, I was Social Security Man. Yes, I rode down Magazine Street on my unicycle wearing nothing but a mask, Depends, and a bath robe for a cape. Anyway, for that 2003 Thoth Parade to honor Aunt Mimi I had a friend carry a 3 by 4 foot enlarged picture of her down Magazine Street to Bordeaux Street. I rode next to the picture on my unicycle dressed in one of Aunt Mimi's Mardi Gras costumes, wore a wig, and had a clean shaved face—the first time I had not had a beard in some thirty years. I looked so like Aunt Mimi that even my wife did not recognize me.

My father Joe, actually my uncle, was a very poor, uneducated, but incredibly kind man who had once been a hobo, riding the rails. This was another part of his life he never talked about. I remember just a few things about my father. He ran a linotype machine for *The Shreveport Times* long before the days of computer printing. He was a good man who often took me and my three cousins to movies on Saturdays or Sundays. To this day, I still love movies and think I enjoy them so much because of those days with my father. He was a heavy smoker and was dying of emphysema the entire time I knew him. One of my last memories of him when I was in my mid-twenties was as a shriveled up old man barely able to walk or talk, coming at me with as much anger as he could muster in his feeble state saying, "You're the worst Goddamn nigger lover in the south."

At that moment I had no retort. The chasm between my boyhood life and the activist I had become was too wide. I only knew it hurt so much because I hurt him so deeply, even though he and the rest of my family raised me Catholic, to believe in the goodness and sacredness of human beings. The day my father died, I had flown in from New Orleans and went directly to the hospital, rather than to our house. I immediately went to his room. As I entered, all the family members walked out. I walked over to him and said, "Hi Dad. It's me." He looked up at me and died. The nurse, who was a family acquaintance and in the room at the time, said, "I knew it, I knew it. He was waiting for you." I never made peace with my father. At his funeral, he was given a military burial because of his military service. When the soldiers folded the flag covering the coffin and approached me with the flag, I ever so subtly motioned for them to give Aunt Mimi the flag. Suffice it to say, I would love to have the flag today, but did not want it then. At that moment of my life I was ashamed of my country's actions. While I regret to this day not having a closer relationship with my father, I will never regret shedding my racist, war-fetish upbringing. Racism runs so deep that it can destroy a family, warp a nation, and relegate humans to non-human status. No, I do not regret challenging racism and an unjust war. The pain and punishment suffered by the victims of racism and war far surpasses the experiences and rejections I have endured throughout my life.

Enough about my family. Let me continue this tale by briefly discussing my education and the political environment in which I was raised. In grade school, the one thing I remember is learning an Irish jig from Sister Ann Patricia, a fourth-grade teacher. The jig seemed complicated to me, but once I learned it, I loved dancing it. Dancing was and is one of my passions. Folk dancing became an integral part of the Free School over the years and I can't help but think that it all started with that jig. The other thing I remember is when I was in the fifth grade a crowd was gathered outside of a classroom door and everyone was peering through the glass windows and talking in a hush about the large word written on the chalkboard. I managed to squeeze through the gathering and see for myself the word "FUCK" in big bold letters scrawled on the board. I didn't know what it meant but it sure caused a lasting memory. In addition to not using coarse language, I did not drink and did not even know that there were such things as drugs until college. I grew up sheltered and naive.

I remember high school being a more intellectual endeavor than grade school, but also being very boring some of the time. My main moments in high school were on the debate team and the drama club. I think my debate team took second place in the state my senior year, though I may be embellishing. In the drama club, I played Cassius in *Julius Caesar*, and in an elocution contest I recited Cyrano DeBergerac's famous nose speech.

Later, the Free School also put on a number of plays throughout our history such as *Ten Little Indians*, *A Midsummer Night's Dream*, and *Trojan Women*. We also had a yearly elocution night in which students performed poetry from memory at the hotel Chateau LeMoyne, our business partner. Students would get all dressed up and recite their pieces of literature or self-written poetry to an audience of parents, friends, school mates, and faculty.

In high school I also spent a great deal of time in sports, although in football I was too light, in basketball too short, and in baseball just not good enough. I love telling the story of my football career. I rarely, if ever, was put in a game—I was simply too small. However, at one practice, the fullback came running through the line and I slaughtered him with a great tackle that everyone started shouting their praise. I watched him jump up and hustle back into the huddle while every bone and muscle in my body was aching. I knew I could do it again, but I didn't want to—the pain was not worth the gain. I took off my helmet, walked over to the coach, gave him the helmet and said, "I quit."

In reality, the Free School was modeled after my Catholic school upbringing and Jesuit influence. I attended a small kindergarten through grade seven school and my high school was a small eighth- to twelfth-grade school. My graduating class was about fifty students. The elementary school was co-ed; the high school was all boys. In high school we were primarily taught by priests and young men—scholastics, studying to be Jesuit priests. They were addressed as mister, rather than father, so I had Mr. Wiltz, not Father Wiltz. Many years later, Father Wiltz performed the burial service for my Aunt Mimi and the wedding for my daughter, Iyana. When he recently passed away I lost an old friend. The Free School, which was kindergarten through eighth grade, never grew to more than 300 students, and many students were taught by Teach for America teachers. These were incredibly bright and very energetic young men and women whose passion and desire to do a great job were very reminiscent of my former scholastic teachers, and also of those of us who started the Free School back in 1971. The Free School was often so reminiscent of my school days that it reminds me of the old saying: the more we change, the more we stay the same. I can only hope that the Free School with its emphasis on small and personal also has had similar influence on those whom we educated.

The Shreveport of my youth was a very conservative and segregated world. The schools I attended were all white, except for a couple of black students who attended Spring Hill College where I did my undergraduate work. My parents strongly supported military service, and my Uncle Neckley served as Commander of the local American Legion Post, which under his leadership achieved the highest membership of any post in the United States. I was caught up in this white, military-supporting world. When I was about eleven or twelve years old, I won an award for the best speech in the city on anti-communism and patriotism. I look back on that earlier self with amazement at how much I have changed.

I can honestly say that I never heard an adult (with the exception of my high school teacher Father Michael Kammer) oppose the military, the government, or support civil rights. I had led an incredibly sheltered life, encased in God, country, apple pie, and the white way. A very good friend of my parents owned a restaurant in Shreveport. While in college I argued in favor of his right to discriminate against African Americans or anyone else. Ironically, I worked for him as a waiter a year or two after I graduated from college, and he fired me for associating with blacks. He resented me for having a white female friend who also worked for him, who was dating a black man. How he knew this, I did not know, but I suspected his close ties with the police provided the answer. He fired us both.

During college, I remember arguing against inviting a black student to enter our then-alternative fraternity, simply because he was black. However, it was in college that I began to get introduced to black people, and that began my transformation. The summer before my senior year I worked laying railroad tracks in east Texas. It ended up being forty-nine black men and me doing the hard labor. Practically every day, the straw bosses, who were white, came up to me and stated that I didn't need to be there. I convinced them that I needed the money, I liked the work, and I wanted to remain on the line.

When I first started, I could barely lift the spike mall, but by the end of the summer through support, sometimes mockery, and much practice, I could swing that mall with amazing grace, speed, and accuracy. I was becoming a little John Henry. I remember a couple of times, when the black workers and I would go into a small town country restaurant, there was obvious objection on the part of the wait staff to serving the first couple of black men. But, when an additional twenty to thirty muscular black men walked in, we were not only served, but served with a smile. All of the men treated me like a son and an equal. For the first time in my life I got to know black people as ordinary people. We shared our life stories, struggles, and became summer friends. These men certainly dispelled the myth that I was raised to believe, that black people were lazy, shiftless, and no good. They were incredibly hardworking and decent human beings with strong family values. They did this hot, hard work day in and day out so that their children could have a much better life. It was men like these that helped transform African Americans from being slaves and servants to a much higher status in life, all the way to the presidency of the United States.

One story I love to tell concerns when we would take a forced break from the sweltering, backbreaking work. While waiting for a train to pass so that we could resume work, one of my fellow railroad workers would desperately say, "God, I hope that train has a flat tire." Often, when a teach-

16

er would send to me a student who was very late for school, I would look up at that student from my desk and ask, "What's the matter, the streetcar had a flat tire?" The student, of course, would look at me like I was nuts, but many did see the humor in it.

In 1966, my senior year of college, I worked as a referee for girls and boys basketball games. That summer, one of the coaches, a black lady whose name I do not remember, hired a number of us referees to be Head Start teachers. I did not know what Head Start was, but the pay was great and I really wanted a summer job after graduation. This was immediately after the loss of my dear friend, which had wrecked my life and crushed my soul. The Head Start summer job, for me, came at just the right time. It forced me to intensely focus on something of grave importance and not to just dwell on my misery and guilt. When I took this job, I had just received my undergraduate degree in history and had never taken or even considered taking an education course.

My Head Start experience began in a black church with a tin roof at the end of a dirt road in Mobile, Alabama. I had no training, my college degree was in history not education, and knew not what I was entering. I walked up the stairs to the office and someone told me my classroom was directly at the end of the hall. I walked to the end of the hall, opened the door and there was an aide and fifteen very young smiling faces looking up at me. My education career had begun.

The thing I remember most about my Head Start teaching experience was the dichotomy between what I was hearing and reading about these Head Start children and what I was experiencing in the classroom. Most everyone I came into contact with, and the literature about these children, constantly depicted them as poor, deprived, even backward. My experiences with these children were so different. I found them to be full of life, intelligent, and very creative. Most people saw needy children, I saw potential. Head Start certainly ignited my interest in education—obviously so much needed to be done but the educational process needed to get there seemed endless. The rest, as they say, is history. Well, that history is this book.

2

Getting Educated After Being Educated

One particular story during my Head Start year grabbed me, though I never knew if it was true or not. The story went as follows: Some bigwig educator was giving a keynote speech at a huge educational conference somewhere in Alabama. He went up to the podium and said, "Hi, I would like to introduce you to someone. This is Jessica, and she is a beautiful, inquisitive, intelligent five-year old. It is sad because I have to send her to you and you will destroy her." He sat down. Marilyn Ferguson, in her wonderful book, *The Aquarian Conspiracy*, stated that we get students as butterflies and release them as cocoons. What we were doing and are still doing in public education perpetuates this destruction. The above story, whether true or not, and writers like Marilyn Ferguson, have truly inspired me and given me the courage to attempt to do schooling differently.

There are two other moments with my Head Start experience that I have never forgotten. I was mostly given kids who were more difficult to handle. One student was responding to nothing I tried. He was constantly having fits, throwing things, and hurting the other students. Out of defeat, I decided to deal more harshly with him than I had been. I put him in a locked room down the hall from our classroom and told him that I was going to leave him there until he calmed down. When I went to check on him about five to ten minutes later, I found him climbing out of the second floor window to escape. I have never known all the answers; I was just inspired by the Head Start experience, though quickly grasping the concept that I had a whole lot to learn.

The second thing I vividly remember during this 1966 Head Start experience was that the adults socialized in a racially integrated group, which was certainly not kosher at the time. We would often go to this black-owned bar with a sign on the wall that I will never forget that read as follows, "We Reserve the Right to Serve Anyone." I was always welcomed in the black community while quickly becoming ostracized from the white community—at least the white community who steadfastly held to the notion of white America and the concept that white is right. My life was certainly changing.

Sometime during the summer Head Start experience, some friends of mine, both black and white, decided that we were going to integrate Wintzell's Famous Seafood Restaurant. Wintzell's was the most popular seafood restaurant in Mobile, and one that many of us, all white, had been going to during our college years. About ten of us, half black/half white, went to dinner one Friday evening when the restaurant was packed. After a long wait, which was not usual for such a large crowd on a Friday night, we were finally seated and treated politely and decently. Our waitress told us that she did not want to serve us but had to and would do the best job she could. She did an excellent job.

We did get a few stares and hush-hush comments from other customers, but nothing more. Wintzell, the owner of the restaurant, who was a great big fat, ultra-conservative man, merely eyed us. He was a big George Wallace fan, and looked just like Bull Conner, at least to me. We left that evening, after a great meal, with truly no incidents. A week later, I went back to the restaurant with just a couple of white friends. After we were seated, I suddenly felt two strong hands around my neck and heard Wintzell, say in a good natured southern voice, "I would like to wring your neck. Now y'all have a good meal, ya hear." He went on his way, running his restaurant. I did not return to Wintzell's until many years later. The restaurant looked the same with thousands of little cards with sayings on them posted everywhere in the restaurant—on walls, on the back of stools, in the bathrooms, etc. On the cards were sayings like, "Oysters—fried, stewed and nude" and "George Wallace sat here." Another read, "On the bulletin board at the weather bureau office: 'We are a non-prophet organization.'" Wintzell has passed on but the original restaurant is in the same place, looks the same, and the meal I had was still very good. The restaurant has grown to eleven restaurants all filled with the ever present sayings. Having recently eaten in one of the newer restaurants, I read the adage on one of the cards, "Ignorance is when you don't know something and somebody finds out." God, I hope this book is not an example of this.

Around the time the summer Head Start job ended, I was accepted into the Peace Corps to be trained in San Diego and sent to an African country. I only lasted a couple of weeks in the training program. I was still grieving the loss of my friend and I could not stay focused on the intense training program. My close college friend, Mike DeGuire, had a teaching job in Havre, Montana, and he encouraged me to come out there. I accepted. I loved Montana with the mountains, wide open spaces and the big blue sky. Staying with Mike proved to be the right therapy for my aching heart and directionless soul. Mike, too, was a close friend of Marilyn; in fact, he had known her long before I met and dated her. Commiserating with such a dear friend over the loss of a loved one helped tremendously. I remember the first time it snowed in Montana not long after I got there. I was like a kid in a candy store. I ran up and down the hilly, iced streets of Havre and woke up the next morning black and blue from falling down on the slippery streets. Shreveport and Mobile rarely had ice or snow.

Shortly after moving to Havre, I began teaching in a one-room schoolhouse with five kids from the same family near a little mountain town called Big Sandy. The parents of the kids were the school board members. I would stay in that schoolhouse from Sunday evening to Friday after school when I would drive back to Havre to stay with Mike and his house-mate. The schoolhouse had two rooms: the classroom and my kitchen, bed, and bath combination. The toilet was a portable one that I had to put lime in and then dispose of the contents as necessary. I no longer remember how I bathed.

I recall a few events that occurred during my stay in that one-room schoolhouse. I would often go into Big Sandy and visit a bar. Montana apparently has lots of bars throughout the state because everything is so far away with little else to do. Anyway, in the one bar I frequented, I befriended the piano player. We often had long conversations or played chess. He was a history buff and I was doing extensive reading on the Vietnam War and on education. He was a very informed person and excellent conversationalist who challenged my knowledge while inspiring my convictions. I thoroughly enjoyed the evenings I spent with him and believe that he was the only friend I made in Montana.

I remember one time it snowed heavily on a Thursday night and the following Friday morning. After school when I was driving to Havre for the weekend I quickly discovered the road blocked with snow. I went back to the ranch and asked the parents to borrow a shovel. They told me that there was no way I could get off the mountain because the road was covered for almost a mile. Nevertheless, they gave me the shovel and I went back to dig. I knew I could not spend the weekend in that lonely schoolhouse—five nights a week was despondency enough. I literally shoveled for about a mile clearing snow so that I could escape that lonely mountain. I was sore but I made it.

I found the children to be very bright and I loved working with them. Each child was in a different grade from kindergarten through seventh or eighth, which meant that each had to work individually on his or her grade level. We did spend a lot of time working as a group, however, particularly on creative projects. The older kids often helped their younger brothers or sisters with their school work. We played a lot outside on the mountainside and in the snow. It truly was like being immersed in song… "The hills are alive with the sound of music."

Then, everything collapsed. I do not remember the order of the events so I may be telling this tale with a few mistaken sequences; but, since I was only there from October 1966 through some or most of January 1967, the timeline is not that significant. At some point in late November or early December, the parents had me over to dinner. They were very conservative politically and lived the isolated rancher's life. At the same time they were very nice and always treated me in a friendly and polite manner. At this dinner two issues came up that particularly disturbed me. The first knocked the breath out of me. They told me that the only reason why the school was still open was that they did not want their kids going to school with Indians. Wow! Did this not show me how naive I was? I knew nothing about American Indians much less where they lived or how they were being treated. I have always lived in a white or white-and-black world. I remember several years later my friend Jeanette asking, as we stood in Los Angeles at a crowded Mexican market, "Where are all the people?"

The next part of the conversation that evening also caught me by surprise. The parents expressed fear that their youngest daughter, who was in kindergarten or first grade, was not learning how to read. This surprised me because she was doing very well with reading while in school. When I asked the parents why they felt this way, they informed me that she could not read the word "father." I had recently read or was reading Sylvia Ashton-Warner's book, *Teacher,* and was already using her method with the younger children. I asked the parents to give me a day or two to figure out was going on and that I would report back to them with my findings. They seemed pleased with my concern and response so the evening ended cordially, though I was still stunned by the revelation concerning the American Indians.

Basically, Ashton-Warner's approach to reading was to use as much as possible what a student knows, feels, and wants to know to develop their reading skills. Each day I would ask the little girl what words she would like to read. She would tell me and then I would help her write them down. Then she composed a sentence or story with the new word(s). We learned four or five new words each day while constantly reviewing old words. I would often ask her permission to introduce a new word or words. She readily accepted them time and time again.

On the day after that family dinner I gave her the word "father." Her sentence was, "My father is sick." That afternoon I asked the mother if her husband had ever been ill or in an accident. She said yes—that he had been ill and that he had been in the hospital for about a week. I explained to her what I had done with her daughter that morning during reading and offered my opinion to the mother that they must have solemnly told her, "Your father is very ill and we have to pray for him." I suggested that her child now equates the word "father" with that illness and therefore has tried to avoid it. I reassured the mother that otherwise her daughter was reading quite well. The mother accepted this explanation and seemed pleased to receive it.

For me, this little incident clearly illustrated how important the inner person is to the acquisition and development of knowledge. The more we externalize the motive for learning through bureaucratic control, massive testing, dependency on textbooks, scripted reading, and grading, the more we lose the learner. It is just like the phrase in the Bible, "What does it benefit a man if he gains the whole world but loses his soul?" What does a student gain if we cram knowledge down the student's throat only to lose the student as a learner? What if the student passes a test but fails to develop a love of learning? Simply put, good education focuses on the needs of the learner and helps the learner create new needs. Excellent education focuses on the engagement of the learner and not the dictated coverage of information.

After the Christmas holidays I brought back a lady friend from San Francisco who stayed with me for a few nights. This lady, the children, and I had a great time, but the parents were upset that a woman had stayed with me. They told me that it was improper for a lady to be there if we were not married. While they did not require me to leave, I could tell that they were not happy. I think we both saw this as my opportunity to leave. I was unhappy about the Indian discrimination and I was lonely; they were not pleased with my decision to have a lady friend stay with me over night. I left sometime in January 1967 and returned to a Head Start teaching job in Mobile. I missed the kids, my piano playing buddy and my close friend, Mike DeGuire, but I never missed those lonely nights spent in that schoolhouse.

Upon returning to Mobile I quickly realized that most, if not all, of my college friends had departed Mobile for graduate school or jobs elsewhere. A short time after returning to Mobile my worst nightmare became a reality. Since college I had been only seeking teaching jobs to avoid the draft. Apparently my habit of constantly switching jobs caught up with me and I received a draft notice to report for a physical. All I knew was that I had to fail that physical. I was not opposed to serving my country or even being in the military, so I could not claim conscientious objector status. I simply felt and still feel that our country was engaged in an illegal, unjust, and immoral war in Vietnam. At this time in my life I had read a few books on Vietnam, kept up with the television coverage of the war, and read every newspaper article about the war that I could get my hands on. At the same time I had never attended a protest, never participated in a teach-in, never organized a march, or ever opposed my government in any fashion concerning this war. I was a neophyte in the anti-war movement with absolutely no support—no political support, no movement support, no peer group support, nothing. I had to face the draft alone and I was scared as hell. I had no one, but I had my convictions. I was not going to fight in Vietnam even if it meant going to jail or escaping to Canada. Remember, I was deep in the South and even though in 1967 Dr. King had come out against the war, support for the war was the strongest and opposition was almost nonexistent. I was no longer a conservative and I was fighting for my life.

I knew that I had one weapon on my side: Few in the south were very familiar with dealing with draft dodgers or seemingly radical hippies. I had to convince them that I was not what they wanted in the military. I planned accordingly, not knowing where or what was going to happen.

I stayed up all night before I was to report for the draft physical to give myself a dazed, worn-out look. I went barefooted and dressed in raggedy clothes. I wanted to look as discombobulated as possible and to absolutely convince them, "Not him!"

The other potential draftees and I were put on a bus and headed to Montgomery, Alabama, as I recall, for our physical. I immediately started anti-war discussions with every potential draftee who would listen. I demonstrated that I knew a fair amount about the war, so many engaged in the discussion while others listened. We all knew why we were being drafted so it was not difficult getting a conversation going. I could not help but notice that the military personnel kept their eyes on me.

When we stopped for lunch, I noticed that the potential black draftees were not getting served. When a small argument between them and the lunch workers ignited, I jumped up and said, "I saw them pass over you." I continued in a much louder voice, "I'm with you, brother. Let's burn this motherfuckin' place down." 1967 was a time when our country had experienced race riots and tensions were high. The black draftees were quickly and quietly served after this ruckus, but I again gained the attention of the army officials. Not only did I look like hell but I was the worst of all political evils—a troublemaker.

Back on the bus I continued the anti-war discussion that had grown in participants and intensity. A couple of the same potential black draftees who were involved in the argument in the restaurant were also very articulate in their opposition to the war and able to express that opposition in well thought-out racial terms. We became a small clique and when we reached the induction center where many more potential draftees were arriving, we initiated fresh discussion concerning our opposition to the war. This immediately drew a larger crowd of participants and listeners.

The army officials dispersed our group by sending us to different lines for our physical exam. The physical was the typical "drop your draws, bend over" experience. At some point one of the officers pulled me out of line and told me to get dressed and follow him. He walked me down the street and took me into an old office building. Both the induction center and this structure were in the older, downtown area. We took the elevator up a couple of floors and he led me into an office where he left me. I felt certain that this was a psychiatrist's office and, sure enough, it was. I was barefoot, clothed in rags, bedraggled, and keenly aware that it was now or never—if I was ever going to get out of the draft, this was my only opportunity. I assumed that the psychiatrist had been informed of everything that had occurred since I first got on the bus that morning. Now began the climax of this drama. While it started with pleasantries, the psychiatrist quickly quizzed me about my personal life, especially covering any tragedies. I told him about the loss of my very close friend, cognizant that he might use this information to disqualify me for the draft. Surprisingly, he did not spend a lot of time on this issue as he quickly turned the discussion to political issues. This summit meeting quickly turned hostile. The doctor discussed modern society, pointing out how far the human race had progressed since the Stone Age. He talked about the marvels of modern society, the advancement of human civilization, and the greatness of the United States of America. I responded that our society was very flawed: our forefathers had slaughtered one race of people and raped another into slavery and poverty. We Americans were dominating the world with our military industrial complex, and we were now waging an immoral, unjust, and illegal war.

The psychiatrist replied that even in battle we were engaged in a much more civilized endeavor because we no longer were fighting face to face or with knives and swords. I admitted that we no longer fight with just knives and swords, but we instead drop bombs indiscriminately from afar, never witnessing the horror being inflicted on fellow human beings. I told him that I refused to call this progress or refer to it as "civilized." I deemed it inhumane and torturous, and in this criminal war, "murder."

He looked at me and, to the best of my memory, said, "I don't think you would be a good fit for the Army." I said, "Yes sir."

As I left his office and began walking down the street, I literally started jumping in the air, kicking my heels. I knew I had won. Just as fast as I kicked up my heels, I stopped. I realized that he could possibly see me out of his window and I wanted to give him nothing that would change his mind.

I received a 4-F classification, which meant that I no longer had to worry about the draft. In honesty, I felt bad about deceiving my government: the bare feet, dress, sleep deprivation, and shouting in the restaurant were all drama. The anti-war discussions and the testy exchange with the psychiatrist were the truth. I have never thought ill of the young men, and now women, who enter the military; it too can be a noble calling. At that time in our history, our soldiers were not my enemy; my government was. Later, in my struggles to save the Free School, I constantly had to remind myself that it was not so much the people we battled but the bureaucratic governance that was our true enemy.

After the Head Start experience, I joined VISTA (Volunteers in Service to America). This, too, proved to be a very mind expanding and memorable experience. I trained in Chicago and roomed with a Jewish guy, a black guy and a Polish guy. I am of Lebanese descent. We joked about, and loved the fact that our little microcosm of the world truly enjoyed one another's company, worked well together, and socialized as if we had been friends since childhood. The VISTA training was excellent. It shattered the notion we held that we were out to save the world. It clearly illuminated that we had far more to learn from the poverty-stricken areas we were to be placed in than we would ever be able to give.

Good educators know emphatically that they have as much to learn from their students as the students have to learn from them. Quality education is about the interaction of human beings; it is not just about imparting information, and it is clearly not just about passing the test.

I eventually ended up working in Gary, Indiana, as a VISTA volunteer with the family planning organization, Planned Parenthood. The women clients and I always giggled when I was required to lead a session on family planning.

While in Gary I met several white construction contractors who were either building or renovating project housing. They spoke freely with me, I guess, because I was white. They explicitly explained that they were using inferior materials and design in building/renovating these projects because "these people" wouldn't take care of them anyway, so why spend their resources or energy building quality structures? What an incredibly racist way to perpetuate the belief that blacks are inferior, lazy, and incapable of taking care of anything nice! The apartments they were given to live in would crumble because of shoddy materials and construction, no matter what they did. The blame for this deterioration, however, would inescapably fall on the black residents, not the white contractors. The "level playing field" supposedly ensured by the Civil Rights Movement has been tilted one way since slavery, and this 1967 incident was designed to perpetuate this slant.

3

From Conservative to Liberal

By the end of 1967, and almost two years out of college, I had become an avid civil rights advocate and a strong Vietnam War opponent. This change was to further put me at odds with my upbringing, education, and most people I knew growing up. A particularly enlightening moment occurred one evening when I traveled with fellow VISTA volunteers to Evanston, Illinois, to hear David Schorenbraum, a professor at John Hopkins University, speak against the Vietnam War at an American Friends church. The audience stood while Schorenbraum spoke from the podium. After explaining that Lyndon Johnson, who promised to de-escalate the Vietnam War, actually escalated it after he was re-elected president, David bellowed, "I'll tell you who the American traitor is. The Great American traitor is Lyndon Baines Johnson!" I had never heard an adult oppose our government so forcibly. I finally realized that there was nothing wrong with me and my thinking about civil rights and the war; there was something horribly wrong with the thinking and actions of almost everyone I had known growing up and with the powerful people who controlled our government. I was transformed and would never go back.

Schorenbraum explained that we could never win the war in Vietnam. He brilliantly articulated the reality that the Viet Cong spent $15 blowing up a bridge we built for $15 million, while we spent $15 million blowing up a bridge they built for $15.

Schorenbraum concluded, "All of you have heard the saying during this war, 'My country, right or wrong.' Well, let me tell you the ending to the saying, which rarely gets said. It goes, 'My country, right or wrong. When it's right, keep it right; when it's wrong, make it right.'"

Near the end of my VISTA year, I jumped at the opportunity to work for Senator Robert Kennedy's bid to become president of the United States. I drove to California with several people to join his campaign. How we got to be part of the campaign, I do not really know. I was immediately made an advance man and was sent to San Bernardino County to unite the factions supporting Kennedy and to set up a county headquarters. I was given a few hundred dollars in cash, a car, told where to go, whom to contact, and where to sleep. It was an exhilarating time, working long hours and meeting lots of people. We were changing the world and, though exhausted, we were having the most glorious experience imaginable.

My world was shattered that evening when Bobby won the California primary and was shot moments after his victory speech. I remember finishing a steak dinner that was paid for by the campaign, then heading back to the Ambassador hotel with my fellow workers. The hotel was a

26

short block from the restaurant. We passed by some Eugene McCarthy volunteers about our age who told us Bobby had just been shot. We replied that that was a mean way to accept defeat, to tell us that untruth. We did not consider what they said to even be slightly possible, much less true. Nonetheless, literally seconds after they spoke, we heard sirens coming from everywhere. As we entered the Ambassador Hotel, I saw Rosie Greer either leading or following Sirhan Sirhan out of the hotel. Policemen were everywhere. A number of us, all Kennedy-paid volunteers (I considered us volunteers despite the fact that we received expense money) were huddled in a single hotel room, glued to the TV and frantically praying for Bobby to survive. As we all know, he did not make it.

A few days later, the Kennedy organization flew me back to Chicago where I stayed with my girlfriend and fellow VISTA volunteer for a couple of months. During this time she and I joined the anti-war protestors during the 1968 Democratic Presidential Convention. We were there when the police rioted and attacked the protestors. I remember seeing the line of police marching toward us in a very orderly fashion and thinking that they were simply cordoning us into a specified area so that the protest could continue. To everyone's horror, some policemen broke ranks and started charging the crowd of protestors. They were wildly swinging their billy clubs, pushing, kicking, and knocking people over. I vividly remember getting separated from my girlfriend, falling to the ground, and watching police swing clubs while running over us.

Miraculously, neither my close friend nor I was injured. I survived the assault, but as a person who had been further transformed. I could never again blindly trust authority. My country had forced us into an unjust war and the Chicago police had willfully, and even gleefully, physically attacked me, my friends, and fellow Americans for performing an American, democratic act. My resolve to change America was deeply cast, and has remained resolute throughout the years. It grieves me that the military industrial complex has, once again, gotten its way, and George W. Bush thrust us into another immoral, illegal, and unjustified war in Iraq, costing lives and billions of dollars, but making billions for the war machine.

Growing up in the white South was an incredibly indoctrinating experience. We were taught to believe that propaganda was one of the worst government evils to be imposed on a society, while simultaneously demanding blind loyalty. We were also instructed to never question authority. Black people were inferior due to natural causes that were beyond the scope of societal or governmental change. Amazingly, we were raised as democratic people believing that "Might and White were Right." Growing up, I was constantly told that black people (with much more derogatory terms in use back then) were lazy, shiftless, poor, uneducated, and stupid. Blacks were weak (not physically, but mentally and socially), dirty, and any other disgusting term whites could think of. In essence, white southern children were raised to believe that black people were somehow less than human. White society did a thorough job of keeping black people out of our lives with segregated neighborhoods, schools, churches, and entertainment. Black people were only to be seen or heard from as our servants, and to perform menial tasks, dirty jobs that no "decent white person" would undertake. Society with its traditions, laws, and power relegated black people to being a shadow people virtually invisible to white society. The white South was masterful in preaching the concept of "Love thy neighbor," all the while subtly, and not so subtly, meaning, "Love thy white neighbor."

The indoctrination concerning our military and our "enemies" was no less captivating. I remember the first time I heard someone question our history by asking the simple question, "Why is it that in our history books, every time the American Indians won a battle, we call it 'slaughter,' but when we won a battle, we call it 'victory'?" We were thoroughly brainwashed in our teachings about American history. It was always the case that the United States was fighting for freedom and the American way of life. We were perpetually opposing tyranny and despotic evil. Growing up, if I heard it once, I heard it thousands of times, "My country, right or wrong!" During the Vietnam War, the irony was that if you opposed the war, you were considered less than an American citizen and even less than human. You were definitely considered a traitor.

Civil Rights and the Vietnam War helped bring together a powerful force of black and white people struggling to help make the United States of America right where it had been wrong for so long. Fortunately, out of these horrendous conflicts causing so much pain and death, so much good has been accomplished.

After Bobby Kennedy's assassination and experiencing the Chicago police riot, I found myself lost, with no job and no true direction. I returned to Shreveport toward the end of the summer of 1968. I headed south because I felt that I could do more good there than anywhere else. I was raised a Southerner and I believed that I could communicate with most Southerners. I was no outside agitator—I was one of them. Southern white people hated "outside" agitators—white or black. This was one roadblock I would not have to encounter.

Much happened during the two years I was back in Shreveport, which continued my education into how deep racism permeated our society and how completely the military controlled our nation. When I returned to Shreveport, I moved in with my parents, and slept once again in my childhood bedroom. I immediately became involved with the underground hippie culture of mostly young white people as well as a civil rights group that included prominent black members struggling to change Shreveport society. Many of us were deeply involved in voter registration and we spent all of our free time together. These actions led to my parents telling me that I had to move out. My Aunt Mimi did the telling, but she indicated the demand came from my Uncle Neckley.

Uncle Neckley acted like he was the head of the family. He always sat at the head of the table, held a law degree, and put down the rest of the family for not being so well educated. He was not mean, although he did expect to be catered to by all members of the family. While we all participated in the charade, I knew that the strength of the family rested with Aunt Mimi and Aunt Rose. He was also very politically connected in the city of Shreveport, with the mayor being one of his best friends. I moved out but still maintained contact with the family primarily with Aunt Mimi.

I moved into an apartment in the black community. I was amazed at both how well I was received and that I had discovered a city within a city. With my new black and white friends, I was living in an exciting time. I helped organize an anti-war march, one of Shreveport's first. Dr. Louis Pendleton, a prominent black dentist, gave the keynote speech and a black lawyer, Jesse Stone, did the legal work to protect our march. While the march drew a nice crowd and everyone behaved peacefully, tensions were high and definitely at the breaking point.

I vividly remember one night when Gregory Tarver, a black funeral parlor owner who eventually became a Louisiana State Legislator, Leman Hawkins, who was a local neighborhood black activist, and I were going to a black power rally in Baton Rouge. Greg had picked me up at my apartment and we were on our way to get Leman when the police stopped us and threw me in the paddy wagon. As they put me in the wagon, Gregory started protesting and shouting to take him, too. The police got angry with him, beat him with their billy clubs, and shoved him in the police wagon. I asked Gregory why he angered the police, effectively drawing them off me. He said that he was afraid they were going to seriously beat me, if not kill me, and he could not let that happen.

When we got to the police station, we were treated roughly and Gregory was again hit by the police. It was now 1 or 2 a.m. and I called home to talk to my uncle. I told him that all my life he told me how "just" and "right" the police were, yet I had just been arrested for simply being in black company. I told him that I had witnessed police brutality with my own eyes. He said, "That's what happens when you have been drinking too much and cause trouble." I told him that we had not been drinking that night because we were about to drive to Baton Rouge. Needless to say, the conversation went nowhere.

I do not remember how we got out of jail that night, but it was probably through the help of Jesse Stone. We went on to Baton Rouge, and I was the only white person in a gym filled with black people listening to speeches, clapping, and singing. It was an amazing moment with hundreds, possibly thousands of black people uniting, growing strong, and struggling to change the United States of America in the Deep South in 1969. The sixties were coming to an end, but change was marching on.

Not long thereafter, I participated in a civil rights march in Shreveport. I did not help organize the march; I was just a participant. I thought I was going to be the only white person there, but there were four others. They were two lieutenants in the U.S. Air Force who were stationed at the Barksdale Air Force Base, and their wives. To my surprise, everyone in the march, including me, was arrested and hauled down to the underground court house parking lot. One of the lieutenant's wives was hit in the head during this forced march into the parking garage. I was placed next to these four other white people. A white police officer, dressed in a suit rather than a police uniform, went down the line harassing people. He told one of the two lieutenants that he, the lieutenant, ought to be in a ditch in Vietnam.

When he came to me, he said, "You're Neckley Ferris' nephew, aren't you!" I said, "Yes sir." My knees were shaking a hundred miles an hour. He then said, "I sure hope he isn't made of the same stuff you're made of." I replied, scared to death, "I sure hope he isn't made of the same stuff you're made of." He looked me square in the face and said, "What did you say?" I responded bravely, but still shaking throughout my body and trying not to let my fear show, "Well, you said, 'I hope he is not made of the same stuff you are made of,' and I replied, 'I hope he is not made of the same stuff you are made of.'" I thought for sure that he was going to hit me, but he simply said, "I think you're made of shit." And then he walked away. I do not remember how we got out of the legal charges for being arrested, but we did. Again, I suspect that Jesse Stone handled the situation.

During this two-year Shreveport stay, I hitchhiked to Washington D.C. with a friend, actually a former high school acquaintance, named Don, to attend the March on the Pentagon. One night in Shreveport when we were planning the trip, we went to the Toddle House on Fairfield Avenue near Jordan Street. While we were in there, a couple of military guys walked in, saw Don, and started screaming at him. Don shot up and started screaming back at them. Before this came to blows, a skinny old waitress got between them and calmed them all down. The guys were angry at Don because he was an anti-war activist and protestor at LSU, where he went to college studying the Chinese language. Apparently, Don led one of the first anti-Vietnam marches on LSU's campus. He led that march because he was the only protestor. I told Don I was surprised at his angered response to these military guys, especially since he was seeking or had received Conscientious Objector status with the draft board. He replied in his nervous, energetic style, "No. No. I am a pacifist, just a violent pacifist."

We went to the D.C. March on the Pentagon together. I somehow ended up in a crowd near Dr. Benjamin Spock, the famous baby doctor and author. Before I could grasp what was really happening, a row of troops started marching right at us. Someone shouted, "Get on your arms and knees to protect your body!" As I quickly got on the ground cramped up in a ball, I remember seeing one of the young soldiers start beating an older woman. A man jumped on the woman to protect her and shouted at the soldier, "Stop that! You can't do that!" The soldier hit him a couple of times and then just stopped. I also remember that I was just frozen with fear and was disgusted with myself for not having the courage to protect the abused lady.

During the Shreveport experience, I went to the Louisiana Department of Employment. The chant went throughout the office that someone said he was willing to work. I do not know why it was such a big deal, but it was. Ironically, the only job they could offer me was making bullets or weapons for the war effort. When I refused the job, you could hear the silence fall throughout the office.

Another side note concerns another uncle and aunt who were not really my uncle and aunt but whom I called Uncle Fred and Aunt Edna. They were part of our extended Lebanese family and were the parents of Woody, the same Woody mentioned above with the kindergarten episode. One evening Uncle Fred took me aside and gave me $50 for the voter registration drive. He said that he supported my efforts and that he thought that I was doing the right thing in struggling for civil rights. How I longed for any and all of my family members to help make our country right after it had been wrong for so long . . . Thank you Uncle Fred and Aunt Edna Nackley.

While looking for employment I received a grant from the Southern Education Foundation based in Washington, D.C. The grant was marketed as a Professional Grant for Southerners to keep people who were from the south in the south and to help change the educational landscape there. In my case, it worked—I have never left the south nor lost my zeal to do education differently and to help make it better for all. I used the grant money to investigate how the federal Elementary and Secondary Education Act (ESEA) Title I compensatory monies were being spent in Louisiana.

Title I funds were federally school financed compensatory funds legally restricted to helping the poor. My findings quickly made enemies and got me kicked out of Shreveport. I had written an article for the Shreveport underground newspaper, *The Other Voice*, in which I detailed abuses of Title I funds throughout the state and lambasted the local Superintendent, Donald Kennedy, for blocking my viewing the records of Title I expenditures in Caddo Parish. He told me that I could only view the records if I paid the salaries for any and all employees who assisted me. Apparently my article had raised the ire of Superintendent Kennedy because he wrote a blistering letter to John Griffin, executive director of The Southern Education Foundation. In this letter he forbade me to enter any public school in Caddo Parish, he claimed that I had misrepresented myself to be a representative of the Department of Education, and he requested a copy of all information I had sent to SEF about the Caddo Parrish School System. He included a letter from the Police Commissioner of Public Safety, George D'Artios, listing my police record and accusing me of being "very much involved in the war moratorium . . . and most anything anti-establishment." In the police chief's letter he also stated I was arrested in 1967 for vagrancy. This was the arrest with Gregory. The police chief did not mention that I was living down the street from where I was arrested, with $40 in my pocket, but he did point out that the charge was discontinued, in a move known as "nol pros."

The second arrest he mentioned was the civil rights march I had participated in when we were all arrested. In the police chief's letter full of the abbreviations of the day, like C/M for Colored Male, he wrote "He was arrested along with B.J. Mason, C/M, Larry "Boo Ga Loo" Cooper, C/M and others who were involved in a disturbance downtown over a black power struggle." Of course he did not mention that two lieutenants in the United States Air Force, W/Ms, and their wives, W/Fs, were also arrested with us. I wrote John Griffin with a detailed response to Superintendent Kennedy's charges and never heard of this matter again, but I did leave Shreveport and move to New Orleans.

Before I discuss the move to New Orleans, I should note that the characters I was in opposition to in Shreveport were not very reputable. Superintendent Kennedy ended up heading an all white private academy. I will let the words of Deno Seder, author of famed Harry Lee's biography, *Wild about Harry*, describe George D'Artois' character:

> But integrity wasn't being restored in many other parishes, because back then, politics in Louisiana was a dangerous business. It could get you killed. In 1976, the state's top political consultant, Jim Leslie of Shreveport, refused to accept a check drawn on city funds for campaign expenses incurred on behalf of George D'Artois, the city's Public Safety Commissioner. D'Artois tried to use taxpayer dollars to pay for campaign expenses, and Leslie wanted no part of the scam. He was scheduled to testify before a grand jury investigating D'Artois, but never had the chance. He was murdered on July 9, 1976, by a single shotgun blast. Months later, D'Artois was arrested for hiring a hit man to kill Leslie, but he too didn't make it to the court room. D'Artois died of a heart attack before coming to trial. (55)

I apparently was dealing with some very unsavory characters and was fortunate to get out of Shreveport unharmed.

In moving to New Orleans, I joined forces with the Lawyers Constitutional Defense Committee (LCDC), a legal civil rights group handling school desegregation suits and voting rights issues, and who were also investigating how Title I funds were being spent in Louisiana. LCDC at that time was headed by George Strickler, and they had a small apartment in the French Quarter that I rented for several months. I continued my investigation of what could only be described as the misuse and abuse of Title I funds in Louisiana. The U.S. Department of Education finally declared the Louisiana Title I funds expenditures illegal. Either the Superintendent of Education for Louisiana, or the head of Title I for Louisiana (I do not remember which one), accused me of being a communist. In those days, if you were not for God, white America and apple pie, you were quickly labeled a communist. Fortunately for me, one of the associate directors of the Louisiana Title I program was my former high school teacher, Father Junkin, who was then an ex-Jesuit. It was weird talking to him somewhat as an equal and as a friend because he was the Prefect of Discipline back in my high school, where I often found myself in trouble. He convinced this top Louisiana bureaucrat/politician that I was no communist—just a do-gooder at best. I guess this story is reminiscent of my kindergarten story. I was not a communist then either; I was just trying to do good.

Working with LCDC not only provided me the opportunity to finish my investigation of Louisiana Title I, it also proved to be an incredibly mind-expanding and exciting experience. I would travel with the LCDC attorneys to the smaller Louisiana towns where they were handling school desegregation suits and voter rights cases. The black community welcomed us with open arms while the white community tried to kill us with stares. I did some work in Bogalusa, where I met former members of the Deacons for Defense. I did most of my work in Tallula, Louisiana, helping to make sure an election for sheriff was conducted properly and legally. Zelma Wych became the first black sheriff of Tallula. In this endeavor, we formed close ties with the black policemen of the town.

Also, because of my ties with the LCDC, I met some hippie, white, anti-war protestors whom the lawyers were defending after they had been arrested in a war protest march in New Orleans. Out of this group six or seven of us formed a commune and lived in a house owned by an activist couple named Susan and Miles. One really big event happened while I was living in this commune. Jane Fonda was coming to town to raise money for the local Black Panther Party to rent cars so that members of this community would have transportation to attend a Black Power rally in Washington, D.C. Jane spoke in New Orleans one night and then spent the night in our commune. Since I was the only single person in the commune, and being the Southern gentleman that I am, I volunteered to let her sleep with me. She brought her boyfriend—no, it wasn't Ted Turner, and I slept alone.

The group going to D.C. needed another car to carry all the people. Since I had a credit card I volunteered to rent the car, which meant that I would have to drive a group of people to the rally. On departure day we picked up the rental cars and drove to the Desire housing project, where the Panthers had taken over one of the apartments, to pick up the community members going to the rally. After a short time, we all loaded up and took off for D.C. We hadn't even reached New Orleans city limits—we were at Chef Highway and Interstate 10 where significant highway construction was occurring—when it seemed like the world came to an end. I was driving the lead car very slowly on one of the construction roads when policemen, on foot, came pointing rifles directly at my head. We were immediately surrounded by what seemed like hundreds of police. News cameras were everywhere. When a police officer handcuffed me, he cuffed my hands very tightly, hurting me. He ignored my pain and complaints but another officer eventually loosened the cuffs. We were quickly placed in the paddy wagons and hauled to New Orleans Central Lockup via the interstate, which was completed but not yet open to traffic. In our particular wagon the driver sped up, slammed on the breaks, and made sharp right and left turns, forcing us to pound into one another. For the first time in my life, I feared I was really going to end up in prison—for what I did not know, but I was going. Our arrest was aired on national television: this had to be serious.

While in Central Lockup, my fears quickly dissipated. The police were running around with one saying, "Let's charge them with this." Another replying, "No, the judge threw that one out." My fear of a long prison stay was diminishing. The officers finally charged us with trespassing because we had entered the project to use the bathroom in an apartment held illegally by the Black Panther Party. I quickly realized that this was all for show and to make the police superintendent look good by arresting Black Panther members and breaking the back of the Black Panther Party in New Orleans. Later that night, the police chief sent a policeman disguised as a priest into the headquarters of the Black Panthers, ending in the arrest of all members found in the apartment. The police chief was successful in destroying the Black Panther Party in New Orleans. The irony of that day was that an older woman in Boston was watching the nightly news covering our arrest when she told her husband, "That looks like our son Miles." Her husband said, "No, that couldn't be Miles." It was Miles, one of my fellow commune members, and also a driver of one of the cars.

While we each spent about four days in jail, including Thanksgiving Day, the charges were ultimately dropped, but we all had to sign a release saying we would not sue the police for false arrest or anything else. I did not want to sign the release, but the mothers of the young black men did not want to take the chance that their sons could end up getting a police record. By signing the release, all charges were to be dropped and expunged from our record. I signed the release.

4

The Free School Opens

Through all of the struggles during those past few years I had come to the realization that if I were to effect major change in our society, I must do it in my own backyard. I had been raised in the South, in a middle class environment, benefiting from a Catholic education kindergarten through college. As someone attempting to be a change agent, I needed to be home. Education in the south seemed to be that venue. I had talked about starting a school with my girlfriend when I was in Chicago. Some members of my commune and other citizens of New Orleans were disgusted with the public education being provided to the children of New Orleans and were eager to bring about change. We were constantly discussing how to start a school and felt strongly that the time was right. Throughout the nation people were starting up "Free Schools," and we wanted to be part of that movement. We had read with excitement and inspiration new books focusing on education such as John Holt's *How Children Fail*, A.S. Neil's *Summerhill*, Jonathan Kozol's *Death at an Early Age*, George Dennison's *The Lives of Children*, and others.

We started a school without any corporate or governmental authority or support. We simply opened our doors and said that we were a school. We did not face the present day charter school paper work requirement for charter status or the necessity of governmental approval. However, Saint Mark's Community Center, on Rampart Street on the edge of the French Quarter, gave us free space on their second floor. The Free School was born and titled, "Rampart Street Free School." The three founders, along with me, were Susan O'Malley, Ann Houston and Kathy McFadden. Susan taught English Literature at UNO and had one child enrolled in the Free School. Ann had a limited educational background and Kathy was a certified teacher. Ann and Kathy were our first two teachers hired; we then hired an African American male, Nelson, to be our third teacher. He also had a limited educational background. The three ladies recruited twenty-nine students in grades K-5. How they did this, I do not know to this day. We opened our door on January 6, 1971, with these twenty-nine students.

We had almost no resources. We operated the first two-and-a-half years on a $10,000 inheritance I had received, my grant salary, donations from friends, and grants and fund-raisers we held during this period. We once received a grant check for about $8,000 with a note stating not to respond and not to ask for more money. I tore up the letter and threw it in the trash. We never knew where that money came from. We also received some financial help from the Southern Education Foundation, which continued to support me and their mission to make educational change in the South.

What we lacked in money and resources, we did not lack in energy and passion. We were one-hundred percent committed and determined to make it work. The first five months at Saint Mark's were high energy, to say the least. It was a struggle mixing black and white kids and families in this urban setting while developing an educational program in these uncharted waters, but we laid the foundation for creating a strong educational community.

We had a number of visitors, including famed educator John Holt, during those first few months. I remember one particular visitor who walked into the school with radiant curly hair that went everywhere, and it was love at first sight. I did not know it at the time, but Sue and I were to become partners for life. One of our teachers was moving in the fall with her husband so we knew that we had to hire a new teacher. We offered the position to Sue's friend, but he refused because the pay was very low. We offered it to Sue, who was a recent college graduate with a teacher's certificate, and she accepted. Back then in our love-struggling days, I would tell Sue, "Forever is a long time." Now forty years later, I tell her, "Forever is not long enough." As our friend Lee Mullikin loves to say, "and Bob Ferris married his intern!"

Let me explain our salary scale back then. We pooled our resources, estimating how much we could pay teachers for the school year, and that became the salary. If public school teachers were making around $10,000 per year, our teachers were making at best about $2,000 per year, without benefits. Teaching at the Free School in those days was truly a labor of love. In reality, there was no salary scale, only a subsistence wage.

By the end of May 1971, our fifth month, we realized that the space in Saint Mark's was not large enough for our twenty-nine students, much less any additional students. Fortunately, we found and quickly rented an old, dilapidated mansion with a front wide stairwell and a huge front porch on Chippewa Street. We started a second commune above the school which paid the rent for the building so that the school could be rent free. Sue and I started dating and just as quickly moved in together on this second-floor commune. She and I did not always have a smooth sailing relationship. We were part of the sixties, lived in a commune, were politically active, and hell-bent on creating different types of relationships, all the while changing the world. It was not always easy, it was not always pretty, but in the end, it has been a wonderful relationship. We did not change relationships; the relationship changed us, particularly me. It helped calm me down, kept me focused on the Free School, and got me through the trying years ahead. We have ended up as homeowners with two children, dogs, and four beautiful grandchildren, Svara, Teagan, Ameya, and Isla. We are together, still in love and still dancing. We are often the oldest couple dancing and, sometimes at a festival or party, the only couple dancing, but dancing we are.

Sue's move into the commune on Chippewa Street and her working at the Free School did not please her parents. They considered me akin to Charles Manson and believed their beautiful daughter was moving into the ghetto. Some of Sue's parents' fears about her new life were true. However, her mother softened over the years, and instantly fell in love with our first born, Mika. By the time our daughter Iyana was born, Sue's mother and I had grown close. Many years later one memorable moment stands out. When I went to visit her in the nursing home where she was staying, she said to me, "Kiss me." So, I kissed her. She said, "Mmm, that was good!" Sue's mother and I ended up close, but her father, though always polite, never really accepted me.

The building on Chippewa was two stories tall—the bottom floor was used as the school and the top floor was our commune. This property also featured a free-standing building that looked like an old railroad station with three large rooms also used by the school. The main building, dilapidated and in need of much repair, looked like a faded plantation from years gone by. The property had a nice-sized yard and was located in the Irish Channel at 2309 Chippewa Street, just off Jackson Avenue. We loved the old structure and spent the entire summer of 1971 fixing it up. We were lead by Frank Boughton, a parent and fireman, who coined the phrase "fifteen-minute job." Every time Frank would say that a job would take fifteen minutes, we knew that was the kiss of death—we were in for a two- or three-day job. But Frank, with our assistance, worked miracles, and by our standards we were ready to open our new location in September 1971. I believe we were up to about forty-five students at that time.

That school year was a most memorable one! During that time, I still worked with LCDC through my grant investigating the use of Title I monies in Louisiana, but the investigation was coming to an end. The U.S. Department of Education found that the Louisiana Title I program was not being used legally because the state and local school boards were not targeting the money for low-income students, as the law so clearly stated. Thus, I was able to spend a considerable amount of time working at the Free School. We changed the name from the Rampart Street Free School to the New Orleans Free School. Students came from all over the city and many were too poor to pay for their transportation. Thus, in our own cars, particularly an old van we had, we picked up a number of students and then took them home after school. We worked hard as bus drivers and educators from 6:30 a.m. until 5:00 p.m. After school and after dropping off students we continued fixing up the old, dilapidated building. The building was truly a hell hole, but we thought it was a palace and loved it. When we first moved into the building there was a homeless wino living in one of the rooms on the ground floor. The disgusting smell of stale wine, urine, and feces made the room impenetrable. I do not remember how, but we managed to get that man out of the room, into a car and dropped him off at Charity Hospital. Throwing all of his stuff away was an equally painstaking activity. Several months later, he returned looking like a ghost, extremely pale, but walking and talking in a sober manner. We informed him that we had to throw his stuff away. Upon hearing our explanation, he thanked us for getting him to the hospital, turned and left, never to be heard from by us again.

Every night, after 7:00 p.m., we ate and drank heavily until the wee hours. Despite our consumption and late nights, we were up and ready every morning for the new day's tasks. I do not know if it was the excitement of what we were doing, the fact that we were young, or both, but those late nights never stopped or slowed us down. It was a magical time and those hard-working days and fun-loving late nights continued all year.

Sometime, either while at Saint Mark's or on Chippewa, a parent introduced us to the clay pits. This was an area about sixty miles north of New Orleans, down a dirt road where the earth opened up, revealing huge mounds of red clay thirty to sixty feet high, maybe even higher. The clay pits quickly became a regular Free School field trip. Kids could fall off the top of these mounds and tumble all the way to the bottom and never get hurt. The clay was mostly powder, and a tremendous amount of fun to play in. We went there many times that year and for the next few years. It was a wonderful experience that the five-year-olds, the adults, and the dogs, (yes, the dogs lived at the Free School too), thoroughly enjoyed. The clay pits and the structure at Chippewa can be seen in my son's award-winning documentary titled, "The Free School," an hour-long documentary about the history of the Free School up to about 2000. To view this video you can search the Internet for "The New Orleans Free School."

Also during this time we took kids on camping trips. We took one while at Saint Mark's and two while on Chippewa Street. These were incredible events that further developed the Free School community and made it a worthwhile experience for students who were usually confined to their urban setting. The adults also had a glorious time on these trips and certainly benefited from the close personal relationships these experiences provided for all. We continued our annual camping trips for about twenty-five years, until the school system stopped us due to bureaucratic interference. However, in truth, we were getting too large for these school trips by then. We were taking over one-hundred kids on our last camping trips and each year it got harder to accommodate our ever-growing crowd.

The first major camping trip I can remember was a week-long trip in the southern mountains of Arkansas. After driving all day in a car caravan with most, if not all, of our students, we literally camped on a spring with no building or running water besides the spring itself. There was no electricity, no bathrooms, just the spring, land, air, and thousands of stars. Some of the kids could not believe what we were doing, but they loved it.

We stayed five nights. We enjoyed swimming in the spring, hiking in the mountains, and even daring to cross a long, swinging bridge. One five-year-old came on the trip with no shoes, but we managed. He, and everyone there, had a glorious time.

The camping trips were a significant part of the Free School for years to come. Once a young student snuck on the bus and went on the trip with no clothes and without his parent's permission. This was only a two night/three day trip across Lake Ponchartrain at Fontainebleau State Park. We were able to let him share clothes with the other kids and called his parents to get permission for him to remain on the trip. He was not to be left out! One student never forgot that we slept on the ground behind a gas station on our way to the Smoky Mountains.

One of the big events on these trips was campfire-story time, which in later years meant sitting around a flash light we turned upside down. With all the lights out in a big open room with screens all around, we actually created the atmosphere of a campfire. Inevitably I would tell gory horror tales, much to the excitement of the older kids and to the chagrin of the teachers of the younger kids who ended up screaming, crying, and huddling around their teachers. These younger kids went to bed long before I got good into my stories. One story particularly captured the heart and fright of the students. I do not remember the details because I told so many over the years. However, the story went something like this.

The Free School went camping on these same grounds a few years ago. While we were sleeping, monsters would seep out of the ground and mutilate two or three of our students. I will leave out the gory details. The monsters somehow communicated beforehand whom they were going to attack. One evening Jeanette learned that three of her children were going to be attacked. She stayed up that night to protect her children and to confront the monsters. Sure enough in the middle of the night, the monsters came. After a bitter argument between Jeanette and the monsters, an agreement was reached. The monsters were so moved by Jeanette's love for her children they decided that they would take one part of Jeanette's body and forgo gorging on her children. Jeanette agreed, not knowing which part of her body she was to lose. The monsters proceeded to chop off and eat one of her middle toes, and then left. This ended the story and we all went to bed. Well needless to say, the next morning practically every student who heard the story went up to Jeanette wanting to count her toes. When they counted her toes their eyes got wide and they immediately counted again. There were only nine toes. Jeanette had one of her toes amputated years previous, which is a story unto itself. From that moment on, students never questioned the authenticity of my ghost stories.

We were certainly an adventuresome group. In the second or third year of the Free School when we admitted students up to at least the seventh grade, I started taking the ten to twelve older students on a special trip and then meeting up with the rest of the school on the annual camping trip. I always had at least one parent accompanying me on these special trips. One year we were headed for the Grand Canyon but only made it to Carlsbad Caverns. No one wanted to get in the van and go another mile farther. On another trip we went deep-sea fishing on the Gulf Coast, on a boat that held about sixty people, where one could just fish from the deck.

Everyone on the fishing trip, with the exception of one student and me, spent the first hour throwing up. But in the end we caught a lot of fish and headed out. The group was to meet up with the rest of the school later that night in the southern mountains of Arkansas. We just agreed to meet, but at no designated place. As we drove into Arkansas, long before the days of cell phones, it was getting dark and we realized that we lacked some necessary communication to find the rest of our school group. Giving up our search, we turned into a camp site, and to our amazement, the school was there. You may not believe this, but it was true. Talk about the luck of the Irish, and I'm Lebanese. We cooked the fish we caught and fed all, basking in our success. We were adventurous and lucky, too.

That first year on Chippewa Street never let up in its intensity. We worked all day and into the night, ate, drank and went to sleep only to awaken to work all day, then the next day, and so on. I became famous, or infamous, for going to parties on Friday nights and falling asleep on the floor every time. Besides the camaraderie, the hard work, and the counterculture life, there were three things that stand out most in my mind about that incredible first year. The first was an old, blue sports convertible left in the yard on Chippewa Street. Children played in that car day in and day out, taking trips to everywhere. It was the symbol of the Free School—free and going everywhere.

We considered ourselves radical educators, but many in the community viewed us as a hippie school, and in many ways we were. The second memory was of a kid who refused to get into a teacher's car to be driven home. He was making quite a scene, screaming and hollering, refusing to get in the car and drawing the attention of a number of our neighbors. Many came over, some admitting later that they did so because they thought we were beating the child. They were amazed to discover that the child was throwing a fit because he did not want to go home; he wanted to stay at the Free School. One older black guy from the neighborhood came up to me, handed me a twenty dollar bill and said, "I thought you were just a hippie school, but you must be doing something right."

The third most memorable thing about that year was the fire department. One day we noticed a fire truck driving by with the firemen eyeing us. A few minutes later, someone came and said he was with the fire department. He told us we must shut down immediately. He offered no documentation, so I told him no, that we would not shut down. He departed. I will let the article, which was printed in the *NOLA Express* (an underground newspaper), written by James Mashburg, a close friend of ours, tell the story. The article is dated March 17, 1972.

NOLA Express 3/17/72

FREE SCHOOL

March came in like a lion for the Free School, as New Orleans officialdom nearly closed it down. At one point during the week the building was declared unfit for human habitation as a school. The school managed to keep going throughout most of the time and in fact only missed two days operation.

The first indication of trouble was the passing of a firetruck past the school at 2309 Chippewa on Monday, March 6. An hour later an inspector named Hughes came by. He told the school that bad news would be forthcoming from the fire department. Later Hughes returned with 2 men from the fire and health departments and inspected the school. They tried to give the school an order to shut down, without written reason, which from one from the school would accept.

24 hours later Hughes returned with another inspector and a police officer. He presented the school with a list of about 29 fire violations, tacked up the "unfit for human habitation" sign and told school officials to close the school.

That night teachers and parents met at the school. They decided not to have school the next day. A meeting was to be held the next day between school officials, with their attorney Lolis Elie and Charles Foti, city attorney and Mr. Fontaine, head of fire prevention.

The meeting was to reach some sort of compromise. Parents, teachers and friends of the school had worked for months trying to make the building and grounds safe for the children. They were, of course, ready to make further improvements. There were, however, basic differences. The fire department tended to label as discared materials and fire hazards many things that were school equipment. For example lumber and an old car had been ordered removed. Both lumber and car were used consistently by the children at the school. Lolis Elie acted not only as attorney but as something of an interpreter between the progressive and the bureaucratic and a compromise was reached. The school agreed to 1) build a wall and door to enclose a staircase between downstairs and upstairs 2) brick up open fireplaces 3) provide fire extinguishers 4) provide a fire bell 5) clean up yard.

Friday and Monday school was held in Audubon Park. This gave Fontaine time to approve the above work which was done on Thursday. There were additional minor things which were done. There has been something of an air of cooperation since the Wednesday meeting at the school between the school and the fire department. The school is open now and can be visited at 2309 Chippewa Street.

James Mashberg

43

I vividly remember, as fire marshals kept investigating the school, we needed to keep one of our commune members out of their sight. He was constantly high on Quaaludes and certainly would have further brought down the wrath of government if they had discovered him. High and drunk though he was, he was a dear friend and a true ally of all of us closely connected with the Free School. I am happy to report that with his parent's help, he sobered up and has remained sober all these years, raising a beautiful family, and having a very successful business career in New York City. I think he has even run in the New York marathon. As he used to say, "You know me— anything worth doing is worth overdoing."

Lolis Elie, the attorney Mashberg mentioned, was certainly the Free School's guardian angel. He was a prominent black attorney with close ties to the mayor of the New Orleans, Moon Landrieu. It is amazing how political support can help you or harm you. Instead of being run out of town like I was in Shreveport, the Free School and I were treated with respect and significance in New Orleans. Lolis also helped us get a few students the next school year and remained our friend for years. As the years have gone by, every time we run into each other, which is not often, he reminds me that he is on the board of the Free School. This is true, he was on the first, and only, board the Free School ever had. This board only existed for the first couple of years when the Free School started.

This experience with the fire and health department taught us that we needed a facility that met all fire and health regulations. We wanted to buy the Chippewa house and fix it up to code. Our landlord, a local attorney, offered us the facility for $25,000. We countered at $15,000. He went up to $27,000, we countered at $17,000. He went up to $29,000. Apparently, he thought we had come into money and would buy his facility at a higher price. Unbeknownst to him, we found a real estate agent and began a search for a new facility. After a two or three month search, we felt like we had hit a brick wall; we could find nothing. We were sitting at a local K&B drugstore counter, eating biscuits and drinking coffee, when our agent said that it was too bad we did not want the nursing home that was for sale. We said, "What nursing home?" It turns out that she had crossed off the property formerly used as a nursing home because it did not appear to have a large enough yard, which was one of our significant requirements. She immediately took us to the nursing home, not far away on Bordeaux Street.

We were amazed with what we found: a structure that had been available all these long and frustrating months, including a raised house, plantation style, with a large attic upstairs, and two outside buildings. One was a large two-story, four-room building with a bathroom on each floor. The other building was much smaller with two rooms, one being a laundry room. The yard space was small but adequate for our needs at the time. Inside the two main buildings were tiled floors and ceiling fans. The structure had a sprinkler system throughout and an industrial stove, dishwasher, and refrigerator. We knew instantly that we had found the facility for the Free School. We bought the building for $25,000. A parent and I signed the note. We moved the commune over there, and the commune paid the note so that the Free School could continue rent free.

It turns out that this building, previous to our ownership, housed the black branch of the New Orleans Home for the Incurables. The reasons the building was in impeccable shape, and code compliant, was that the Home for the Incurables tried to make it "separate but equal" to the main facility, located on Henry Clay Avenue. After "separate but equal" was ruled unconstitutional and segregation had to come to an end, they simply moved the black patients to the main facility and left everything at the Bordeaux structure intact, including the hospital beds, window units and, most importantly, a working fire sprinkling system, which meant no more problems from the fire department.

We found the perfect building, bought it, relocated in just one week, and started our second full year of schooling. It was now September 1972. The first year at Bordeaux Street was very similar to our time on Chippewa Street—lot of play, extreme high energy, continuous efforts at conflict resolution, great strides in defining and refining our educational practices, and the further building of a strong school and cultural community.

One last side story about this building—in its history, it was once a black honky tonk known as The Green Lizard. Apparently, it was a very hoppin' place and, according to lore, a house of ill repute.

Shortly after moving to Bordeaux Street someone approached us about having Professor Longhair play at the Free School for a fund-raiser. Always desperate for money, we quickly accepted, though at the time I did not know who Professor Longhair was. I quickly found out that he was a fantastic piano player whose music packed the house with everyone jumping and shouting. I stood outside and watched as our porch floor went up and down.

At some point that evening, one of the promoters of the event came to me and said that they wanted a bigger percentage from the sale of each ticket since far more people were coming to this concert than anyone had imagined. I politely told him that we had a deal and we were sticking to it. I am not sure but I believe that this man was Quint Davis, who became the CEO of Festivals Productions, Inc. New Orleans, and the producer and director ot the New Orleans Jazz and Heritage Festival. It's a good thing that I did not try to go into the music business in New Orleans.

Two things happened in that 1972–73 school year that proved monumental in enabling the Free School to thrive until maturity. First, we hired Jeanette, and second, in 1972, we started conversations with the Superintendent of Orleans Parish Schools, Dr. Gene Geisert, to become a public school. We became a public school in August 1973.

5

Jeanette

When we moved to Bordeaux Street, Jeanette was one of the first people in the neighborhood to register her three school-age children at the Free School. Jeanette, in her early to mid-twenties and the single mother of five children (Michelle, Trina, Wayne, Stevie, and Ray), proved to be very instrumental in getting the school ready in the short time from our move into the building to opening our doors for school that September 1972. She was young, black, intelligent, and high energy. She was just what the doctor ordered. Jeanette told us that she had a high school diploma, so we hired her as a teacher. In those days we were not concerned with credentials or certification. After all, we just opened our doors one day and said, "We are a school!"

Jeanette's previous employment was as a cashier at a nearby neighborhood grocery story. Just like that, she became a teacher. Her pay scale remained pretty much the same, from a minimum-wage earning grocery store cashier to a teacher, both paying a subsistence wage. While Jeanette wasn't making any more money, her professional status changed radically. She not only was a teacher at the Free School, she quickly earned the respect and a reputation as an excellent and highly effective teacher. Overnight, she became a creator and builder of the Free School.

Now, stories about Jeanette are so numerous that she should write her own book, so I will just describe some of the more memorable moments. First, I should state that we became fast friends, deeply committed to making the Free School all that it could be, and we never ceased fighting, bickering, or loving one another the entire forty years we have known one another.

You must understand that Jeanette was very poor and a single mother raising five children and, as we learned later, she did not have a high school diploma, as we'd thought. She was able to teach at the Free School because she was also able to bring her two youngest children to school each day, who were treated just like they were students at the school. I can remember to this day, her son Stevie running up to us every time we went on a field trip, or anywhere for that matter, shouting, "Me too, me too!"

Sue and I spent almost every Sunday afternoon eating dinner with Jeanette and her kids. Jeanette was an excellent cook and there was no way we were going to miss one of those Sunday meals. Over the years Sue would get agitated with me whenever I would call Jeanette and invite ourselves over to dinner at her place. I still do it today, though not as often. Anyway, when we were not at Jeanette's, she and her kids were with us in our attic living space at the Free School. We always drank too much, laughed too loud, and had the best of times; we would not have it any other way. We also played a lot of Scrabble, but no matter who was winning, the losing person would knock over the board, never to finish a game.

I need to reiterate that from day one Jeanette demonstrated her teaching and leadership abilities. The students, parents, and faculty loved and respected her. She was, and is, the Free School. But, Jeanette and I had our moments, particularly in the first few years. It seemed that almost every other day Jeanette would get mad at me over something and then tell her kids to get their things; they were going home. It happened so often that I started telling her kids to get their things before Jeanette and I got good into the argument.

Her other thing was the bathroom. Whenever one of her own kids misbehaved or got in trouble, primarily one of her boys, she would tell him to "go to the bathroom." She was taking him in there to give him a whipping. I would jump in and tell her she could not do that. Jeanette would say, "That's the way 'we' do it." I said, "Not here!" She said, "Here!" I think she managed to get her misbehaving child in the bathroom sometimes, but not always, and this would often lead to one of those, "Kids, get your things." Thank God Jeanette never left, and those many spats only brought us closer and closer.

There will be much more to say about Jeanette as this tale unfolds. Let me end this section by simply saying that she got her GED, in three years graduated cum laude from college, taught for Teach for America during two or three summers, and had some of the highest eighth grade high-stakes testing math LEAP (Louisiana Educational Assessment Program) scores in the City of New Orleans.

6

The Free School Becomes Public

Now let me move to the second major event that occurred during that first year on Bordeaux Street: The discussion and actualization of becoming a public school in the Orleans Parish School Board (OPSB) system of public schools. Let me say from the start, the Free School would not have survived its many years had it not been for the funds provided to the school through the system. It was just too much work for us to be full-time fund-raisers and educators. The money we raised was never close to the funding provided by the school system, nor was there any guarantee that we could continue to raise enough money to keep the school alive even though we spent very little. Some few parents made a voluntary monthly donation to help out. We did not want to charge tuition because we did not want to exclude anyone due to monetary issues. We had tax-exempt status because we could clearly demonstrate an integrated community with an obvious non-discriminatory policy. Ultimately, the school system's financial support with bureaucratic control that came with it proved to be the drowning pool we initially feared. Over the years we kept the little school afloat, however each storm the Free School endured from bureaucratic control chipped away our program and the constant frontal attacks of proposed closings of the Free School did their damage.

Let me not get ahead of myself; let's return to the discussion and actualization of becoming a public school. During this 1972–1973 period, there was a local educational activist group called the Innovative Education Coalition, headed by a young man named Graham Wisner. He was a friend of Dr. Gene Geisert, who was superintendent of the Orleans Parish Schools. Graham approached us about becoming a public school while stating that the superintendent really wanted to liberalize the school system. He had a number of open classrooms and wanted a more radical approach to counter the educationally conservative schools that dominated the school system.

We definitely wanted to be a public school to demonstrate unquestionably that you could do education in an urban setting differently from how the traditional school was structured. At that same time, we were very concerned that joining the system would end our freedom and destroy our program. The school, while less than two years old, was already gaining the reputation of being far out on the traditional educational spectrum, but something worth considering for parents and the public sector, in particular. But in becoming part of the school system, we wanted to maintain our autonomy, like present day charter schools enjoy.

Graham and Superintendent Geisert kept assuring us that their only goal was to open up the school system to new ideas, and that they did not intend to destroy our school. The superintendent gave us a copy of the rules and regulations of the OPSB and told us to go through and see which regulations we wanted to be exempt from. The book was huge and intimidating. We thought for sure that this was the end of the negotiations. After much scrutiny of the book, to our surprise, we only desired to be exempt from a few things: dress code, grades, standardized testing, field, trips and transfer policies.

We presented to Dr. Geisert an eight-page proposal including a $26,000 budget. This was our first concession in becoming a public school. Teachers would be receiving teacher salaries and aides would be receiving aide salaries, comparable to those working in the public schools. Pooling of money for salaries as we practiced in the Free School would no longer be required but some of us pooled nevertheless. Jeanette and I were hired as the aides. Dr. Geisert immediately accepted the proposal and said he needed the name of our leader so that he could present the proposal to the school board. We received that request like getting hit with a sledgehammer. Our group had been very careful not to have one leader. We shared money, power, and all decisions up to this moment. All of us realized that we had already agreed to dissolve our pooled money practice and we were now being requested to abandon our shared power structure. We refused to give him a leader. After some discussion, we could not reach an agreement and stood up to leave. Dr. Geisert threw up his hands and said, "Come on, just give me a name. I don't care if that person is the leader or not." Someone from our group said, "Martha Howden." Martha was a parent of three children in the school and a teacher at the Free School. I believe she had her Louisiana teaching certificate. In essence, she was the perfect person to name. Martha quickly agreed, and gave Dr. Geisert her name. The meeting ended. Our proposal was going to the board.

The one major hurdle we encountered in our attempt to get Board approval was getting the support of the area superintendent, Dr. Everett Williams. Dr. Geisert instructed us to work through Dr. Williams to get the proposal to the board. After two or three months of not being able to get Dr. Williams to move on the proposal, we went over his head straight back to the superintendent, Dr. Geisert. As I stated above, he was willing to meet with us and eagerly pushed the proposal through.

Our going over Dr. Williams' head was not motivated by any animosity toward him; it was motivated by our need to get our proposal approved as the school year was rapidly approaching. We were told that "personal reasons" prevented Dr. Williams from helping us in an expeditious manner. I do not know for sure that we made an enemy of him, but we most definitely earned the unintended reputation of not being team players—the absolute kiss of death in a bureacratic institution. Our battles began and we may have inadvertently, and certainly unknowingly, thrown the first punch in our numerous survival struggles with the administration.

In August 1973 the Orleans Parish School Board approved the adoption of the New Orleans Free School into the system as a satellite school connected with McDonogh No. 15, an existing creative elementary school in the district. We were to be an independent entity while reporting all data through McDonogh No. 15. However, the principal of this school was responsible for our teacher evaluation. We were now a public school.

Our first year with the system went flawlessly except for one incident that I caused and then inflamed. In March 1974, toward the end of our first year as a public school, I engaged in a minor conflict where I, again, sent the message that the Free School and I were not team players. A man in the school system, whom I had never met, sent me an evaluation form to fill out. I found the form to be incredibly insensitive and completely irrelevant to my teaching position at the Free School. It was concerned more with dress and emotions than with education. The teacher-aide evaluation form covered issues such as the following: "The type of grooming which reflects neatness, attractiveness, and appropriateness of attire…Posture and bearing which gives evidence of energy and vitality in daily responsibilities…The degree to which this person exhibits social adjustment and control of his or her emotion." I wrote the following words on the form and sent it to him: "This form is ridiculously impersonal. One of the major ideas of the Free School is to personalize living. If someone wants to know who I am or what I am like, then they can come work with me or have me over for dinner."

I learned from another source that this man took my comments as sarcasm. I wrote him a letter clarifying that sarcasm had no purpose in my note and that I was just trying to emphasize that the evaluation form had absolutely no relevance to my work at the Free School.

While I never received a reply from the man, I did find in my files a written comment made by him to our satellite principal, stating, "Would you please 'play the game,' as Mr. Ferris puts it. If I had to 'play the game' like this with all aides, etc. I don't believe I'd get past the first quarter." For him, along with most bureaucrats connected to the school system, the system was more about compliance, forms, and making the system work than about education.

Many in the school system performed their jobs well. The nature of a bureaucratic school system, however, emphasized efficiency and compliance over teaching and learning. It was believed that if the system would work, then schools would work and kids would be properly educated. Nothing could be further from the truth. It is not surprising that my argument for personalization fell on deaf ears and all that mattered was getting the forms filled out in a timely manner. Nothing came of the incident, but little did I know that I was poking holes in the side of the monstrous ship, slowly but surely, turning its bow directly towards us.

I took the 1974–1975 school year off and toured the country, visiting all types of public and private schools, and especially free schools. I took Jeanette, one of her kids, and another student with me on the first half of the trip. Jeanette made it as far as Los Angeles and then demanded to be flown home. She was with me to witness the accidental death of a student at one school, she was offered marijuana by a ten-year old at another school, and had to sleep in a mud home with a large Dixie flag. She was homesick and wanted to go back to New Orleans and the Free School. Jeanette was never a hippie. While she was fascinated with us, this more in-depth counter culture experience was too much for her. One interesting incident happened in Taos, New Mexico. We were in a restaurant/bar one evening when we suddenly heard a loud scream from across the room and saw a man come running towards us. He was quite possibly the only other black person in Taos and was overjoyed at the sight of Jeanette.

Sue and two other students joined me in San Francisco to continue the journey. While I was influenced by much of what I saw and I learned many new things in visiting so many different types of schools, I was most impressed with one school where a teacher was teaching folk dancing to the students. I said to myself, "I love to dance, I can do that." I went back to New Orleans, went to the Jazz and Heritage Festival, found the NORD (New Orleans Recreation Department) folk dancers who were headed by Pat Jessie, joined the group, and the next year started teaching folk dancing at the Free School. I ended up having fifty to seventy students each year performing folk dance at the Jazz and Heritage Festival. Our Jazz Fest performances progressed yearly to include our sixth-grade teacher Woody Penouilh's student band, and Jeanette's sign language and tap dance performing groups. In the last few years of the school, we had about 130 performers who participated in one or more of the activities. Students even started choreographing their own dance routines. This means that we had one out of every three students voluntarily performing at the Jazz Fest. The performances were so moving that they often elicited tears from many in the audiences.

Two other events during my year of travels also greatly influenced the Free School. Toward end of the school year one of the teachers had an incident with one of the students that made the teacher want to transfer schools. Also, Ann, one of the original founders and our last remaining initial teacher, seemed to be burned out. When I returned from my travels, she seemed very upset most of the time. I forced her out, though I'll never know if it was the right decision. We lost two excellent people and learned early on that turnover would always be a problem threatening our stability. We had three major growth spurts that required new teachers each time, and we inevitably would lose one or two teachers each year. Then in 1990 we started hiring Teach for America teachers with great success, which greatly helped solve our teacher vacancy problem.

Even with the loss of the two important teachers, the years on Bordeaux Street, from 1972 through 1980, were some of the best years for the Free School; at least they were the most like what we had envisioned the Free School to be. It was a well-integrated school made up of low-to-middle-income students with a few students coming from wealthier families. It was small: we never got above fifty-five students and we had created a strong educational plan that seemed to work well with the students, though we were far from one hundred percent successful.

During these eight years we were moving slightly away from the hippie radical school concept that anything goes, to a more organized school program that required students to attend classes that were individualized with little or no dependency on textbooks. Our small size and our low teacher to pupil ratio made this possible. Remember, even though some of us were hired as teacher-aides by the school system, we were full-fledged teachers carrying the same load as those who were hired as certified teachers.

It was at Bordeaux Street that we embedded the arts into our school curriculum through our sign-up program. Monday mornings each teacher offered a class or an experience he or she wanted to provide the students. Students then signed up for the class that most appealed to them and attended that class for the remainder of the week, usually the final period of the day. Thus, when teachers prepared an activity, they were assured students would attend. This worked well when teachers prepared properly. The more popular classes over the years were folk dancing, sign language, band, tap dancing, perspective art, photography, brain teasers, drama activities, creating a haunted house, movies, juggling, school newspaper, and most sport activities, particularly volleyball and four square. I even had students sign up for jogging when I was a jogger—you know, when I had legs and knees that could move and not hurt. A few even ran with me in the Crescent City Classic, a 6.2 mile local race that drew thousands of runners and walkers.

Over the years, as I mention before, we performed a number of plays such as *Ten Little Indians* and *Trojan Women*. Because of the large crowds that these plays attracted, we usually had to perform them for two nights in local churches or some public domain. One year, at the Community Arts Center, we performed Shakespeare's *A Midsummer Night's Dream*. Jeanette played the jackass—ah, my life has meaning!

We put on a solar fair a couple of years, demonstrating a variety of ways to use solar energy. I think we baked cookies, cooked hot dogs and hamburgers, but we were not successful cooking a roast. We built a solar green house and attached it to a window in a little alcove in the main building, growing plants there for a number of years.

Reading was always a part of the Free School. Our library was filled with books, a dining room-like table, and a couch. We wanted to make sure reading was enjoyable, not an arduous task. Sue painted a mural in the room with the words of Kahil Gabran's *The Prophet* from the section titled "On Education." This reading room was called "The Quiet Room" and even students enforced the quiet rule. Some students read books above their age level, others read not as well, and some truly struggled with mastering reading. Regardless, each student had a teacher who encouraged them, taught them, inspired them—whatever was necessary.

Writing was also an integral part of the school day. It was incorporated in just about every lesson. Students wrote plays, stories, diaries, poems and incorporated writing with much art, math and science work. Writing, reading, science study and discovery, math computation and complexes were viewed as an extension of the child but also included teacher-presented lessons to present traditional school material. The goal was always to broaden the child's knowledge base and to introduce new concepts and ideas to the students. From early on, most teachers at the Free School shaped the education to the needs of the learner and helped the learner create new needs. I say most teachers because throughout our history we were not always able to hire teachers who had a passion for innovation and creativity. Many did but a few had no desire to be in an innovative environment. Some loved the Free School but were more traditional in their practice. We had some say in whom we hired but little say in whom we needed to let go. Fortunately, most teachers who had no love for the Free School did not stay long. They could not handle the freedom, even what was left of it as the years went by, so few of them lasted more than one year. We did have one teacher transferred to another school, but we had to go through the area office and the teachers' union. Both groups were helpful and supportive in this endeavor. I am excited about charter schools having a major say over who works at the school; I am somewhat ambivalent about teachers' rights under this arrangement. I do know that our school would have been a much better place had we had much more say over the hiring and firing of our staff.

Textbooks were rarely used in early Free School history, except by those students who actually requested them. As time went on, textbooks became more and more of the lesson format for math and English for all of our students. Standardized tests forced this on us. However, textbooks rarely dominated the social studies and science classes. We were able to keep these classes more open-ended, project-based, and closer to the Free School philosophy. I hate to see science and social studies become part of the high-stakes testing frenzy; we have way too much "teaching to the tests" already. I will get to the subject of tests at the end of this book.

The whole school camping trips were a major part of the Free School in those years from 1972 to 1980. Not only were they fun and a good team-building experience for staff and students, they were part of the educational experience, as well. One experience provided a teachable moment we had not planned. When I drove a group of students to the mountains in Arkansas, I was pulled over by a cop in Tallulah, Louisiana. This was the city I had helped monitor the election where a black sheriff had been elected for the first time. When the cop recognized me and I recognized him, we both started laughing. He admitted that he was instructed to pull over anyone in a Volkswagen van—apparently anti-hippie sentiment was hard to kill. Anyway, the kids were fascinated by the experience and loved that I was friends with the Tallulah police.

It was during these years, in fact on June 11, 1974, that Sue and I had our first baby, Mika. Sue had a very difficult labor and we had to rush her from the midwife's home to Charity Hospital. I remember crossing the Mississippi River Bridge with Sue screaming and me thinking she would give birth in the car. When we arrived at Charity, someone rushed Sue and our midwife upstairs. Immediately thereafter, someone else took me upstairs as well. I saw my new baby boy and was told that Sue was fine. I cried like I was the baby.

A year or so after we had Mika, Sue became tired of living above the school, living in a commune and, thus, moved out taking Mika with her. We were not married so there was no issue of separation or divorce. However, shortly after her moving out, I went to her like a wounded puppy and begged her to let me move in with her and Mika at her Arabella Street apartment. Thankfully, she agreed and we continued living together.

It was also during these years that Sue convinced me that I needed to get teacher certification if I was to stay teaching at the Free School and to help the Free School continue on its educational journey under the OPSB. By then I had received my Masters in Alternative Education from the University of Indiana but had no undergraduate education courses, nor had I ever done student teaching. I needed to go before the State Board of Education to get courses and student teaching waived. I went before the board shortly after they had passed the requirement that a person must pass the National Teachers' Exam (NTE) before achieving certification. The board had taken much flack over this requirement because many felt that it was a tactic to prevent minorities from obtaining certification. On the day I went to Baton Rouge to appear before this board, I was terribly sick with the flu. I went anyway because it had been difficult to schedule this meeting to obtain the waivers I needed. I could not miss this opportunity. I sat at this board meeting from the early morning hours to the very late afternoon hours. Sick though I was, I spent some of the time preparing my presentation. When I was finally called up, one of the board members said something like this: "This man is from New Orleans and says that he will take our tests. I say if he passes this test, give him what he wants." All the board members agreed with him, and I was granted the waivers if I passed the NTE. I now just needed to pass the NTE. I took the test and then waited for my results. I received them one morning while at school. When I looked at the score, I saw I had not passed. I actually called the testing agency and they informed me that the score was correct and there was nothing they could do about it. I was crushed. My dream of being a life-long educator was over. That became one of the loneliest and most frustrating days of my life. I was a defeated human being. Then, around 3:15 that afternoon, I received a phone call from the testing agency informing me that the score I had told them I had received was only part of the score. When added to the other part of my score, I passed the tests. If I didn't believe in miracles before getting this phone call, I did now.

In the spring of 1978 Sue and I were married in a hippie wedding in Audubon Park attended by Mika (now almost five) and a few friends, officiated by our friend, Dave Wells, who had a minister's license with the state. Then in 1979, Sue and I had our second child, our beautiful daughter Iyana. We recently had bought our first house, a small shotgun single on Jeannette Street where Iyana was born on our dining room table in our kitchen, delivered by the same midwife who had assisted Mika's birth. Iyana still has the table to this day. When she popped out of Sue's body and heard Mika's voice, she immediately became wide-eyed, trying to focus on him.

I tell you these stories because the Free School was, in so many ways, home to our students and our own kids, Jeanette's kids, Martha's kids, and many other teachers' kids. A lot of parents became our very good friends and many are still our close friends. But, this very closeness shattered the Free School and changed it forever. A student, an older black girl, got mad at our most prominent parent-volunteer, and hit her son, a younger white student, at the Free School, in the face in an extremely hostile and forceful manner.

The son's parents were as much a part of the Free School as I, Jeanette, or anyone else was, and they had co-signed the loan for the building. They were now demanding that the girl be expelled. This was at a time when the Free School was functioning really well. We had a well-integrated, small student population with students involved in all types of projects and activities. We had discipline problems but never of such a serious nature. This incident started tearing us apart.

We had meetings over this issue night after night. The parents who were demanding expulsion were very calm but consistent in their demand. They never raised the race issue and they even could deal with the violence issue. It was the revenge factor that they were most concerned with. If a student was mad at a teacher, parent, volunteer, or anyone, and they took out their anger on the adult's child, especially in such a violent manner, then that student had to go. They agreed that this was not the only violent action that had occurred at the Free School, but the revenge factor, and the violent nature of the action, crossed a line that we should never tolerate. The girl never denied hitting the child and doing it because she was mad at the mother.

In the end, the other parents, faculty, and I decided that a week's suspension was a sufficient penalty. We were still young, naive, idealistic, and thought that we could save the world. The parents of the boy disagreed and took their child out of the school. This left us in a very awkward situation: What to do about the next school year in that building. We had a lease with the school board for that year, but not for the next. To their credit, the parents of the boy never threatened to not allow the school to use the building—this issue was never brought up to my recollection.

I met with the area superintendent, Dr. Norwood Roussell, whom I only slightly knew. I explained the situation to him. He immediately had the girl transferred to another school and suggested that we look at a building at 3601 Camp Street that had a vacant third floor. We did this, and immediately fell in love with the building, even though that floor was trashed, with holes in the wall and flaking paint. The building was three floors tall with the ground level floor called the basement. This basement housed one classroom, a small cafeteria, two small rooms, large separate bathrooms, and a large open area with a stage. We had outgrown Bordeaux Street, and had already considered the possibility of moving, even though that building worked well for our now, slightly crowded, fifty-five students. The incident over expelling the girl and the availability of space which was fairly near the Bordeaux Street school clinched the move. We moved to 3601 Camp St. the summer of 1980.

The school system moved our furniture and supplies to the new building but offered little other support. The building was in incredible disarray. Trash was everywhere and on the third floor peeling paint predominated. The second floor was supposed to continue as a school for "push out" and "drop out" high school students. Thus, we were to use only the third floor and share the basement floor with the other school.

At the last second, the school system did not allow the school for drop outs to be in the building. Apparently, this was a good move, because reportedly there had been a number of serious fights in the school in the previous years, and on more than one occasion students had started fires in the building. This was not the kind of school environment to share with an elementary school. Instead, the system placed a small school for special education students on the second floor. The system was closing that school at the end of the school year. The things I remember most about that school were that we got along well with each other and I made a life-long friend, the principal, Mike Lynch.

To get that third floor ready for the school year, I paid a friend to paint the large hall while teachers, parents, and I painted several of the classrooms. The school system supplied the paint. This third floor had six classrooms, a small office with a bathroom and a large hall. It had very tall ceilings and large windows in every room. There was no air conditioning or ceiling fans, but we loved it.

But, again, let me not get ahead of myself. What about the building on Bordeaux Street that we had also loved very much? While we were not enemies with the parents who had cosigned for the building, there was tension. I remember when a group of us moved a piano out of the building—not an easy task—and were about to put it in the home of one of our other parents. The co-signing parents said, "Wait a minute, this piano belongs to us!" Well, cooler heads prevailed and we gave them the piano, even placing it back in the school building. The mother had been the school's music teacher and it seemed only appropriate, whether the piano was theirs or not, to give it to them.

When we bought that building, we all had agreed that if we ever sold it, we would somehow share the profit. Since the building was no longer used as the Free School, I insisted that we sell the building. The father called me and asked how much I wanted for my half. I told him I had to honor our commitment to somehow share in the sale of the building. He said, "How much?" I found out how much the building would probably sell for and asked for half. They would have to pay off the note, but they were still getting the building for a very good price. I then divided my half with the parties who had been most involved with creating the Free School. The money was divided proportionately according to years involved, effort put in, and other factors.

To this day I believe we did the right thing when we sold the building, but I have never convinced myself that we made the right decision in not expelling the girl. We were just still too darn idealistic and did not want to give up on any student. We quickly learned, in our new public school building, that while we were good, we were not miracle workers. The school had morphed over the years into a creative urban school fighting the bureaucratic system and educating primarily poor, black, urban youth. Once we moved to Camp Street, the change and the bureaucratic experience began.

7

The Principal Position and Superintendent Charles Martin

Our first year on the third floor at Camp Street, 1980–1981, proved incredibly difficult. Our enrollment increased from fifty-five students to ninety students, so we had to increase our staffing. It was necessary but difficult adjusting to having student bathrooms in the basement while the school operated on the top floor. The biggest adjustment, though, was to the new reality. Our little oasis school had instantly become urban, locked in an engulfing tide of bureaucracy. The never ending bureaucratic attacks started that year.

Things were difficult the first couple of months. On September 4, 1980, Dr. Roussell, our area superintendent at the time, ordered Ellen Peckman, head of the testing department, to test our students with the CTBS (California Test of Basic Skills). Ironically, a year earlier, she had called me and wanted to know if I wanted to give our students the CTBS. I told her, "No. We are not interested." She jokingly replied, "Thanks, you know how to make a person feel good."

Now, we were ordered to give the test and there was nothing we could do about it. The slow but painful dissolution of our program had begun. I disagreed with the idea of standardized testing then and I detest it even more now that we have made the tests high-stakes. The first time our students took the tests they scored at the very bottom of the nation, even our very brightest students. I knew this couldn't be a true evaluation of their abilities, and I immediately suspected institutional sabotage. Apparently, Dr. Peckman noticed some major irregularities with the tests, and she quickly invalidated all of our students' tests although she never informed us what those irregularities were. I was amazed at her honesty, but I never found out what caused the problem—human error, machine error, or human malice.

The second time our students took the tests, this time with the entire school system, they did very well. Over the years, our school has performed fairly well on these tests when compared with other Orleans Parish schools. Some teachers in our school almost always had above average test scores among their students, even occasionally scoring higher than the state average for that grade. I always hoped our test scores would remain just above the Orleans Parish average so that the administration would leave us alone and that we would demonstrate that our program was beneficial. Even though the scores were there, this strategy never worked—the system never left us alone.

Testing was not our only problem that first year on Camp Street. We were struggling to get use to our much larger enrollment, our much larger faculty, and our very large school building. Inevitably, things quickly got worse. I do not know if the initial poor test results, which had been quickly invalidated, had initiated a look at our program or if it had just happened by chance, but a couple of months later, in December 1980, our satellite principal visited the school for two or three days. She then wrote a twelve-page report on her observations, condemning just about every aspect of the Free School. In her report, she pitted faculty members against faculty members, attacked some of our personalities, attacked our expectations of children, the quality of work produced by our children, the behavior, or lack thereof, by many of the students, the quality of our teaching, and more.

Dr. Roussell called me to discuss this report and asked why I had not responded. I told him that many things the satellite principal said were correct. For example, it was true we were having a difficult time adjusting to our increased student population and faculty, and to our new building, which was not conducive to allowing children freedom to walk around. The yard and the student bathrooms were two stories below the classrooms, which certainly aggravated this situation. I also told him that we found the document much too vindictive to respond to and much too personal to be objective. As one teacher said, "I find it hard to believe that anyone can spend three days here and not see one positive thing to comment on or record." This made a response seem useless. But, I also told him that we were struggling to make things function the way we wanted and had already scheduled a consultant to meet with us in January and present to us a non-textbook structured approach that truly allowed reading, writing, social studies, and science to occur in a school in a very organized, but open-ended manner.

Dr. Roussell requested that I put in writing what the Free School was and what it was all about. I responded in a succinct manner, but he insisted on a more formal definition of "Free School." I think he wanted a very academic definition, which I was hard pressed to write because the Free School was a personal institution and was truly an extension of ourselves. His written request was very bureaucratic and professional in nature. My response was very personal. I did not know how to mix the two.

In retrospect, I think the satellite principal's critique of our program did much good. We successfully made some changes that were in the works before her visit, continued adjusting to the new building, and quickly made sure that the next person who entered our building could not accuse us of poor quality work from our students and teachers.

By the end of the year, we had corrected many of our problems by adding the "Success for Reading and Writing" program. We learned how to somewhat control movement of the students, replaced a staff member who was hired at the beginning of that year and was very critical of the school, and hired a new staff member, Jim Charbonnet, as her replacement. Jim was one of the original parents of the Free School and was considered a superior educator by many of his peers. Included in his long list of achievements was his Harvard education. He loved the school. The other teacher's exit and his swift entrance quickly dissipated the tension that had built up the first four months of the school year. These changes enabled us to have a much more pleasant and successful second half of the year.

In the spring of 1981 we began to hear rumors that the system was placing the Montessori School in our building. A supervisor from the system, whom I will call "Ralph" (fictitious name) came to inform me that the Montessori School wanted to move into the building with us and demanded that I support the move. He insisted that I say that I wanted the Montessori School placed in our building, in a way I found obnoxious. Quoting from a letter I wrote to Dr. Sam Scarnato, Deputy Superintendent, on April 2, 1981:

> Ralph repeatedly asked me if I would support them coming into the building. I continually answered that we would like to use the entire building, but I also assured him that we would be most cordial and cooperative to any group placed in the building. I also said that if they were placed in the building, that we really needed the seven classrooms we are presently using plus one additional classroom. Anything less would curtail the type of program we offer. If this were agreeable, it would leave us with eight classrooms for approximately 160 students and leave the Montessori group with four classrooms for their 80 students; this based on the Ralph's statement that over the next year or two they would be bringing in 80 students. We definitely use the entire basement, but would certainly be willing to share it on a proportioned basis.

Continuing in the letter, I then informed Dr. Scarnato that neighbors had received letters stating that the Montessori School was definitely moving in.

Dr. Scarnato called a meeting with Ralph, Dr. Roussell and me. Before Dr. Roussell arrived at the meeting, I met with Dr. Scarnato and Ralph to discuss putting the Montessori program in our building. I got my one jab in, stating that I had no trouble with the Montessori program sharing the building with us, but that we would appreciate being involved and informed of all decisions. The neighbors had all received a letter confirming that the program was coming in—we were not sent a letter. Ralph said there was no need to send us a letter because we already knew through his and my conversation. I said no, that he had only told me that they definitely wanted the space. No one had ever confirmed it.

Dr. Scarnato cut the conversation short by asking which space each program needed. Ralph began the conversation by granting us the two rooms on the second floor. We were to remain on the third floor, but maintain two classrooms on the second floor, which was to house the Montessori School. Our students were to use only the front stairwell; the Montessori School was to use the middle stairwell. Dr. Scarnato took out a floor plan of the building and marked whose room was whose. The conversation ended with Ralph reversing himself, once again trying to get those two rooms on the second floor from us, but Dr. Scarnato firmly stated that we had already agreed on the classroom space and to move on. At this point Dr. Roussell arrived and, to my surprise, Dr. Scarnato dismissed Ralph—boy was I relieved. I remember thinking, "He doesn't trust him any more than I do."

I knew I was in trouble when Dr. Scarnato began our three-person meeting with the words, "You know, there are some people who do not think that we should be in this business" (meaning the Free School). I replied that I was aware of that, but I felt that they were very prejudiced and that we had an excellent program. He asked me what I thought of putting a principal there. This was the first time I was presented with the idea and did not hear it again until the summer, when rumors started circulating that a principal was to be placed over the Free School and the Montessori School. I told him that it was fine if that person was me. It wouldn't work otherwise. We briefly discussed what I lacked in credentials to be a principal. I also told him we were willing to allow anyone to look at our program, study it, evaluate it, whatever; but, please don't let it be someone connected to our satellite principal or her friend, Ralph. We felt that we deserved a fair, unbiased opinion. Dr. Scarnato made no reply to the suggestion.

During the course of the conversation, Dr. Roussell mentioned that I didn't handle criticism very well; for example, when I objected to the remarks of a principal sent by him to look at the school. This principal was also friends with our satellite principal. I explained to Dr. Scarnato and Dr. Roussell that this principal came on a day when some classes had been dismissed because of play rehearsal, and we had to move junk from the basement, which the school board had failed to move. It was two days before the Christmas holidays and the Christmas performances were that night.

When the principal talked to me alone upstairs, he started making sweeping generalizations about our school, which I told him were completely unfounded and I didn't appreciate him making such a broad critical evaluation on so little or no evidence. His critique went something like this: He saw no evidence of learning, he saw little or no Christmas spirit, and the strong ruled over and bullied the weak. I felt that he was just parroting what the satellite principal had told him about the school, especially since he was close friends with the satellite principal. He even went to the same teacher who had sided with the satellite principal and told her that he would never put his kids in our school. She, of course, was looking for support since she had taken her kids out of our school only two or three weeks earlier.

I went on with my explanation. When the principal returned after Christmas and repeated his criticisms, I did not want to deal with him. Before I refused to answer any of his questions, I told him that one of our parents had been by to visit his school the last day before the Christmas holidays and one class was so loud that this parent was sure it had to be disturbing the class right next to it. He told me that he did not care what my parent thought of his school. I told him very calmly that he should. He started asking me questions about our school, which I refused to answer. He then started shouting at me. I interrupted his tirade by simply saying, not loudly but forcefully, that I did not know who he thought he was, but that he could not shout at me or try to scare me. He replied, "Then this conversation is over." I said. "Yes!" And, I left my office.

I told both Drs. Scarnato and Roussell that it amazed me how during both of these encounters this principal was so saccharin in dealing with me and the staff when we were all together, but then so bitter when dealing with me alone in my office.

After hearing much of my above defense, Dr. Scarnato was surprised and he asked Dr. Roussell in my presence, "You mean the principal went there?" Dr. Roussell replied, "Yes, didn't I send you a copy of his letter, I'm sure I did. Now, he said that there was room or a need for this kind of school in the system. I'll have to get you a copy of his letter." Needless to say, no copy was ever offered or presented to me.

The meeting ended cordially. The process to absorb the Montessori School into our building was to begin. I always found Dr. Scarnato to be a very fair and honest person, whom I believed would always try to do the right thing. Dr. Roussell also treated me well and honestly. While I perceived that we were in for a difficult time, I felt that we might just get a fair hearing. Shortly thereafter, we were back under Dr. Everett Williams as our area superintendent and we had no further contact with Dr. Roussell. Dr. Williams was the area superintendent whom we were to work with to get our school accepted by the school board—the same area superintendent whose head we went over to reach Dr. Geisert, in order to push the proposal through.

Unbeknownst to us, Superintendent Dr. Gene Geisert left the system to be replaced by Dr. Charlie Martin, whom none of us had met. We were all so wrapped up in running our school that we literally knew nothing about system politics, hiring, firing or changes at the top. This would change.

I and some of our faculty met with the two teachers from the Montessori School and with Ralph. One of the teachers came on to us, parroting Ralph. She was making demands and telling us what she would accept and would not accept. Both of them argued that since neither school had a principal, the system had to place a principal over us. She also made it abundantly clear that she would not tolerate any turmoil in the building—I guess that she considered us to be a rowdy bunch. Our response to this teacher and Ralph was always friendly and welcoming. The teacher who had been in a huff finally calmed down and even encouraged me to get into the administrative pool to be considered for a principalship as quickly as possible. The other teacher, Jill Otis, who ultimately became the principal of the Montessori School, was initially accepting and willing to work together with us. Jill and I become strong colleagues and friends during our career with OPSB.

By the end of the 1980–1981 school year we had survived moving into our larger building, the significant increase in our student enrollment and faculty, the critique from the principal of our then-satellite school, and the initial struggle over our two classrooms with the incoming Montessori School. We now had a strong faculty, a very creative, open-ended reading, writing, English, social studies, and science instructional program, and our strong, creative sign-up classes. We thought "all's well that ends well." I do not know if our naiveté hurt us or helped us.

In the summer of 1981, rumors circulating that a principal was to be placed over the Free School became louder and more convincing. Our voice, our personalization, and our practices were in for electric shock treatment, if not execution. Needless to say, though not appreciated by our opponents, we would not abandon ship easily or quietly. Don Van Loo, a dear friend and parent at the Free School, described our struggles with the central office administration in the following paraphrased declaration: The central office thought they were going to run over slow-moving, dope-smoking, peace-loving hippies. What they never realized was that they were unleashing wild lions and tigers ready for battle. Don always had a way with words.

On July 18, 1981, I wrote the following letter to Dr. Charles Martin, Dr. Gene Geisert's replacement. I had never met the man and knew absolutely nothing about him. I just knew we must tackle this issue head on or have the flood waters of bureaucracy quickly appropriate our last breath. The rumors were now mammoth waves. Now, instead of fighting for co-operative leadership, which once almost prompted our not joining the Orleans Parish School System, we found ourselves fighting for the captain of our ship. Martha Howden had moved to Rochester, New York, many years earlier and I had taken over as spokesperson for the Free School.

I am including this letter to Dr. Martin in its entirety because it, along with many other such documents, so clearly and forcefully tells this tale while passionately defining and explaining what the Free School was all about.

Dr. Charles Martin
Superintendent
Orleans Parish Public Schools
4100 Touro
New Orleans, La.

Dear Dr. Martin,

I am writing to you because of a great injustice about to be forced on the New Orleans Free School community. An injustice which if not stopped now will end a beautiful and successful educational program. It seems that the powers to be, and I only heard of this through rumor, plan to place an outsider as "principal" of the New Orleans Free School. Sir, I have served as principal or director or whatever you want to call it of the New Orleans Free School for the past ten and a half years. I nor anyone else from our community was contacted or informed that such a decision was in process.

Dr. Martin, we gave birth to the New Orleans Free School, nursed it through infancy and raised it to adulthood. Now we will prematurely bury it rather than see it so defamed, so abused. There is no way we can allow so personal an experience to be so impersonally treated. We will struggle to save our school, but we will not allow this to happen.

I realize that you probably know little or nothing about the New Orleans Free School. This was so exemplified when I called your office for an appointment and your receptionist very politely asked, "Is the Free School affiliated with the Orleans Parish Schools?" Sir, I doubt that there is one person in the Central Office who has the slightest idea of what the New Orleans Free School is all about. This amazes me. You have in your own backyard one of the most unique educational experiments going on in the country and we are only looked at bureaucratically. Only one person, Dr. Ellen Pechman, has come to us out of curiosity and interest, to find out what we are all about.

Dr. Martin, I am now going to briefly explain to you what the Free School is all about. In this letter, I can give you just a few pebbles of sand on a beach of information. Unfortunately, brief words cannot capture the experience. I am going to quote to you at length from a letter I wrote to Dr. Roussell. It was your words which motivated me to write the letter. I felt that you were saying that your leadership was going to move Orleans Parish Public Schools to a more humanistic and relevant educational system even administratively. I did not complete nor send this letter to Dr. Roussell. I did not feel it was what he wanted. I think he wants a more marketable explanation in more scholarly terms. However, for me, the Free School is a very personal experience and I can only relate it as such. I am not criticizing Dr. Roussell; it is my inadequacy that I am unable to respond to his needs. Anyway, the letter:

> Dear Dr. Rousell,
>
> I have been motivated this morning to write to you a letter. I was motivated by reading Dr. Martin's statements in this morning's paper:
>> "We can hardly sit here and beat our chests and proclaim success in this school system. We have to make some changes that I think need to be made. We don't give enough flexibility to schools. The administration is too regulatory, and does not provide enough support (to individual schools). We have to move more control down to the school level."
>
> I am not writing you because of your lack of support. Sir, you have been excellent in this regards. Your concern and support certainly helped me and my staff to get through a very unfortunate experience. Nor am I seeking more autonomy. Your guidance, nudging, suggestions have always proved helpful. I am using Dr. Martin's

statements because they are what got me going. I feel that
this is an excellent direction for the school system to
be moving in.

I am writing you because of my frustration over what I
feel to be your frustration--i.e., why the Free School?
why does anyone, white or black, want to put their kids in
our school? why do they want to stay? why is the Free
School in a privileged class?

The Free School exists to offer a wealth of experiences
and an academic approach which challenges and feeds the
natural curiosity and organic nature of the human being.
Our program is not primarily an individualized programmed
approach whereby every student is learning the same thing
but at their own individual speed. Our program is a
highly structured approach which better allows for
individuality, creativeness, spontaneity. Each student
takes the direction in his or her way and hopefully
utilizes the instruction for their own personal growth
and development. Our approach does not eliminate textbooks or workbooks--they just become part of the whole
instead of all of the whole. In addition to our individualized but cooperative learning approach, our program
offers a wealth of in-depth experiences--art with our
artist-in-residence, pottery, improvisational theater,
photography, folk dancing, acting, travel, woodworking,
creative writing, leather, science experiments. These
are the kinds of experiences offered in the best of
schools--usually rich private schools where learning
is viewed as an enrichment experience. Give the student
a chance to breathe, to stand, to fall, to explore, to
experience, to conquer, to win, to lose, to question, to
think.

Our program also offers a more personal approach. We
have smaller class sizes because we prefer to put adults
in the classroom rather than in an office. We tie ourselves
to programs that can offer us top quality teachers at a
reduced rate. We gain--the teachers gain. We have always
been willing to do extra work so that our resources can
place more adults in the classroom. We also offer fairly
close contact with parents-- calling on them to help with
activities, requiring conferences when needed, inviting
them to social events to keep the community close. It
seems to me that in this age of single parenting and/or
both parents working there should occur a major revolution
in the schooling process which guarantees closeness and
personalness. If we want to have a healthy society we
must not sacrifice attention and care. The Free School
has a deep commitment to smallness and closeness.

Dr. Martin, there are a number of other relevant facts about the Free School which I should bring out.

Our student population is approximately 50% black and 50% white. We started off with 100 students last year; we would like to begin this year with somewhere around 140 students. We would not like to get much larger than this. As I've already stated smallness is a very important part of our program. Our students come from all over the city.

Our student body is made up of students who are incredibly bright academically, many who are average and some who are in great need academically. This is the first year we gave the CTBS test. We did this under pressure and also because we decided it would be another valuable learning experience for our students. From what I know about the test our students did fairly well. As I compare our scores for this year with scores of other schools from last year we are in the top 25% both for grades K-6 and 7-8th.

Dr. Martin, we have a school which is attracting people back into the public schools. We have a well-integrated school. We have a school where teachers love to teach. We have a school with high test scores. We have a school with a very supportive parent body. We have a school that children love.

I feel that we have been able to develop this school through my leadership though I would never claim sole responsibility. It has been a collective process. It makes no sense to disrupt our community or to hamper the many fine educational and creative experiences we offer to our students. I think that my leadership should be formally accepted; it has been accepted since the Free School joined the public school system in September, 1973.

Thank you very much for your time and consideration. If you have any questions or need more information, please do not hesitate to call me. (home phone 899-5311, school 899-0452).

Sincerely,

Robert M. Ferris

Robert M. Ferris

New Orleans Free School

Simultaneously, a group of our parents organized around this issue and set up a meeting with Dr. Martin. About thirty-five of our parents, both black and white (about half of the parent population) went to meet with the superintendent. Our large entourage sent shock waves through the system. I do not remember if Dr. Martin met with all thirty-five or a select few, but in that meeting, Dr. Martin assured our parents that no action would be taken on the Free School without Free School community input. He gave his word that he did not want to interfere with our program and that he would abide by the original agreement with OPSB's non-interference of the program. We were all greatly relieved.

Our relief was short-lived. On August 12, 1981, we received a memo from Dr. Everett Williams, stating that a principal would be chosen for the Free School/Montessori School, and that we were to elect one staff member to be on the nominating committee to recommend a candidate. We were to submit the name by August 17, 1981.

We chose not to comply. We knew compliance was our death knell. We did not submit a name. Instead, I drafted my second letter to Dr. Martin pleading with him not to disrupt our program, make me acting principal for one year, study our program during this year, and only then make more permanent decisions about the future of the Free School. Even if we were to win this battle, we had lost much decision-making power over our school.

A day or two later, Ralph, who had harassed us over the Montessori School, showed up at our door, told us he was acting principal, and started barking orders as to what we could and could not do. Since he had no documentation that he had been placed over our school, we ignored him and went about our business. He was mean in his dictates and condescending in his attitude toward us and kept repeating that he was in charge now and that we were just teachers. I heard he'd been saying we all left him in the building at the end of the day and he ended up in the school yard locked out of the building and had to climb over the school fence to leave. Anyway, he showed up about a week after his arrival with a memorandum from Dr. Scarnato which stated that he was the administrator in charge of the Free School during the duration of a possible teacher strike.

Ralph again started growling orders, and even accused one of our teachers of committing fraud because he came in ten minutes late but signed in for being on time. He kept telling us that we were just teachers, and that he was in charge. He demanded my keys to the school. I told him I would go across the street to Harry's Ace Hardware to get a set of keys made for him. He told me, "No, I want your keys now! You are just a teacher and no longer in charge." After some hesitation, I said: "This is what I am going to do. I am going to give you my keys and then I am going to get keys from all the staff and get my set made." I gave him my keys and we, the faculty, left and went to see Dr. Scarnato.

Dr. Scarnato met with us immediately, and we quickly explained to him how rude, demanding, and demeaning Ralph had been. There was no way we could work under his authority. Dr. Scarnato replied that we had all abandoned our jobs and would be fired if we did not immediately return to work. We were dumbfounded and silent. Then Jim Charbonnet said, "My God, man, Bob Ferris tells us that you are an incredibly decent man and we come to you for help in dealing with this tyrant and to preserve our school, and you threaten to fire us!" Silence again. Dr. Scarnato finally spoke and told us to go back to work, and that he would take care of it. We trusted him and went back to work. Ralph was nowhere to be seen.

In the meantime our parents continued to pressure Dr. Martin on behalf of the Free School. On September 1, 1981, our parents wrote Dr. Martin the following declaration. The original, which follows, is too faded to read.

September 1, 1981

Dr. Martin,

When we met with you this past July, you assured us that no action would be taken concerning the Free School without our input. In fact, you gave us your word. This commitment was not upheld. Something was done without our consultation whatsoever. Not even the decency of a phone call was made to inform us that an acting principal had been appointed. We feel betrayed.

We do not wish to war with you. We only want what is best for our children. We are shocked and dismayed that you have waited until the opening of school to attempt to force this decision on our community. We feel that this administrative action is completely irresponsible. We will not be bulldozed into accepting a decision just because school has opened.

We are disgusted that your administration can so use and abuse our children. What we want and expect is really very simple. We do not want the New Orleans Free School changed. We want Mr. Ferris to remain as chief administrator of the school.

We think that you should be proud of the Free School as part of the Orleans Parish School System.

Sincerely,

Parents & Staff of the Free School

Dr. Martin —

When we met with you ~~in~~ July, you assured us that no action would be taken concerning the Free School without our imput. In fact, you gave us your word. This committment was not upheld. Something was done without our consultation whatsoever. Not even the decency of a phonecall was made to inform us that an acting principal had been appointed. We feel betrayed.

We do not wish to war with you. We only want what is best for our children. We are shocked and dismayed that you have waited until the opening of school to attempt to force this decision on our community. We feel that this administrative action is completely irresponsible. We will not be bulldozed into accepting a decision just because school has opened.

We are disgusted that your administration can so use and abuse our children under its responsibility. What we want and expect is really very simple. We do not want the New Orleans Free School changed. We want Mr. Jerris to remain as chief administrator of the school.

We think that you should be proud of the Free School as part of the Orleans Parish School System.

Sincerely,

Parents & Staff of the
Free School

Claudia Newton Jurney
David Harold Jurney
James A. Charbonnet
Jamie C. Charbonnet
Adrienne Knighten
Ann C. White
Sandra Elkins
Charles Peters

Lisa S. Ray   U. J. Commuto

D. O.   M. Parker

R. W. Martin   Agate Lawson

Janette Boulet   Gwen Clement

[illegible]   _[illegible] Clement_

Alice E. Fort   Alice Rolfs

Bonnie Van Loo   Andrea Naundorf

Gail Taylor   Frank R. J. Arnold

Donna Myhre   Debra Johnson

Bill Mickles   Joyce M. Davis

Eddy Marshman   Mr. & Mrs. W. F. Shipman

Lesley Baker   Fred Clement

Lynette Jerry   _Mary [illegible]_

Elaine Johnson   Leander Roberts Sr.

Geo Simmons   June Roberts

Kate Simmons   Connie Taylor

Don Van Loo

Rhonda Ford

Sue Buser

Mrs Elizabeth Ann Ash

Mrs Norman Dalon

Mary Gonzales

LCDR John Ray

Mrs Betty Granger

Laura S. Kauffman

Sandra Gomaz

Somehow, in September, Dr. Martin had communicated to our community that he had removed Ralph as our "administrator in charge." He assured us that Ralph would have no say over our program and that he was forbidden to enter our building. Before this happened, sadly, Ralph had wreaked havoc on our program. He somehow found out that Jeanette was hired as a teacher's aide and not as a teacher. He went into her classroom, and in front of the students, told her that she could not be teaching because she was just a teacher's aide and to get out. I found Jeanette in the hall crying. I do not remember how we got through that day, or the days immediately thereafter, but we solved this problem by placing a certified teacher in Jeanette's classroom while Jeanette taught the class. As I stated before, Jeanette was an amazingly capable woman. Shortly after this incident, she took the GED, passed, and enrolled in college. As I mentioned before, she received her college degree in three years, graduated cum laude, and passed the NTE (National Teacher's Exam) on her first try.

The removal of Ralph did not improve things. On October 5, 1981, we received a memo from Dr. Williams stating that another person had been placed in charge over the Free School and the Montessori School. Then on October 19, 1981, we received notice that a principalship for the Free School and the Montessori School had again been advertised in the Superintendent's Bulletin.

After the October 19, 1981, advertisement came out, we received a memorandum dated November 11, 1981, from our new administrator stating that the deadline for applying for the vacancy for principal for the New Orleans Free School and the Montessori School had been extended and to please submit our concerns and suggestions for this position in writing as soon as possible.

Our parents immediately responded in a letter to Dr. Martin asking for clarification. They pointed out that he, Dr. Martin, had assured them that no principal would be placed at the Free School until I had an opportunity to apply for the principal's pool, the bureaucratic structure for one to be eligible for consideration as a principal. Many principals of today's charter schools avoid this system requirement and start and/or are hired by the school itself. It is interesting to note that many principals of the charter schools presently operating in Orleans Parish have no administration certification. Bureaucracy is about control, not quality or innovation.

Shortly thereafter, on the day Thanksgiving holidays were to begin, at 1:15 p.m., we received two memos from our new administrator telling us our improvement objectives and our written input for the principal's position would be due immediately after the Thanksgiving break. We all felt intimidated and frustrated by being treated so abusively—no work days were allowed for preparation or production of these documents and the information demanded on the principal position was still in contradiction to what we had been promised by Dr. Martin. I spent the Thanksgiving break writing to Dr. Martin, knowing full well that I was not endearing myself or our school with the bureaucracy.

I sent him a three page, single-spaced letter because, as I stated in the letter, "But you said it yourself—you receive much more feedback from others than you do from me." I held nothing back. I decried the timing and timeline afforded to us by these memos literally only allowing our holiday break to deal with these issues, I raised the issue of fairness and objectivity in the handling of our evaluations and I suggested that the problem was not us but a bureaucratically run school system. On this matter I will share with you my actual words from the letter dated November 29, 1981:

Dr. Martin,

What started out as a questioning of my leadership has rapidly evolved into a questioning of public education. Is a program that is working, that is drawing people into and keeping people in the public school system to be crushed because of petty jealously, in-fighting, etc.? Is a program which demonstrates that it has the ability to draw students or face the specter of being closed to be crushed? We are a true school of choice. We have accomplished what the critics are screaming for: happy kids, learning kids, happy parents, a highly motivated staff. This is not to say that we have no problems. We are simply seeking relief and support from administrative harassment. To put this idea another way, I would like to quote Neal Peirce from his article entitled "Let's try school voucher" in *The Times Picayune* Monday, October 12, 1981:

> *Philadelphia Inquirer* columnist Dan Rottenberg put the issue succinctly: "It's time we recognized that institutions were never intended as a substitute for individual initiative. At best, bureaucracy is a necessary evil. When its tasks—and consequently its size—multiply, then it becomes unresponsive and counterproductive. In each case, the solution is not to strengthen the bureaucracy, but to break the problem down to human scale. ... the key to urban education is motivation—which can be achieved only by giving parents and children (not to mention teachers

and principals) more freedom of choice and more control over the schooling." (Section 1, p. 11)

So, here it was in black and white, an open attack on bureaucracy and a plea for humanization and school-site control for schooling. Obviously, I was not making any friends and was probably making many enemies in the bureaucracy during our struggle to preserve our little school. At the same time I felt that Dr. Martin was listening to our pleas and arguments. This was the direction he was trying to move the school system. Members of the entrenched bureaucracy, however, were going to resist his every move.

I sent the letter to Dr. Martin on the day we returned from the Thanksgiving holiday. On December 1, 1981, a few days later, we received another memorandum from our second administrator. This extended the principal input information until December 10. I again wrote Dr. Martin on December 2 because of the memo and because Ralph, whom Dr. Martin had banned from entering our building, was there on December 1. He was observing one of our classes and conferring with the second administrator placed over our school.

In my letter, only four short paragraphs, I asked why Ralph was still stalking our halls and classroom. I wanted Dr. Martin to know demands were being made of us concerning the principal position when we were still waiting to hear from him whether we were talking about a temporary or permanent position. On the same day of my letter to Dr. Martin, on December 2, he wrote to one of our parents, Lynette Jerry, and informed her that the principal vacancy announcement for the Free School was "inadvertently published." Then, on December 8, he met with members of our parent representative group and stated that the December 10 deadline for our parent input had been postponed. Additionally, on that day, after he met with our parents, he wrote a memorandum addressed to Dr. Williams and to our second administrator stating firmly but nicely that an extension had been granted for our input and that he was determined to resolve this issue "to the mutual benefit and agreement of all parties."

Our parent group, on December 8, sent a brief note to Dr. Williams confirming this postponement of the deadline for our input into the qualifications for the principal position for the New Orleans Free School. We never included the Montessori School in our discussion of this issue. We were always clear and steadfast that we were only talking about the Free School. However, Dr. Martin referred to it as the "principalship at the Free School and the Montessori School." Dr. Williams referred to it as "the principal for the Howard Montessori/New Orleans Free School." Both of our schools were located in the old Howard #2 school building.

On December 10, 1981, Dr. Williams responded to our parents' letter. He let his frustration show over having been overruled by Dr. Martin. In his letter addressed to Don Van Loo, another one of our leading parent representatives, he wrote the following:

> I understand that the parents have now requested an extension to the middle of January and the Superintendent has approved the extension. While I have great difficulty understanding why it should take you two months to offer suggestions that might be included in the job description of the principal for the Howard Montessori/New Orleans Free School, I shall abide by the direction of the Superintendent. The Montessori parents met our requested deadline.

For the first time since this issue began, we felt a ray of hope surrounding this issue of principalship for the New Orleans Free School. Sometime in January 1982, our faculty and parents submitted our qualifications for the New Orleans Free School principal to Dr. Williams. If my memory serves me right, it was Jim Charbonnet, after consultation with faculty and parents, who drew up the following qualifications.

Qualifications of the New Orleans Free School Principal

To administer and supervise all the activities and personnel of the New Orleans Free School.

CHARACTERISTICS AND FUNCTIONS

1. The principal should demonstrate a refined ability to engage the judgment and opinions of parents and interested friends in the working of the school.

2. The principal should know how to allow the parents and guardians to determine the ends of their children's education and to judge the efficacy of the means by which the school arrives at those ends.

3. The principal should foster a climate of open discussion and tolerance in which no one's view is sacrosanct and all views are respected.

4. The ethical responsibility of the principal must be to educate the child to take possession of her/himself, adapt to changes and have the power to shape and direct the course of her/his life.

5. Since the school is an instrument of society, the principal must maintain a broad view of social conditions and directions to insure that the curriculum is not insular, stultifying or hopelessly out of touch with reality.

6. The principal must honor flexibility and innovation. S/he must be ready to consider, test and try variations and innovations as they occur to the faculty, students, and parents.

7. The principal must appreciate the family model of the school and of the classroom, rather than the office or factory model so commonly seen today.

8. The principal should make the New Orleans Free School a part of his/her life and not leave it behind when s/he walks out the door in the evenings.

9. The principal should truly practice the art of loving.

10. The principal must be someone who likes children and who is dedicated to working with the students and not just the adults of the school.

11. The principal should be willing to accept the traditional role of principal-teacher as well as administrator.

12. The principal should be a student of education and of life.

EDUCATION AND TRAINING: Masters degree in Alternative Education. Elementary Principal Certification. Minimum of five years direct experience in a free school. Prefer first-hand contact with alternative schools throughout the country.

On February 11, 1982, Dr. Williams, in a memorandum to the second administrator appointed to our school, acknowledged the receipt of our parent input for the principalship of the Free School and stated that no principal would be appointed for this school year, but one would be in place for the 1982–1983 school year.

Just when we thought we were going to survive the appointment of an outside principal being placed at the Free School, we received from our second administrator a copy of an anonymous letter sent to Dr. Martin.

March 2, 1982

Dear Dr. Martin,

As a concerned parent of The New Orleans Free School, I am
writing to you to inform you of the following concerns I have
about the present administration and leadership in the school.
1. The children are taken on "fieldtrips" without proper
   supervision and chaperons.
2. Rumor has it that those children who attend the annual
   camping trip are exposed to and allowed to indulge in
   certain drugs and alcohol.
3. Children who are sent to the office for misbehaving in
   the classroom are left to do as they please due to the
   fact that there is no one there to supervise their actions.
Action must be taken to remedy the above problems and to
insure the safety of my child and the other children who attend
this school. I feel you are the man to take the action !

                        Thank you,
                        A Concerned Parent

3/9

Bob
For your information

On March 25, 1982, I replied, in writing, to this anonymous accusation in a rather lengthy letter to Dr. Martin. The letter clearly articulated my position on these accusations and the need to respond to this anonymous letter. I defended our students' behavior on their numerous field trips. I told him that I knew of two trips when our students did misbehave and how we quickly and effectively handled the situations resolving both issues. I took particular umbrage to this anonymous author's putting in quotes "field trips" to ever so subtly imply that our field trips were unusual and suspicious. I listed the many field trips that we often took our students on: "the Audubon Zoo, brown bag concerts, the Clay Pits (a natural land phenomenon some sixty miles due north of New Orleans), museums and parks in the area." I informed him that we had a planned trip to visit and tour the Amtrak station and to view the Creativity exhibit at one of the museums.

I tackled the issues of alcohol and drugs head on by responding that I knew of only one time when I witnessed a parent in a home allowing her thirteen-year-old son to have a drink. On drugs, I wrote the following:

> Drugs. Dr. Martin, I am not stupid. I know the Free School came out of the sixties. I know that many people think of us as hippies, crazies, etc. But, sir, I came out of the political sixties. I knew then and know now that if we did not have a strict policy of 'no drugs' in our school or at school functions that we would simply be committing suicide. In all honestly I did think drugs were going to be a huge problem for the Free School. However, I am happy to report that our school has been surprisingly free of drugs. In our 11 year history I remember finding drugs on students only four times.

I then explained how we dealt effectively with each drug situation and concluded my remarks on drug use at the Free School with the following: "I feel that for a school that evolved out of what has been called the 'counter culture' our low-keyed and consistent approach to drugs has helped prevent drugs from being a major problem at the Free School."

I conceded the fact that students were sometimes sent to an empty office (we had no secretary or administrator), but I pointed out that the office was connected by a door that was always left opened to my classroom, making it fairly easy to keep an eye an any students sent to the office.

I will say that the second administrator handled this situation extremely well. He certainly put an end to the situation by writing to Dr. Williams and stating that field trips were being properly supervised and would continue to be so in the future, that students would not be sent to the office and left unsupervised. "Students are to remain under adult supervision at all times," he wrote, and "A proper field trip request will be required for any and all future camping trips and the rules and regulations of the OPSB are to be followed." While we were able to properly handle this situation, all field trips now became bureaucratized, meaning we had to get approval from this second administrator.

That was the last I ever heard about the anonymous letter, but the pressure to limit the Free School and to curtail our strength only intensified. Apparently, because it seemed we might win the principal issue, we were now again being placed in conflict with the Montessori School over the use of space in our shared building. It should be noted that during this first year sharing the building with Montessori, our two schools worked in harmony throughout the year. On March 12, 1982, Dr. Williams sent Dr. Scarnato a memorandum stating the following: "It is anticipated that due to an increase in enrollment at the Howard Montessori School it will be necessary to house primary children in two classrooms previously occupied by the New Orleans Free School." He then went on to request a meeting at my bequest concerning this matter.

A couple of things struck me about this memorandum. These were the same two classrooms that Dr. Scarnato had granted us at the beginning of the school year, so I wondered why we were confronted with this issue again. Our argument remained the same as when we first argued for the classrooms. Our program—with also increasing student numbers though not mentioned by Dr. Williams—would use and need eight classrooms for our increased enrollment to 160 students. This would give the Montessori School four classrooms for their increased enrollment to eighty students. Dr. Williams referred to the two classrooms as "previously occupied by the New Orleans Free School." In fact, we were presently using the two classrooms.

Going after our classroom space was not enough. Our bureaucratic enemies started targeting our faculty. On May 19, 1982, Jim Charbonnet received a termination notice effective on June 2, 1982. No explanation was given—just a termination letter with the word "Terminated" typed on it. We had no idea why they targeted Jim. Then on May 27, we received a memo from the second administrator, ordering us to give up the two classrooms we were using to the Montessori School, effective June 7.

Needless to say, I was frustrated and distraught. We all were. The school system's top administrators, not including Dr. Martin, were coming at us with cannon fire and our little boat was taking hits. I quickly, but reluctantly, wrote once again to Dr. Martin. This, too, was a most impassioned plea for help with little or nothing held back. The letter included numerous other ways our opposition whittled away our authority to operate our school and to make us function just like every other ordinary school in the system.

May 30, 1982

Dr. Charles Martin
Superintendent
New Orleans Public Schools
4100 Touro
New Orleans, La.

Dear Dr. Martin,

Almost a year ago I and members of the Free School community first approached you to help us preserve our school, our community and my leadership. At our last meeting in mid-December of 1981 you personally assured me that this issue would be resolved sometime in the spring but certainly before school was out. I made this request so that teachers and parents would have adequate time to adjust and relocate if they were not satisfied with the resolution.

Since that December meeting the harassment of me and our program has definitely shifted gears but in essence continued. We bore the burden of these insults hoping that any day the major issue of our school would be settled and that the attacks would end. They have not ended; they have only intensified.

I have been called into conference a number of times this semester. I was called in once to inform me that it was being recommended that we lose two of our classrooms to the Montessori program because they are increasing in number. We are increasing too. Why are we insulted? The only thing in writing concerning this issue mentions the Montessori increase. Nothing mentions ours. We are to have about 160 students. They are to have about 80 students. We are supposed to put our 160 students in the exact same amount of space reserved for 80 students. I think it is pathetic that one program is used to try and get at another.

Less I be misunderstood, I applaud the Montessori staff. They are most cordial, talented, and enjoyable people to work with. My objection is to abusive management.

I was called into conference where it was implied that I had without authorization signed for several hundred dollars of requisitioned materials. The repeated statement by the party was, "I hope it was I who signed for the equipment." The implication was perfectly clear: You, Bob Ferris, are no longer powerful. If you are not absolutely careful, we are going to get you. We are either going to whip you into shape or we are going to destroy you.

This entire experience is nightmarish. Instead of a very personal, close, family-like lifestyle, you enter a world where jealousy and ambition rule, where vindictiveness and visciousness dictate.

I was called into conference to be informed that we may lose two of our teachers next year. First our classrooms, now our teachers. I figured that must be in great shape after all this chopping. However, it was agreed that this dismissal would be tabled until after the issue of principalship was settled. I am about to learn another lesson. No sooner did we return from our whole school camping trip--an experience elevating us all--that one of our teachers, Jim Charbonnet, was greeted with a termination notice. Just one word on the notice "terminated". No consultation, no personalness, no humanity.

Dr. Martin, I was not going to write you any more letters. I was simply going to keep these and other issues inside of me. My thinking was that some people had a need to flex their muscle and I wanted to show them that I was truly willing to work with them. But this last action is so utterly cruel, so nasty that I feel I must say no to their tactics. You have come out publicly saying that you would like the best school system in this country by the year 2000. I asked Jim to jot down some of his background for me. I am enclosing what he gave me. Can our system so easily and insensitively dismiss such quality? There seems to be a hiatus between rhetoric and practice.

I hope that you will personally look into this matter and help rectify any wrong doing and get Jim immediately reinstated.

I appreciate that my writing such a letter will support those who feel that we refuse to play by the rules. But I feel that we have been most cooperative and have complied with all of your demands. I think our books are in order; I do not sign for equipment. We have subjected ourselves to the evaluation process (an issue that would require a letter by itself) which was held over our heads since October and to this day has not been finalized. I now fill out all necessary forms for field trips; we did not react when our request for the annual 7th and 8th grade trip that would have taken us this year to Baton Rouge to visit the state legislature in session was denied. We no longer use our cars. We have been totally cooperative but it seems that this is not enough. Some people want our souls, our spirit, our persons--this we can not, should not and will not give. We have suffered abuse, insults, and now attempted annihilation. Let it be noted that our crime was a struggle for freedom, a struggle for humanity. All we want is the right to offer a different educational program that works for most of the kids we touch. For this we plead, "Guilty."

There is one last issue which I feel you should be aware of. John Holt in his book, How Children Fail, made the following statement: "There are very few children who do not feel, during most of the time they are in school, an amount of fear, anxiety, and tension that most adults would find intolerable." This quote is relevant for two reasons. First, at the Free School we try to minimize the fear and anxiety on the part of our students by providing a more open-ended approach to education and by providing a wide range of fun and educational experiences for all the students. Second, the adults in our environment have had to work with this fear, anxiety and tension all year. This was simply cruel. No one could possibly continue to teach under such threatening circumstances.

Please, let's jointly resolve this issue and then hopefully go on to create a better school and a better school system.

I am looking forward to some type of reply.

Sincerely yours,

Robert M. Ferris
New Orleans Free School

Someone from Dr. Martin's office called and requested information on our anticipated enrollment for the 1982–1983 school year. On June 8, 1982, I supplied the information Dr. Martin had requested, again sought help in reinstating Jim, and requested help in finding a solution to the conflict over the two classrooms.

We heard nothing more from anyone on these issues for the rest of June and all of July. I spent the time focusing on getting into the administrative pool so that I could apply for the principalship at the Free School. The first time I applied I failed to get in. I feared that I would not make it in because this would be the perfect bureaucratic way to prevent me from becoming principal of the Free School. However, as it turned out, a number of other people who did not get in also felt that they were unfairly treated and subjectively prevented from being placed in the pool. We wrote a joint letter to Dr. Martin claiming that the entire process was overly subjective, unfair, and in violation of Orleans Parish School Board policies regarding the selection process.

Dr. Martin must have agreed because he had the entire process completely revamped so that it became more objective and much fairer. I believe all of us who had signed the letter of protest and asked for changes were accepted into the administration pool the second time and, interestingly, ended up as principals and/or high level administrators in the Orleans Parish School System. Dr. Martin had proved, once again, to be a very fair and honest man who seemed determined to correct the many ills plaguing the Orleans Parish School System trapped in this sea of dishonesty, subjectivity, harassment, and cruelty.

When I tried to get into the pool that first time, I took a test known as the Perceiver. This is a subjective analysis as to leadership capabilities conducted in a one on one question and answer session. My questioner asked me what my main goal was for the next five years. He did not ask me what my educational goal was; he simply asked me my major goal for the next five years. I answered him truthfully, even knowing this was not the answer he expected. I stated, "It is to run the Crescent City Classic Race in under forty minutes." To accomplish this feat, I would probably be in the top 500 runners out of a 25,000 person race. I saw his mouth drop; but, I answered his question the way he asked it. I received a low Perceiver score from him. On the second go around, Dr. Williams gave me the Perceiver and I received a very high score from him. I also got accepted into the administrative pool.

Just so you know, I never ran the race in under forty minutes, but at forty years old I ran it in forty-two minutes and some seconds. I was very proud and satisfied with this time even though I missed my goal. For me I ran that 6.2 miles like the wind and I never stopped running until I crossed the finish line. I salute all runners, bikers, hikers, swimmers, and exercisers.

Running was very therapeutic for me during the many years the Free School struggled with the bureaucracy. The constant undertow of taking our teachers, our space, our building, and threatening us with closure was akin to drowning. Throughout those years we kept coming up for air only to be quickly and strongly pulled under water again, never sure if we were to resurface. Running kept me breathing. At the same time, I cannot convey how many times over the years the parents, students, and teachers would ask me during these struggles over staff, leadership, space, and closure, "Will the Free School remain open? Will we have the school next year, tomorrow? Should I look for another school for my child? Do I have a job? Do I need to look for another job? What will you do?" When I ran, I did some of my best thinking, which usually ended up on paper. I kept running until my knees gave out and then I took up cycling.

With the advent of August our problems almost instantly resurfaced. I received a letter dated August 9, 1982, from Dr. Williams, ordering the Free School to vacate the two classrooms so that the Montessori program could take them over and set them up for the coming school year. He ended this dictate with the following sentence: "This meets with the approval of the Superintendent."

Obviously we felt as though we had been blown out of our little boat. However, a life raft was thrown to us that certainly buoyed our spirits. Ralph, the supervisor who first smeared us with orders, dictates, and insults, but who was ultimately banned from entering our school, resigned from the school system, as reported in the August 11, 1982, *The Times-Picayune*, "in a flap over credentials." The article reported that there was something about his stated educational background that did not prove true. This was a small vindication but vindication nonetheless. We breathed freely, if only for a moment.

Our easy breathing was extremely short lived. On Thursday, August 12, 1982, Jeanette received notice that she had been transferred to another school in the system. Also on that day, around 3 p.m., I received a phone call from one of the two leading Montessori teachers (not Jill). I no sooner said, "Hello," that the ten to twenty minute harangue started. The speaker said something like this: "Bob Ferris, I have had it with your underhanded tactics. You think you have Dr. Martin over a barrel because your parents are organized and will make a stink if you don't get what you want." I set down my coffee cup and tried to reply but couldn't think of what to say. "The whole system is aware of the clout you have," she continued. "Dr. Martin is scared because he wants his contract renewed, and doesn't want a big flare-up before this happens."

There may have been some truth to this last statement. Unbeknownst to us, the Free School may have been in the middle of a battle for the superintendent's position. Dr. Martin did not want to throw the school system into turmoil, causing a community explosion. He did not want to make a mistake by too quickly rushing to judgment on the issue.

The other theory circulating was that Dr. Williams wanted to be superintendent. He was a black man in a system that had never had a black superintendent, but he had a lot of white support in the Lusher and Montessori schools. If he could get Dr. Martin, who was white, to make a mistake on the Free School issue, the Free School could be crushed and Dr. Martin might lose a lot of his white support.

I never knew if either or both of these scenarios were correct. I religiously avoided city or school system politics. I was always too busy swimming and floating, trying desperately to find land to save the Free School.

My caller's diatribe continued. "Bob Ferris, I've watched you. You don't get along with anyone. You just want to have it your way. Well, I'm going to tell you, we're going to have an onsite principal and you may not like that. It's because of us that the school system spent $90,000 to improve this building."

Now, this was true. The school system did spend $90,000 to fix up the building; i.e., to fix up that part of the building housing the Montessori School. Not one penny was spent to fix up our part of the building. Not one penny even though the major reason for spending this money was because the Montessori School was bringing in kindergarten and first graders into the building and all lead-based paint had to be removed. The Free School had kindergarten and first grade students as well, but no money was spent to rid our portion of the building of lead paint. I suspect we did not count. I knew we were not welcomed.

My caller continued arguing vociferously for the two classrooms given to us by their spokesperson, Ralph, at the meeting with Dr. Scarnato and thus granted by him. I informed her that during the last school year, the second administrator who was appointed by Dr. Williams to oversee our two programs stated he was going to authorize that we give up the two classrooms on the second floor to the Montessori School. I then told him, "Oh, you mean because we didn't fight for them, a fight has to be manufactured." He stated that he would drop it for then.

I explained to my irascible phone caller that a few months later, this second administrator, Jill, and I met again over this issue. I took the same position of not wanting to give up the classrooms. Jill offered a compromise, stating that they would only take one of the classrooms. The second administrator replied for me that we would still view it as a crushing blow; a little bit here, a little bit there. I nodded in agreement. But in that spring meeting, I did offer to go in and take down, free of charge, the partitions in the back two rooms on the Montessori floor, creating two more classrooms for the Montessori School. I stated that the only thing I could not do was replace the flooring; the school system would have to do this. Jill said that

I should get paid for my labor. I told her I was not interested in the money and I made sure that the second administrator understood that I was serious about this proposal. I never got a response; I ultimately received an order to vacate the two classrooms. On Monday, August 16, 1982, I met with the same Montessori teacher who had raked me over the coals on the phone. She was much calmer, but still adamant about the two classrooms and securing an onsite principal. This teacher informed me that her parents had written Dr. Martin, demanding this action. She also was angry with me because she thought I was secretly trying to get Dr. Martin to visit the school building. She was surprised to learn that it was Dr. Martin's idea to visit the schools and that he had tried to reach her but her son had apparently failed to inform her that he had called.

Shortly after August 12, 1982, our parents were granted a meeting with Dr. Martin. The agenda contained the principal hiring-process, Jim's termination, Jeanette's transfer, and an order to vacate the two classrooms. On this last issue, our parents reiterated that we were not fighting over territory, but for a program to be allowed to function and to be treated fairly. Our parents left the meeting believing that these issues would be resolved favorably.

On Wednesday, August 18, 1982, I went to a staffing meeting with Juliet Robertson, teacher placement director for elementary schools. As I feared, she had nothing from Dr. Martin stating we needed six teachers, not five, due to our increased enrollment. She was very helpful in filling the five positions, however, giving us everything we needed, including keeping Jim as a teacher.

I went to see Eric Boyd, the man in charge of paraprofessionals, about Jeanette's transfer. Jeanette was still classified as a teacher's aide. He confirmed the transfer stating that he had received a call from Dr. Everett Williams earlier in the summer to have Jeanette placed on the surplus teacher aide list.

I then went to see Dr. Martin who saw me immediately. I began the discussion of the classrooms and told him of the Montessori teacher's phone call. I presented to him the two letters I had written to Dr. Scarnato because I wanted to clearly show that I had never been underhanded in dealing with this issue. I explained that they could have the two classrooms if we could have the back room behind the large basement. He said he thought that we had the two classrooms and that we, or someone, was taking partitions down to make two more classrooms for the Montessori School. I told him, "No, no one had approved that idea and now we were willing to forgo the two classrooms—they're not worth discussing or fighting over anymore."

He stated that the Free School kids were just as important as all kids, that he had told Everett his opinion, and that this whole thing should be looked at again. He asked me if the arrangement to give up the two classrooms on the second floor and get the back basement room was truly agreeable to us. I told him yes. He then told me that he had cleared with the director of personnel the six positions, one being an intern and another an aide, and that he was working on getting me a part-time administrative assistant. I kept asking him what that meant. He finally stated that it could be something like an 03 (the code name for an administrative assistant) who could be used for instructional relief.

I informed him of Jeanette's pending transfer and explained to him that we were not able to get an intern. Could we use the funds for having ten students over our allotted 150 students to pay for Jeanette? He looked at me and said either, "This whole thing has been a mistake" or "This thing has been a mistake from the beginning." I answered, "Amen." He said he would immediately look into the situation and get back to me within two days.

Fighting over this leadership issue, begging to keep staff we absolutely needed, and being entangled in turf wars clearly illustrated our diminished power. Even if we won all the issues, we had lost. We were no longer in control of our school's direction. We were at the mercy of the bureaucracy. Power no longer resided at the school site; it was being engulfed by the bureaucrats who always believed it belonged to them. Winning these battles may have been essential for survival but they also added to the pain of drowning. Bureaucracy is suffocating education and should be dismantled if we are to revitalize our urban schools. The school house, not the state house or the boardroom or the administrative office should make all crucial educational decisions for the operation of the school and the education of the children. Those closest to the education of the students should be the decision makers. Bureaucratic meddling reverses this simple rule and places decision making at the top, erroneously removing it from the school site. The classroom and the schoolhouse are where education occurs.

I once again met with Juliet Robertson, the personnel director of elementary schools, on the afternoon of Monday August 23, 1982. I would be remiss not to mention that she was always helpful and polite with the issues facing the Free School. Decent bureaucrats help a bureaucracy function more humanely, but they do nothing to diminish the power stranglehold of an entrenched bureaucracy. She knew nothing of the part-time "03 position," that Dr. Martin had mentioned to me. I immediately met with her supervisor, the director of personnel, whom I had never met before. I explained to this lady what Dr. Martin had told me. She said, "Listen, a teacher type 03 person has been approved for two-thirds Free School, one-third Montessori, who is to perform all the administrative duties. This person is not to teach." She went on, "And don't sic your parents on us. All they do is jam up the phones and we can't get anything done here. Don't have them bother us just because you don't get what you want." I calmly told her that I begged to differ with her about parents—we should be accountable to parents. She replied, "I am accountable to parents, but I do not report to parents—I report to my supervisor. I am going to see who Dr. Williams wants in the position and that's the way it's going to be." I again told her that I had received different information from Dr. Martin, and asked if she would go with me to see him. She declined.

I excused myself and went to see Dr. Martin by myself. I had to wait about an hour because he already had someone in his office. It was after 5 p.m. when he finally came out. I asked him if he had a minute. He said, "A minute, I've got two minutes." He asked about Jeanette and I told him everything was fine on that matter. I then explained to him what the director of personnel had said. I left out mentioning the attack about parents. Dr. Martin said, "Damn it! I'm going to get this thing straightened out, no matter what it takes." He told me to call him at 10:00 the next morning.

I phoned but was never able to reach him. At 3 p.m., I decided to go out to the school board to meet with Juliet Robertson who was meeting with the director of personnel at the time. Both returned a short while later. The director then confirmed that I was to get a part-time person to relieve me so that I could contend with administrative chores. She then put her face right next to mine and said, "You want to be principal of the Free School, don't you? Well, you will never get to be principal unless you fill out all the forms exactly the way Dr. Williams wants them. You are going to be watched really closely while you are in this position." My only retort was that I had always only acted with permission. Some people may not have liked what we did, but we had always been granted permission. She said, as she was leaving, "Well, as long as you have permission." I felt incredibly insulted and intimidated but I got the staff I wanted.

During the second day of school for students, the director of personnel surprised me by showing up at our school. She asked me how many students we had the first day. I told her we had 160 plus. She said, "No, how many noses actually showed up?" I said 150 but that about ten parents had called and stated that they would not show up until next week. I saw her a little later during her visit and she asked me how many students were present today and I told her 154 or 156. I think she was trying to prove that I was lying about our enrollment in order to get extra staff. I also think she was surprised to see so many students, especially so many black students, and realized that I was not lying.

She also asked me about one of the new black teachers. I explained that Dr. Williams approved her being on substitute status until the teacher forms went through. She asked twice, "Dr. Williams approved this?" She also wondered if this was the teacher I wanted. I replied, "Oh, yes." It was only later that I learned that she asked Ann White, who is black, if she was comfortable working at the Free School. Ann told her yes. She then asked Ann if she was new and Ann told her no, that this was her third year.

I think she came to check on two things: whether we really had the numbers we claimed and if there was racial tension and/or racism at the school. She was able to prove nothing negative. When she was leaving, I invited her to come back in a month when our program would be fully underway. I told her I thought she would really be pleased by what she would see. She told me, to my surprise, that she was already pleased: teachers seemed happy and everything seemed calm. I thanked her as she left.

If I was surprised by that administrator's visit, I was traumatized by our next visitor. That day, another principal walked through the door unannounced and said he was the new supervising principal for the Free School. He said, "Didn't Everett tell you?" My heart dropped to my feet. I stood there paralyzed with my brain shattered and my soul wounded, listening to this man make nice, while I wanted to explode into oblivion. Despite my numbness I agreed to meet with this man the following week.

I survived this initial encounter but to this date that brief uncomfortable meeting remains hazy. Anyway, I met with him the next week and gave him the history of the Free School, concentrating mainly on the present struggle. He responded by sharing some of his experiences and saying that a lot of our problems stemmed more from bureaucratic ineptness than conspiracy. He said he viewed his role in three ways: (1) To be supportive, (2) To make sure the program met state standards, and (3) To evaluate the staff. I told him this was not the message Dr. Martin had given us. He agreed to meet with Dr. Martin, or whoever was appropriate. When he said that he wanted to meet with our staff, I invited him to join our meeting on September 8, 1982.

At this meeting, he laid out the following arguments for his position at the Free School:

(1) Our school was certified by the state and must have a principal. As supervising principal, he could offer our school administrative support regarding things like the budget, school nurse, building maintenance, etc.
(2) To make sure that our school meets the standards set for it by the state.
(3) To evaluate staff
(4) To coordinate our meeting as a group on a regular basis.
(5) Open communication

Not many questions came forward even though he kept trying to drag them out of us. In the discussion I repeated that what he was saying was not what Dr. Martin had told us. He presented the following scenario. Suppose some upper administrator did not like the Free School. Suppose that by the end of the year they were saying that the Free School was really together and a very fine place—wouldn't that be great! One of our teachers said that we felt the Free School was really together now and that it was a fine place and we would feel insulted if, a year from now, it was finally decided that we were a really fine place.

In talking about the evaluations he said that he wanted to make it a matter of record whether or not we were doing a fine job. I again pointed out that we had been chopped to pieces twice by this evaluation process. We went through the whole process last year, agreed to it, cooperated with it, and then became frustrated because it never happened. I pointed out that there were other ways to record doing a good job. One was by our test scores another was by our growth. He said he had never seen our test scores. How convenient!

Later in the discussion, he said he wanted to meet with us bimonthly. We had always kept meetings to an absolute minimum. I asked him, "How do you expect us to run this school, to accomplish what we want to accomplish, and meet with you twice a month?" It was at this point that the discussion really heated up. He said while he was coming here with an open mind, some of us were setting this up for failure (I'm sure he meant me), that his meetings were no different from ours—their purpose was to run the school, to take care of its problems, etc.

Then he dropped what he thought was his bombshell. Did we know what our attendance rate was? I knew he was on to something then. He heatedly said, "It was the lowest in the system. It was 65 percent. Your students only attended two out of three days." Here it is again. Find the negative and attack with it. Never come and discuss a perceived problem. From my view, we did not have a major attendance problem. First of all, a few of our students traveled a good bit—we strongly encouraged this—I personally did not consider them absent, but we usually marked them absent just because people would probably have a fit if we didn't and they found out about it.

Secondly, ours was an elementary and junior high school. On really nasty, cold, or rainy days, a lot of our students stayed home. They came from all over the city, including across the river; and most rode the city buses, even some of our kindergarten, first, and second graders. We did not get upset when this happened; we appreciated that they were coping with inconvenience. Also, on half-days, when no breakfast or lunch was served, many of our students stayed home. We did not worry about this either—it was not worth them coming long distances for three hours and then not being fed. (Years later, the system started serving breakfast and lunch, even on half days.) Finally, a number of our students were tardy because of the long distances they had to travel, often on city buses. These students were typically marked absent. We did not amend the office records because that would mean teachers would have to deal with attendance two or three times a day. In those days we were never big on pushing paper. This too would change. The rest of the absences we did worry about. I asked him if our students were scoring fairly high on their standardized tests, why he was so upset about our attendance. He said that if they were high with 65 percent attendance, think of how high they could be with much greater attendance. I told him that maybe it didn't correlate.

The point of this discussion was not our attendance rate, rather it was this man who came to our school claiming to be open and stating that there would be no surprises from him. The first time he got hot under the collar, he dropped this bomb. Now, I had never seen our attendance record published anywhere. I had seen our test scores in the newspaper. He knew our attendance count, but not our test scores. He was supposedly coming to us with an open mind? We did not have a prayer!

The conclusion of the meeting came when he finally realized that we had had enough and he began to leave. As he was walking out the door, one of our teachers said under her breath, "Now, can we take care of the things we need to discuss?" This new supervising principal also said, in relation to his taking care of problems, that he was to deal with nurse, textbooks, equipment, toilet paper, etc. We should not have to worry with these things. In other words we were back to Ralph's statement, "You are now just teachers."

In a private conversation this supervising principal also told me that he was getting a little bored being principal at his other school. He had been there some seven years and he had the program running the way he wanted it to run. He said he somewhat volunteered for the job of supervising the Free School because he thought he might learn something and that it might be a feather in his cap. He gave me a tour of his school, and frankly, the place seemed incredibly boring, dead, and absent of any vitality. Here is an "educator" who has the chance to create a really fine, alive, creative institution but who avoids this energetic undertaking by saying, "We run a very traditional school." His "feather in his cap" statement convinced me that he wanted to rise up the chain of command and use the Free School to do it.

On Tuesday, September 7 or Wednesday, September 8, 1982, we got notice that Jeanette had been placed on part-time status. I called the bureaucrat in charge of teacher aides to find out why. He told me that this was the director of personnel's order. I called this director who confirmed that's what she was told as well. I informed her I was sure this was incorrect. I asked whom I should call to get this straightened out. She told me to call the same person I always call to get things straightened out at the Free School.

I met with Dr. Martin on Thursday. This was the third time in almost as many weeks he had met with me without an appointment. He didn't seem pleased to meet with me. However, he said he definitely would look into Jeanette's situation. Then I explained that the new principal had said that he was our new supervising principal and was already making demands on us. I recounted to Dr. Martin that I tried unsuccessfully to explain to this man that this was not what we were led to believe and that our conversation had become a little heated. At some point, Dr. Martin blurted out, "Damn it! He is not the supervising principal! I am going to get this thing straightened out. You will have to turn your numbers in to him, that's all." Man, was I relieved.

On Friday, Jeanette called his office because she was still concerned about her status. Dr. Martin actually came on the phone, apologized, and assured her that he would take care of the situation by Tuesday. He seemed to be an amazing man, and I still believe that about him to this day.

Also on Friday, the new supervising principal came by and was friendly, saying he requested another custodian for our school and that he may have an old water fountain for us. He then said he needed to meet with our faculty to discuss the evaluation process, and "would we like to do it at his school in the air-conditioned library?" I explained to him that I had met with Dr. Martin, who reaffirmed what I had already told him. He informed me that he had written to Dr. Martin requesting a meeting between the three of us. He then suggested we wait and see what happened. I agreed.

On Monday, this supervising principal managed to upset me. He had the Montessori secretary (we, of course, had no secretary even though we were twice as large as the Montessori School) go to each of our teachers, me included, in the middle of class and tell us that he wanted a copy of our schedules. I felt this was inappropriate and a mild form of harassment because this lady had no position in our program. Also, the supervising principal had indicated that no further action would be taken until we heard from Dr. Martin. Further, this request came in the middle of instruction, which I felt was purposeful disrespect. I created a copy of my schedule but I did not turn it in. No reason was ever given for the request.

On September 8, 1982, this newest supervising principal sent a letter to Dr. Martin listing what he perceived to be his duties as supervising principal of the New Orleans Free School. These duties included "administrative support in such areas as maintenance and custodial needs, budgeting of school funds, purchasing process, etc. To correlate the instructional program with Bulletin 741, State certification standards, the Pupil Progression Plan...To evaluate all members of the Free School's instructional staff" I was very glad that he put this in writing so all to see, because I believe that his information was the exact information each supervising person had been provided. It clearly illustrated that someone was trying to place a principal over the Free School and, in essence, take over the Free School. At long last, Dr. Martin could see for himself that someone was altering his directives and that I had been telling the truth all along. At the school board meeting on September 27, 1982, Dr. Martin, with board approval, appointed me acting principal of the New Orleans Free School. I still needed to get into the administrative pool, that infamous bureaucratic hoop, to even be considered for the permanent principal's job. This was the next best thing Dr. Martin could do to administratively resolve this problem.

On November 29, 1982, I wrote Dr. Martin a thank-you letter stating that our struggle now shifted from surviving to creating. This was my first official letter as acting principal, but I forgot to use the title in my letter. You see, for us, the battle was never over creating a principal position; it was always over preserving our right of self-determination. We were the stalwarts of our ship, never wanting bureaucrats who would mold us into the system's image and set our directional path. Dr. Martin had proved to be a remarkable man who was hell-bent on doing the right thing, in spite of being entangled in bureaucratic machination. We survived due to his greatness. As I suggested earlier, it is my belief that the powers that be were using the Free School controversy to force Dr. Martin to make a mistake. By appointing someone over the Free School other than me, he risked certain negative publicity and the destruction of a very well-liked experimental, community school. If he appointed me as principal, he risked being viewed as weak and as kowtowing to parental wishes. He took his time, studied the problem, listened to all involved, and after two long, grueling years, made his decision. We will always owe him a debt of gratitude.

It is ironic that my appointment as acting principal of the Free School, Jill's appointment as principal of the Montessori School, and Dr. Martin's renewed contract were all published in the September 1983 issue of the school system's newspaper, *Applause*. The principalship of the New Orleans Free School had been resolved and we were now given the entire building. The Montessori School had their independence with their own building and principal, and Dr. Martin had not only survived the bureaucracy, he now controlled it. Or, so I thought.

Being appointed the acting principal, and ultimately the principal, proved more like winning the battle, but losing the war. I never dreamed how much control over principals the Central Office exercised. The meetings they required us to attend were truly too numerous to document and too meaningless to discuss. Suffice it to say that in my twenty-three years as principal, I never attended a principals' meeting that was helpful, useful, intellectual, philosophical, or educational. They almost always were about regulations, forms, compliance and tests scores. I longed for relevancy and meaningfulness; I got rules, regulations, orders and compliance mandates. I hated those meetings.

I feel I did have some influence over principals' dress habits, even though it took years to achieve this. When I first attended those meetings, I was always underdressed. I made attempts but never made it as a "dresser"—I always looked out of place. The male principals dressed in expensive suits, shiny shoes, matching ties and handkerchiefs. Some twenty-three years later, some came in sport coats, shirts with open collars, and sometimes no jacket at all. Dress-wise, I finally fit in, at least with a much larger contingency; philosophically, I never made it but I did earn the respect of some of my fellow principals.

I should note that when I was finally appointed principal of the New Orleans Free School in September, 1983, school board member Woody Koppel (now deceased), who was always very helpful in our struggles with the school system administration, told me to be sure to wear a coat and tie the night I was to be appointed principal. After such a long struggle with this principalship issue, we made little fanfare over appointment as principal. We were not fighting for a principal, per se; we were struggling to preserve a program. I did wear a coat and tie.

One other incident of dress comes to mind, not mine, but of a young attractive female Free School volunteer who taught Spanish. I passed by her classroom one day and noticed all the students huddled in a mass. This was not a huddled group chanting "fight, fight, fight" with everyone competing to see; rather, it was a mass of rapturous attention. I always thought, and certainly wanted, the Free School to capture student interest in learning, but I must say that this seemed a little unusual. I went to the excited crowd and pulled one student out to ask what was going on. He was wide-eyed, and practically panting, said, "Her tits are hanging out!" I walked through the crowd and took the young lady, breasts and all, to my office, hit my hand on my head and asked. "What are you doing? You can't have your breasts hanging out like that." Buttoning up, she innocently replied, asked, "This is a Free School, isn't it?"

This attitude that the Free School was "loosey-goosey" was one that haunted us throughout our existence. Many people thought that anything went, rules were nonexistent and the Free School was a place without discipline. Nothing could be further from the truth. At the Free School, freedom meant that you had a right to experience knowledge and learning constructively, experimentally, and joyfully. Freedom guaranteed you the right to be actively engaged in the learning process and that you, the learner, were a discoverer, laborer, inventor, actor, builder, and lover of learning, not just a passive recipient in the learning process. Freedom guaranteed that you had the right of voice and movement, and not just quiet and desk-sitting, though too much of this went on in some of the Free School classrooms.

The Free School was not without rules. We were an urban school dealing with poor, urban students. Woody Penouilh, who taught sixth grade and band, once said, "Just as we expect our students to do quality work and perform well academically, we must also expect them to behave properly and to function as well-disciplined children." We were not a simple permissive environment. Fighting was not allowed, disrespect was not acceptable, failure to complete one's schoolwork and/or homework was not permissible. We had our share of students who fought these expectations. Detentions were held after school and on Saturdays. There were parent conferences and we had parents spend time in the classroom observing their child. We had suspensions, and occasionally, expulsions. Any student suspended three times in one year was not allowed to return to the Free School the next year.

We were so rule-oriented that I once heard someone playing a horn on the third floor during more structured class time. I went bounding up the stairs to capture this student in his or her heinous act of disruption, ready to pass out the harshest punishment I could think of only to find Logan Crowe, one of our seventh-grade teachers, playing the horn. He looked at me, smiled, and said that one of the students had brought in the horn for band practice and he just had to try it out. Logan is now a school principal.

No, we were not without rules. At the same time, we did not force students to be controlled, quiet, or blindly obedient all of or most of the time. Ours was a quest for what we called reasonable discipline. We encouraged movement and student participation in the classroom through projects, cooperative learning, presentations, art, drama, and dance activities. There were times when we expected quiet, for students to be seated at desks, paying attention to instruction, silently reading, completing drill sheets and, of course, practicing test taking. In all honesty, it was a struggle expecting and maintaining voice and quiet, motion and obedience, calmness and excitement, all in the same day. Welcome to the Free School.

Many people outside, and a few inside the Free School community, felt that we were laissez-faire in our approach to discipline, dress, and academics. Some critics argued over the years to change name of the New Orleans Free School, especially getting rid of the word "Free." Others, including me, argued that people needed to seriously consider a different urban public school concept than one based on non-stop control, where quiet was the definition of good and sitting passively was viewed as engagement of learning. If "free" helped force a consideration of what schools should be and could be, then we should not change our name.

I should note that in the early, first few years of the Free School from 1971 to 1973, the school was very much a hippie school focused on freedom, even the freedom to do nothing. However, this concept of freedom dissipated as the school became older and more urbanized. Our emphasis shifted from freedom to "freedom to learn." This was not defined in absolute terms;

rather, it occurred through closeness, open-mindedness and multiple options and experiences. In other words, freedom at the Free School evolved to become the option to do many things and experience many opportunities; less and less it meant to do nothing and more and more it meant to do everything. For us freedom did not mean license; it meant responsibility. It was worth fighting for. "Free" remained in the name.

Another criticism our school continually encountered was that we and our students were on a first name basis. For many, particularly those outside the school and, again, even a few inside the school community, the fact that students called us, the adults (staff, teachers and principal alike), by our first names solidified the notion that we were an out of control school maintaining little or no respect. For many of us at the Free School our use of first names was a serious attempt to personalize a child's education. This policy was not an opening for disrespect, but an institutional opportunity for closeness, communication and community.

I should note here that when I received my "Doctor of Education" (what I have jokingly called "Doctor of Bureaucracy") from Peabody, Vanderbilt, 1989, local school officials began to have even more difficulty in addressing me—Bob, Mr. Ferris, Dr. Ferris, Dr. Bob. Sensing this confusion and wanting to preserve our first name basis, I starting calling myself, "Dr. Bob." The more I used "Dr. Bob" by signing all memorandums and letters with that nomenclature, the more people started calling me by that name. The title became formal, even though I'd started it as a bit of a joke. It was at this time that some teachers started addressing themselves and others with titles—"Miss" this and "Miss" that. They encouraged their students to use the "Miss" title. Even though the male teachers and a couple of female teachers kept using only the first name, I unintentionally was moving our school away from our first name basis. This went on until about the end of the 2004–2005 school year when I requested all to go back to first name and I dropped the "Dr." from my name. I had created this lapse in school culture and I wanted to end it.

Another misconception was that our school was intended for troubled students, students who were failing academically and/or having serious discipline problems. We could never shake this belief, either. It was true that we accepted almost every student who applied to the school, which meant that we accepted students who were academically behind and/or who had caused trouble at their former school(s). But, we also accepted students who were academically advanced and who behaved beautifully, and everyone in between. I can honestly say that most, though not all of the students who came to the Free School academically behind or who caused trouble in former schools, greatly improved as a result of the type of program we offered. We were not a school for troubled students, but we seemed to have success with most students who fell in that category.

Not only had Dr. Martin resolved the issue of the principalship for the New Orleans Free School, he also changed the political landscape of the administration of the school system. By the fall of 1983 he had Dr. Everett Williams removed as area superintendent and put in charge of the Maintenance department. Dr. Carol Allen took over as our new Assistant Superintendent for the Elementary Schools. This was a new title given to her by Dr. Martin in his rearrangement of the bureaucratic structure and the proverbial line of command. Most, if not all superintendents who followed Dr. Martin, did similar restructuring of the organization's power holders. These moves always proved to be little more than window dressings and were like rearranging deck chairs on the Titanic. Dr. Allen proved to be a most intelligent and progressive educator who only lasted a couple of years because she too found her power was viewed as a sham to those above her. However, she was helpful in making the principal process work for our school and instrumental in getting us essential resources. When she visited the school for the first time, she immediately noticed that we did not have a secretary and instantly created the position. No administrator below superintendent ever helped our school as much as she did.

A significant thing happened shortly after I had been named principal of the New Orleans Free School. Someone or some group of people wrote an anonymous letter severely criticizing Dr. Martin for patronage, fraud, and vindictiveness and sent the letter to all board members as well as other prominent community members. In the letter, Dr. Williams was portrayed as a victim of Dr. Martin's wrath. Dr. Williams, remember, had been removed as area superintendent and placed over maintenance.

I never knew what ramifications, if any, occurred because of this attack on Dr. Martin. I did know from my own experience that even an anonymous letter could wreak havoc on your psyche and certainly put you on the defensive whether the attack was justified or not. It was not long thereafter that Dr. Martin took ill and died. Sometime in the summer or early fall of 1985, Dr. Everett Williams became the Superintendent of Orleans Parish Public Schools.

8

Dr. Everett Williams Becomes Superintendent

The two years from the time I was made principal in 1983 to the summer of 1985 were conflict-free. However, in the fall of 1985, shortly after Dr. Williams took office, the institutionalization of the New Orleans Free School intensified. One of our teacher aides received notice that she had been "terminated due to surplus"—meaning too many teacher aides were on the system's payroll—and her last day was to be November 22, 1985. This issue was extremely important to us and most poignantly illustrated the dichotomy between school site autonomy and bureaucratic control of schools. For us, finding and hiring people who understood our philosophy of education—that learning best occurred when it was based on the needs of the learner and creating new needs for the learning—was a decisive ingredient for the success of our program. This aide epitomized this personalization of learning. Losing her would be both a blow to our community and a slap in the face to our power.

Our community quickly and powerfully took up the charge to save her. Parents started writing letters and making phone calls. I drafted a letter to the assistant director of personnel, my acting area superintendent, and to the school system employee relations officer who dealt with the union. In my letter to the assistant director of personnel, I made the following three points. The first centered on the personalization of knowledge. Our aide was a capable and caring educator who enabled our school to offer a very strong and responsive school climate. Second, our school had no guaranteed clientele. We survived on our ability to be good educators and to offer parents something they wanted. We could not survive by just hiring anybody; we needed instructors who not only lived our philosophy but could also help us implement it. Our aide, who was also the mother of two children in the school, was just such a person. Third, we must move our schools toward more decision-making at the school-site level and push the system to serve the individual schools.

The assistant director of personnel did respond in a very personable manner, but, in essence, stated that she was unable to help us. She stated in a letter to me that the system "had been flexible in dealing with us in the past, but was under a negotiated agreement with the teachers union which allowed no flexibility in the matter of reduction of force." We must therefore lose our aide and take the next person on the list waiting to be hired who had more seniority than our aide. Not satisfied with losing her, parents kept up the phone calls and letters to central office, and at the suggestion of my acting area superintendent, I wrote and met with the employee relations officer, who requested proof that we had been exempt from the surplus rule governing teacher aides. This was the document originally agreed to by the OPSB that enabled us to become a public school. Even though I supplied him with this proof, I only heard from him after the aide was dismissed.

I also wrote Superintendent Everett Williams, but did not receive a reply. The door to the Superintendent's office was closed forever.

In the meantime, a new area superintendent, whom I will fictitiously call Dr. Bill Macey, was appointed. When he called me into his office on November 15, 1985, his demeanor was friendly, but he was very clear that he wanted the phone calls and letter writing to stop. He stated that I was shooting myself in the foot by refusing to lose and constantly running to parents every time I did not get my way. All further discussion on the aide and future personnel matters were to only go through him. He reminded me that he had to evaluate my performance as a principal.

I left Dr. Macey's office feeling very intimidated, not certain what actions to take. Three days later, I recorded the statements of that meeting because in no uncertain terms I had felt threatened and did not want to lose these threatening remarks to the passing of time. The next day, November 22, 1985, was the aide's last day.

Having gone to every possible power person in the school system's administration and ending up with threats, frustration, and a feeling of powerless, I still forged ahead. I wrote to Nat Lacour, president of United Teachers of New Orleans (UTNO). I heard verbally from other sources that he would not grant an exception in our case. Here they are, two giant bureaucracies, the management and the union, locked arm in arm preserving their power, but crushing a small school in the process. This is not the way schools should be run. Only school sites should determine who their employees are. These decisions should never be made from power removed. We must stop treating schools as though they are factories needing management and unions, and cease viewing them as though they are in the business of producing merchandise. Schools should be in the business of human development and the transformation of lives. If we truly want to change America and end the slaughter of our urban youth, we should be encouraged to create small schools organized on a family model, not an institutional model. The solution is to break the back of the bureaucracies, dissolve them, and create small independent schools of no more than 300 students for elementary schools and no more than 500 students for high schools. (These suggested numbers actually come from John Goodlad's book, *A Place Called School*.)

Think about this for a second: one high school of 2000 students versus four high schools of 500 students each. All of a sudden, we have four quarterbacks, thirty-two cheerleaders, four Hamlets, four debate teams, four bands, four yearbook production teams, four prom queens and their dates, four valedictorians and the list goes on. Along with these greater number of success stories, we greatly increase the possibility that every student will go through school well known, putting an end to the anonymity created by large, impersonal schools, and therefore weakening a student's need for identity and yearning to become a gang member, a dropout, or on the payroll of criminals.

Would such a move create nirvana? Of course not, but it does not take a rocket scientist to appreciate that such a change would move us in a direction of much safer, more just, more successful, and better educated urban youth. At the same time some larger schools could and would exist but at the behest of the people, not of some monolithic bureaucracy hell-bent on controlling the schools' every move.

One thing my appeal to the union president did that surprised me at the time, but not in hindsight, was that it ruffled management's feathers. On January 10, 1986, I received a reprimand from Superintendent Everett Williams for personally contacting the union president. On January 13, I received a notice from my area superintendent subtly criticizing me for contact with the union president and again directing me to go only through his office for any personnel exceptions to contract agreements.

The president of the Principals' Association of New Orleans Public Schools, Inc., whose invented name will be Marie, also wrote Superintendent Williams a strong criticism of my actions but did not have the decency to send me a copy. However, the employee relations officer forwarded me a copy of her letter.

Marie's letter was "the unkindest cut of all" because she, Jill (the principal of the Montessori School) and I had become friends during the 1985–1986 school year and oftentimes went out drinking on Friday afternoons. Her letter was like a knife in the back for two reasons: She never expressed to me such strong reservation about my actions and she failed to send me a copy of her letter to the superintendent. When I saw her not long after seeing the letter, I asked her why I was not sent a copy of it. She replied, "Oh, didn't I send you a copy?" We both knew that our friendship was at an end and I would never trust Marie again. Jill and I maintained our friendship throughout our careers with the Orleans Parish School System.

After receiving these three negative letters in January from top school officials, I felt I was drowning in shark-infested waters. I was called into a meeting with my area superintendent, Dr. Macey, on February 5, 1986, ostensibly for an evaluation conference. However, I was afraid that the sharks smelled blood because of the loss of our aide and my attempt to seek union relief. Over the weekend, I had drafted two very similar letters, one to Dr. Williams and one to Dr. Macey defending my actions for going directly to the union president, and listing the threats I felt Dr. Macey had directed toward me at our November 15, 1985, meeting. Here are a few of the salient points he made in our meeting on November 15, as I noted in my letter:

> He, Dr. Macey, then stated the following: the only way he wanted things to operate from now on was that I was to come to him with our problems and then, regardless, he did not want to be getting phone calls from parents. He went on to say that he had to evaluate me on how well I implemented board policy. He went on to explain why no phone calls. The first reason was because he did not want them—I was to come to him and that was it. The second reason was more philosophical, more within the nature of advice. His statement went something like this: If you go to someone for help and you don't get what you want and then you go over their heads, i.e. parent calls, then all you will get from those people is pleasantries and, as soon as you leave, you will get nothing. You may go to the superintendent and he will be nice and supportive, but as soon as you leave, nothing. Then he got personal, but, I think, trying to be helpful. You (meaning me) may not know it but what people say is that as soon as you don't get your way, you go to your parents. You don't know how to compromise. You don't know how to lose.

> He talked about the need to compromise, to be a good loser, not to push people to get them to do what you wanted. He talked about the system having brought in outside administrators who tried to push the system, whom, he implied, wouldn't readily compromise and who, thus, became very ineffective because nobody would do anything for them. He implied that he got to where he was because he could compromise and cooperate.

> In the conversation, he stated that even if something was absolutely morally correct, he would not pursue it if expediency and compromise could get the results he wanted.

I gave my area superintendent his letter and showed him my letter to Dr. Williams—again, both of which were very similar. Upon reading the letters, he became very nervous but managed to explain, in a calm voice, that this is not exactly what he said, and, if he were me, he would not send the letter to Dr. Williams. For some reason I trusted him and told him I would not send the letter nor would I destroy it. To my knowledge, Dr. Williams never saw the letter.

The area superintendent responded the next day, in a brief memorandum, to what he described as disagreements and inconsistencies with my written recollection of our November 15, 1985, meeting. He requested that I inform parents that the area office is always available to them and that they are happy to accept phone calls. However, he wrote, "As I mentioned to you, it is unethical for managers to use parents in redressing administrative conflicts." He went on to say, "We expect all school board employees to operate according to high moral standards. We could never recommend the compromising of morality for expedience." I responded in writing that, "I not only acted ethically, but I also acted with sound professional and educational judgment. I also believe that when an effective educator is dismissed from a school for any reason, parents have an absolute right to be informed of the situation and to seek whatever remedies necessary to attempt to rectify bad educational decisions which directly affect their children."

In that meeting, I appreciated that my area superintendent had told me exactly what people were saying about me and what I must do to make it in the system. The problem was that my loyalty was to the New Orleans Free School community and not to management. I had no desire to make it in the bureaucratic structure. My passion, my dedication was to the New Orleans Free School and educating our students, nothing else. Fortunately, many other people, faculty, parents, and friends, also felt this strong loyalty to the Free School.

I should note that the bureaucratic argument for cooperation and compromise too often means acquiescence and obedience rather than struggle for the higher good. Bureaucratic education leaves little room for independence and inventiveness. It bolsters rules and has little tolerance for deviation from those rules. Bureaucratic education means doing it "their way." This means that they expect uniformity and obedience. Attempting to do something different that does not flow from the bureaucracy rapidly gets one labeled as a non-cooperative pest. Being a gadfly in this environment is tantamount to career suicide. Except for closing the school, the bureaucratic structure won virtually every battle as they whittled us down towards compliance.

When trapped in a bureaucratic environment and struggling for air, one must confront the bureaucracy on every issue central to preserving one's program. Being a quiet enabler only drowns oneself and the program. The irony is that drowning is probably inevitable anyway.

As a result of my meeting with my area superintendent, I did not, as stated above, send Dr. Williams the letter. Instead, I wrote him a short one page letter defending my letter to the union president. He replied, on a copy of that letter with the following handwritten remark: "Thanks Bob. I understand your concern. I am only sorry that contractual agreements prevent our being able to help you. Everett."

Dr. Everett Williams was a very personable and impressive man. He was tall, good looking, intelligent, extremely well-dressed, polite, and sociable. Everyone I knew really liked him, myself included. To this day, whenever I see him (his home is only a block away from my daughter's house), he is very friendly and never fails to ask, "How's the missus?"

I will never know if his desire to corral or end the Free School was personal or simply his bureaucratic need to have all his ducks in a row, quacking the same tune and smoothly following directions. He probably had to become the quintessential bureaucrat to rise as far as he did. Heroic is probably the best word to describe his achievement—becoming the first black superintendent of Orleans Parish Public Schools. I have nothing but admiration for the man. Regardless, I felt then and now that his position and its bureaucratic structure should be eliminated. Too much power above drowns too much initiative below.

Dr. Williams was the third and last very personable superintendent I ever knew. The one from my past in Caddo Parish, (Shreveport, 1968) proved to be a segregationist jerk. The next four Orleans Parish superintendents after Dr. Williams fell more into the category of egomaniacs. They were capable of leading few, intimidating many, innovating nothing, spending a lot, and sailing a sinking ship to nowhere. I will discuss these four later on.

No sooner had the loss of our aide died down when we started hearing rumors that the administration was going to close the Free School. The administrative proposal was that we had to grow to 300 students by August 1986 or close. This meant that we must enroll 120 new students, almost doubling our enrollment, within a four month period while simultaneously confronting a rumor that we were closing. We realized that these numbers were the kiss of death. The Montessori School had moved into its own building, leaving us with the entire building to immediately fill or close. Once again, they were using the building against us.

Needless to say, we started having meetings, writing letters, and making phone calls. I remember one parent-faculty meeting when doomsday seemed inevitable. I got choked up and couldn't speak. I heard one parent ask, "What's the matter with Bob?" I heard Don Van Loo, my dear macho friend reply, "He's a grown man and doesn't want you to see him cry."

Yes, I lost many tears, much sleep, and hair, but not weight, during the many struggles with the school system's administration; but giving up never seemed to be an option. My love for what I was doing was more powerful than a bureaucratic machine hell-bent on preserving a system rather than devising educational strategies that could alter lives. Fortunately, once again, many folks connected to the Free School had that passion, love, and willingness to take on the bureaucracy.

In one sense, we lost the battle even before we engaged in the struggle. The system was demanding that we grow significantly in a very short time frame, so we knew that we were in for a major change. How much growth and in what time frame became the points of dispute. The administration had shrewdly put itself in a position to alter the Free School no matter what the outcome.

In our struggles to save the Free School from being hacked to pieces or placed on the chopping block, I wasn't suggesting here that we were better than anyone else. I knew even then that we were far from perfect and were filled with blemishes, but we were different. For example, I would often get too angry with students. Jeanette would have a student in tears or she would be in tears. Sixth-grade teacher Woody would put students in detention every day and then take them out over and over again. Fifth-grade teacher Logan, who later became one of our seventh-grade teachers, and is now a principal at the Wilson Charter School here in New Orleans, would demand the removal of a student "or else." Some teachers were too traditional in their educational approach. Seventh-grade teacher Mary came to me at least twice because she had been hit in the face breaking up fighting seventh-graders. One parent screamed at me for forty-five minutes straight and I never got a word in. The funny thing about this incident is that I only remember the ringing forty-five-minute harangue; I no longer have any idea what the lady was screaming about. We even had to ban a couple of parents from entering the school because they had threatened students.

There is no doubt that we, as a school, had our problems. However, what we offered students and what worked for the vast majority of our students was our philosophy and implementation of education. We afforded children the opportunity for success without the constant fear of failure. For almost our entire existence, we offered them a non-graded program using anecdotal reporting instead of letter grades. We personalized our grading system. I always explained to our incoming parents that in our written, non-graded student reports, we were giving them a document that read more like a letter from a friend to a friend about a friend. We afforded students a very warm and personable educational experience without loneliness or the alienation of anonymity. Remember, students from kindergarten through eighth grade called faculty members by their first name because we wanted to operate more on a family model of schooling and less on an institutional model. We took kids on trips every year, had them to our homes for lunch, and partied with many of their families. We provided children with many opportunities and choices on how they could spend much of their school day. To many people, concern and closeness, academic freedom and rigor, flexibility and creativity, all seemed worth fighting for.

So, in spite of having lost the battle over keeping our aide, our school community jumped into the rapidly rising waters to save our little school. We did not have a lot of time. We learned of the "double or die" proposal around February 20, 1986. The final decision was scheduled for March 24, 1986, barely a month later. In their efforts to crush the New Orleans Free School, administrations often allowed as little time as possible for our school to mobilize for battle. What I think they failed to realize was that our loss of the aide would not elicit the kind of struggle and support the Free School would garner as would a proposal to eliminate the school.

In this sea of contention our community did numerous things that helped our case tremendously. All parents, business partners, and community support people were sent names, addresses, and phone numbers of the board members and superintendents, and asked to write or call in support of the school. Many did. We were also aware that most people in New Orleans did not know that the Free School existed or they had only heard of us peripherally, usually through word of mouth or some favorable news feature. Even though we always had good coverage of our school's many accomplishments from the media, we still felt the need to make the community more aware of our existence. We also knew that we had to counter the school system's argument that we were too small and that at 170 students we were a luxury they could not afford. We produced a detailed letter touting our school's accomplishments, focusing on the necessity of small schools, and elaborating on what the Free School was all about. We sent this open letter out to board members, CEOs, press people, educators, citizens, parents of the Free School, just about anyone we could think of. We sent out almost 100 copies, photocopied by our business partner, Ira Middleberg.

The second thing occurred when a parent took some of our students to a New Orleans City Council meeting to seek council support. The Council unanimously adopted a resolution sent to the school board, the superintendent, and the director of facility planning to keep the Free School open. Normally, city government stays out of school board business, but in this rare case, the city council joined forces with our community. Our students were featured on the nightly news making their presentation seeking city council approval. The resolution read as follows and was printed in *The Times-Picayune* in its entirety the next day.

RESOLUTION
R-86-81

CITY HALL: March 6, 1986

BY: COUNCILMEN SINGLETON, BARTHELEMY, BOISSIERE, EARLY, GIARRUSSO
WAGNER AND WILLIAMS

WHEREAS, the New Orleans Free School is unique in it's
personal approach to education, believing that the educational needs
of children should not be separated from all other parts of their
lives; and

WHEREAS, the school offers an alternative to the traditional
classroom and provides a nurturing atmosphere for all students, from
the "gifted" to the "slow" learners, without making obvious
distinctions between them; it encourages active participants instead
of passive recipients in the learning process; and

WHEREAS, all teachers assigned to this facility are there by
choice and are dedicated to the Free School philosophy of teaching;
and

WHEREAS, it is of note that there is no appreciable
difference on achievement test scores between black and white students
evidence that integration can succeed; and

WHEREAS, Dr. _ Director of Planning for the
Orleans Parish School Board has indicated that unless the enrollment
increases to 300 students, New Orleans Free School would either be
consolidated with another facility or closed due to budgetary
reductions; and

WHEREAS, school faculty are confident that New Orleans Free
School's enrollment can be increased to 300 students but it is also
believed that increasing the enrollment will severely dilute teachers'
effectiveness thus affecting the quality educational experience which
is currently being offered; and

WHEREAS, this City Council joins the Parent Teacher
Association asking New Orleans Public Schools, "why get rid of
something that works?"; based on the merits this school possesses,
every effort should be made to keep this school open and utilize it as
a model for other schools in the Orleans Public School System; now,
therefore

BE IT RESOLVED BY THE COUNCIL OF THE CITY OF NEW ORLEANS,
That this Council does hereby urge and request the Orleans Parish
School Board to reevaluate its position regarding the New Orleans Free
School and take the appropriate steps to keep this institution open.

BE IT FURTHER RESOLVED, That the Clerk of Council is hereby
requested to transmit a certified copy of this resolution to the
members of the Orleans Parish School Board, the Superintendent of New
Orleans Public Schools, the Director of Planning New Orleans Public
Schools and the Parent Teacher Association of the New Orleans Free
School.

THE FOREGOING RESOLUTION WAS READ IN FULL, THE ROLL WAS
CALLED ON THE ADOPTION THEREOF AND RESULTED AS FOLLOWS:

YEAS: BARTHELEMY, BOISSIERE, EARLY, GIARRUSSO, SINGLETON, WAGNER,
WILLIAMS - 7

NAYS: 0

ABSENT: 0

AND THE RESOLUTION WAS ADOPTED.

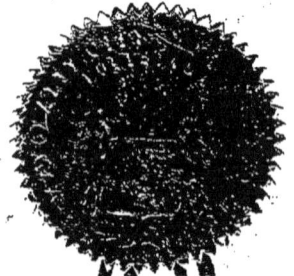

108

As I mentioned above, the timeline between the administration's proposal that the Free School enrollment practically double by the fall of this 1986 or close, and a vote by the Orleans Parish School Board, was incredibly short. Fortunately, we had organized our supporters and achieved enough positive press that a compromise was worked out requiring us more time to increase student enrollment to 300 students by the beginning of school year 1987, instead of 1986. This gave us two enrolling periods to achieve the goal, not just one. Did we win or did we lose? We were still alive but in our struggle to remain a small school we were being chopped to pieces. At the same time, a student body of 300 would fill our school building to capacity, protecting us from having any other school or program being placed in our building. We felt that we could make it as a school of 300 students and that this was still small in terms of most urban schools. We were happy.

Our euphoria was short lived. That summer I attended, "The Institute on School Climate and Governance," a conference sponsored by Harvard's Graduate School of Education and conducted by Lawrence Kohlberg, who was a leading expert on the theory of moral development. Sometime near the end of the conference, I received a most debilitating call from my wife concerning school business. Without any fanfare or public announcement, hidden away in the administration's proposed budget for school year 1986–1987, was a one-line sentence proposing to close the New Orleans Free School. One of our parents had noticed this sickening situation and immediately called my wife. Fortunately, the Institute was drawing to a close and I was able to return to New Orleans from Cambridge to deal with this new calamity.

We were caught off guard and incensed over being chosen for closure after just having won the right of continued existence if we could almost double our enrollment within two years. We were not the only one. Some of our parents and faculty wrote a three-page letter supporting the Free School, which we photocopied and mailed to numerous recipients, again thanks to our business partner, Ira Middleberg.

Many people in the community were just as perplexed as we as to why the Free School was targeted for closure. On August 7, 1986, our City Councilman, Jim Singleton, even wrote Dr. Williams, with copies to all board members: "When I appeared before the Board on August 5, 1986, I was not aware that the Free School was included in the closures. We fought this battle last year (school year 1985–1986) and I thought it was settled once and for all."

This time was scarier than the previous struggle over enrollment because the administration was trying to close the school without pretence. On July 30, 1986, I sent a letter to parents and our closest supporters. The fear I felt can be readily seen in these paragraphs:

I am sure by now that most of you have heard that once again the New Orleans Free School is being threatened. I have been told by many of you, "Oh, come on. It has happened before. They won't do it. They are not serious." Well, in the past the issue was over leadership and size; this time it is over existence. THIS TIME THEY ARE VOTING TO CLOSE THE SCHOOL! Remember, death occurs only once.

If you are satisfied with the Free School and want and expect your child there on September 2, there is very little time left – the final vote will be August 18, 1986.

Fortunately, for both of these battles, the issue over size and now closure, we received excellent press coverage and tremendous community support. This time we even received front page coverage in *The Louisiana Weekly*, a major African American newspaper serving the New Orleans area.

In the end, we won again: we were removed from the school closure list, but I knew for sure that we could never trust the administration. They were out to get rid of us. Our struggles were not ending; they were just going to intensify. The administration removed the Free School from the closure list, only to confront us with internal and bureaucratic discord.

One incident during this 1984–1986 period certainly did not endear us to the administration or the school board. Dr. Williams had two or three schools make a presentation before the administration and the school board before each board meeting. This usually meant some type of song, dance, or award presentation. When our school received his call, we readily agreed and requested to perform the Pledge of Allegiance in sign language, one song in sign, and one folk dance. Meetings were held in a small board room and these student/school presentations were much ado about little.

However, we received a second phone call from the Superintendent's office informing us that the meeting had been moved to a large school's auditorium to accommodate an expected large turnout. This was because the Superintendent was proposing to dismiss all of the aides in the system due to a budget shortfall. We knew nothing about this controversy but could not have asked for a better forum because the large auditorium also had a large stage. Our students began the meeting before a standing room-only crowd reciting and signing the Pledge of Allegiance. The applause was tremendous. Two other schools made their presentations but their performances were low-keyed and certainly not ready for the stage. Our students took the stage in their folk dance costumes and brought down the house with their performance. They performed a dance called Sestorka, which is a complicated dance that gets faster and faster as the dance progresses. Our ten students danced excellently and the cheers and applause were deafening. Some fifty students then joined the stage to sign the song, "Ebony and Ivory." It was a beautiful sight and sound to behold. The silence during the performance was astonishing; the shouts with applause at the end of the performance were astounding. Our students had beautifully represented the Free School and certainly elevated our status in everyone's eyes. Then I did a very controversial thing. I grabbed the microphone to thank the board and the Superintendent for having us showcased at the meeting.

I then thanked Jeanette, who was still classified as a paraprofessional for having taught our students sign language and conducting this performance. When I mentioned that a teacher's aide was responsible for that incredible performance, pandemonium took over. As Jeanette walked down the stairs to enter the auditorium, she was literally mobbed by the crowd shouting her praise. I also heard someone from the administration or the school board say, "Get that microphone from him!" As the excitement in the hall was ebullient, the stares from the big-wigs were murderous. One board member angrily told me, "You don't know when to shut up." We left the meeting shortly after our performance and the ensuing chaos we had created, only to read in the paper the next morning that Superintendent Williams had withdrawn the proposal to dismiss all of the paraprofessionals in the system. In spite of our student performances, I certainly exhibited little tact in this encounter with the power brokers and definitely did not gain the respect for our school I had hoped for.

Now that we had survived the attempted closing of the Free School in the summer of 1986, internal strife reared its ugly head. Due to quickly accepting so many new students and teachers, we encountered difficulties. One of those was discipline, which became a much greater concern for us. We were forced to suspend many more students than we had in the past. We lost our strongest parent ally, who fled because she felt we had abandoned too many principles in trying to accommodate so many students. She concluded that chaos, more than creative endeavors, ruled the school day.

During the two years of this rapid growth, the school became a true New Orleans public school with a 95 percent black population and over 90 percent free lunch student participation. There were no remnants of us as a hippie school. We were urbanized. There were still strong characteristics of our progressive program: first name basis, anecdotal reporting, open-ended assignments, emphasis on projects and presentations, and a strong creative program. But sadly, discipline took center stage. We first relied on suspensions alone, and then we developed a policy based on warnings, detentions, parent conferences and then suspensions. We adopted the rule that students who were suspended three times in one year could not return to the Free School the next year. As time quickly passed, suspensions dropped and detentions rose accordingly. During the first year of this two-year period we created Saturday detentions and successfully implemented them for several years. I would go every Saturday morning and hold detention. Each week my wife would lovingly tell me that I needed to behave so that I would not have to go to detention. I somehow ended up in detention almost every week.

At some point after becoming a school of 300 students, we received a grant to implement the Resolving Conflict Creatively Program (RCCP), which was operated out of Loyola University. The program complemented the Free School philosophy of encouraging responsibility and engaging students in the atmosphere of the school. Students were trained in conducting conflict resolution sessions with peers involved in disputes. This grant program provided a small amount of funds, which aided us in holding detentions. Thus, teachers oftentimes supervised detentions on Saturday, giving me much needed relief. I should note that some teachers also volunteered to hold detentions even when funds were not available.

We survived the growth of 300 students with discipline problems ebbing and flowing over the years, but never reaching the intensity they did during those two years of rapid growth.

9

A New Area Superintendent

The years 1987 to 1991 proved to be more of a nightmare than a threat of closure. The strategy seemed to shift from ripping our heart out to tearing us apart, limb by limb. Sometime during the 1987–1988 school year, the school board hired two new administrators. One was a very conservative black educator who became our area superintendent. The other was a progressive white educator in charge of curriculum development. After a few encounters with both men, I jokingly told friends that if our area superintendent outlasted the curriculum developer, the system was moving to the right. If the developer lasted longer than the area superintendent, the system was moving to the left. Ironically, they each lasted almost two years and exited as if they were a team—they practically came together and left together.

It was also during this time I began working on my doctorate at Vanderbilt University. I was in a weekend program that also required me to attend two summers if I hoped to graduate in three years. For four to six weekends per semester I would fly to Nashville, leaving on Friday mornings and returning on Sundays. I would go to school on Friday, conduct the morning assembly, take care of any necessary business, leave school by 9:00 a.m., go to Mothers Restaurant to get their famous Ferdie Special sandwich to go, drive to the airport, always board the airplane as the flight attendant was closing the door, and then thoroughly enjoy my sandwich on the plane ride. Bless the days before 9/11, I never missed one flight.

Almost the entire time I was working on my doctorate, I had to deal with the new area superintendent, with whom I jousted during his tenure. Having this area superintendent—whom I will call, Dr. Joseph Theadore—was like knowing that someone had put out a mark on us and, worse, knowing the assassin's identity. In this case it was one and the same. To say that this man frightened me would be an understatement; to say that I resisted him with everything I possessed would be the absolute truth.

The 1987 school year began with an immediate problem over a teacher who was placed at our school against our objection. Right before school opened we had an unfilled teacher vacancy position. A lady teacher was surplussed and placed at our school. I immediately turned to the new area superintendent, Dr. Theadore, for help. The teacher was placed in our school by the voluntary transfer agreement between the administration and the union. Once again, we were trapped in the vice-grip of two powerful bureaucracies with little or no voice. The lady showed up the first day that teachers were to report, left early, but skipped the three to five planning days before school started. She then missed the first seventeen teaching days of that school year.

This teacher reported on August 27, 1987. On September 9, 1987, seven teaching days later when she still failed to show up, I wrote the area superintendent for immediate relief and sent a copy to the director of personnel. I also sent copies of all correspondence to the president of our PTSA. In my letter I unequivocally argued for school site autonomy in the hiring of staff: "Just to send any staff member to teach in a school without taking great pains to make sure of that person's compatibility with existing school philosophy is to certainly dilute and weaken said school's program. Randomly placing staff members in a magnet school is to blatantly deny the magnet school concept." I included the magnet school concept only because the New Orleans Free School was listed as one of the few magnet programs in the Orleans Parish School System. I included all schools in my final paragraph in this plea to my area superintendent: "I am asking for two things: First, immediate relief in this particular teaching situation. Either dismiss [this teacher] or place her somewhere else where no negative feelings have developed. This will allow us to quickly find a replacement. Our students have been without a teacher long enough. Second, I am soliciting your help in securing a policy and/or practice whereby staffing is not done systematically; i.e., allow all magnet schools to have a major say in who teaches at that school. I would even suggest that all schools have a veto power in all staffing assignments – this would include voluntary teacher transfers."

While I never had a response from Dr. Theadore on either of my requests, the director of personnel (this was not the same director of personnel whom I dealt with over the principalship issue) did write me on September 16, 1987, defending the school system policy. Apparently this lady teacher was already encountering administrative difficulties and was now being terminated. The director informed me that the lady would be terminated and criticized me for not filling all positions with certified staff. She made the following point: "All schools currently have the right to select their staff until July 1, when the surplus procedure begins. The key to avoid accepting surplus teachers is to fill all vacancies by July 1." She also made the following comment somewhat challenging the magnet school concept: "Magnet schools also share the burden of absorbing surplus personnel if the occasion arises. To exempt certain schools from this procedure would lead to a climate of elitism among the schools." She then ended the letter with the following statement: "I am also soliciting (your area superintendent's) help in assisting you in filling all positions with certified teachers since you have had and continue to have non-certified personnel in your school."

On September 24, 1987, I responded at length to her letter in which I defended my attack of the school administration's surplus transfer policy, responded to her charge of potential elitism on the part of magnet schools, and once again, made my case for non-certified staff being allowed to teach. Concerning the policy of allowing surplus teachers the right to choose any school, including magnet schools having a vacancy after a certain date, I took the following position: "First, this argument is dangerously close to the attitude that if some schools have cancer they all should. Attack the problem, don't spread the disease. Secondly, some magnet schools like ours serve no district and have no guaranteed audience. We survive only by our ability to attract clientele. I question the ethics of sending someone into a situation that they know nothing about, since this increases the possibility of their failure. What about the children who are affected by this process?" I ended this section of my letter by quoting John Goodlad in his excellent book, *A Place Called School*:

> What I am proposing is genuine decentralization of authori-ty and responsibility to the local school within a framework designed to ensure school-to-school equity and a measure of accountability...The guiding principle being put forward here is that the school must become largely self-directing. (152)

I included this quote in the letter because, while arguing for the au-tonomy and uniqueness of magnet schools, I clearly wanted her to under-stand that I was strongly advocating freedom of operation for all schools. Most magnet schools in New Orleans were considered elitist. They had a much higher white student population than other schools in the parish, while they had a much lower student population on free lunch. The New Orleans Free School was definitely an anomaly regarding our student pop-ulation and our classification as a magnet school. Our numbers, of close to 95 percent black students and over 90 percent on free lunch, were compa-rable to the non-magnet public schools in Orleans Parish public schools.

I then took on the issue of having non-certified staff at our school. I defended the few uncertified people teaching at our school as excellent ed-ucators who worked beautifully in our program as they fostered "trusting relationships over controlling relationships" and who "first taught people, then the curriculum." (These quotes were paraphrased from *A Blueprint for Success: Principles for Dropout Prevention* by the National Foundation for the Improvement of Education.) I then continued quoting the authors of this document who went on to state that we needed "new approaches to staff-ing." I then cited the 1985 California Commission on the Teaching Profes-sion's booklet titled, *Who Will Teach Our Children? A Strategy for Improving California Schools*. Its first recommendation to improve the teaching profes-sion was to implement flexibility in certifying educators. Thus, in this letter to the personnel director, I included the following statement: "All we are asking for is flexibility and appreciation that we offer a different approach to education. This difference demands that we be viewed and treated differently. This is the essence of alternatives. To demand absolute standardization is to negate and smother the concept of different approaches to education...our program requires a frame of mind, a philosophical vent which theoretically will never be institutionalized." I should note here that just a couple of years later, Teach for America was created, which offers an entirely different path to teacher recruitment and certification than the traditional school of education model.

I spent a lot of time composing these three letters because they would reveal how strongly I was willing to fight for diversity and uniqueness, even as the system continually eroded our power and minimized our program into being just another public school. We wanted to be a public school but as part of a system that operated on the principle of school-site autonomy with bureaucracy minimized if not extinguished. We should have the power to immediately dismiss any teacher who could not function or who abused our school. Wading through bureaucracy should never be the process in a situation like this—not if you want quality educators in an urban school. The irony of this story is that in bureaucratic time, this issue was resolved quickly. The improperly hired teacher only missed seventeen teaching days. But in educational time it was still a travesty and should have been resolved much sooner.

Dealing with this teacher afforded me introduction to my new superintendent, Dr. Theadore. I never felt support from the man on this issue and even felt intimidation, though I initially could not put my finger on how or why. In the midst of trying to get rid of this teacher who failed to show up, we engaged in an even more intense struggle with the area superintendent over our assistant head custodian, Michael Smith.

To tell this story I must go back to last school year. In April 1987 our assistant head custodian (we only had two custodians—a head and an assistant head), Michael Smith, was our school chess coach. He would hold chess class during our sign-up time and almost thirty students signed up with him on a weekly basis. By April the number was down to eight major players whom we entered in a city-wide chess tournament. The contests were held on Saturday mornings at different schools and whenever our students, with Mike as their coach, entered the tournament area, there were obvious looks of surprise from the other teams and their supporters. The other teams were well dressed, often in uniforms, very reserved and, I believe, all white or mostly white. Our group was racially mixed, came with a black coach, dressed in street clothes and exhibited group excitement that stood out like a sore thumb. However, aside from the stares and initial snickering, we were always well received and treated respectfully. When it came to the final tournament, our eight students stood out once again as they swept the tournament and took first place city-wide. Mike was an instant school-wide hero. The next school day, students and faculty lined up in two rows facing one another from the street to the upstairs office, and clapped as Mike arrived and walked past them. This entrance made the nightly television news and *The Times-Picayune* ran an article about Mike and the school's chess victory.

I knew that this notoriety would bolster us in the public's eye while fostering more resentment from the administration. Throughout our history we often received such excellent press coverage: our eighth grade student internship program received front page coverage in the Living section covering our students performing volunteer work at city hall; our older students who conducted a citywide presidential poll with amazing accuracy every four years received articles in the Metro section of the paper and sometimes received TV coverage; and, of course, we were always in the news over proposed closings or modifications of the New Orleans Free School. Throughout this excellent coverage, we never once received a word of praise or a congratulatory phone call from one Orleans Parish school administrator higher than a teacher or principal. When I ran into a school board member (the same one who told me that I did not know when to shut up) shortly after Mike and our chess club received such excellent press, he was genuinely surprised that no one from top administration had acknowledged this accomplishment. He immediately arranged for Mike and the chess members to be presented to Superintendent Everett Williams and the school board members for congratulations. While we went to this honor, I knew that this too would be another kiss of death.

Between the chess victory and sometime during the first month of school year, 1987, I had convinced our head custodian to retire. He was elderly, had been ill, and when he returned after a lengthy illness, he seemed to have diminished capacities. Retirement versus getting the man fired seemed the perfect option. He retired.

I then expected Mike to be named head custodian. Principals usually had the last word on such a decision, even if we had to interview others for the job. Mike did not get the job. The area superintendent, against my arguments and protest, placed another man of questionable character as our head custodian.

I fought this decision with every breath I had. The timing of this battle was unfortunate, occurring just as the struggle over the teacher who never showed up was ending. On September 23, 1987, I wrote Dr. Theadore a very impassioned letter essentially begging him to reconsider his decision to place an outsider as head custodian at the Free School. In this letter I made the following statements and arguments:

Michael Smith, assistant head custodian, is more than a custodian at the Free School, he is a school hero. Maybe you are unaware of the significance of this man's contribution. I hope so. Should not excellence be rewarded not chopped down? Should not real life black heroes be elevated? Our students, who are at risk students, look up to this man – and they should.

As you and I both know, we were never consulted in this decision. John Naisbitt and Patricia Aburdine in their book, *Re-inventing the Corporation*, quote Professor Bennis who has studied CEOs of major corporations. I am going to share with you some of Naisbitt, Aburdene and Bennis' thoughts even at the risk of alienating you. I do this not out of disrespect but because I believe deeply that your decision to place a head custodian in our school, while it may make sense bureaucratically, is a bad education decision. 'Successful CEOs see themselves as leaders, not managers,' says professor Bennis. 'They were concerned with their organization's basic purposes, why it exists, its general direction… not with "nuts" and bolts"…not with "doing things right" (the overriding concern of managers) but with "doing the right thing." (156)

I believe wholeheartedly that what we are experiencing is sacrificing 'doing the right thing.' In our case, doing the right thing would be to place Michael Smith as head custodian as (sic,) the New Orleans Free School.

You have spoken of the individuality of schools. Our individuality has been lost. Will you please re-consider your decision.

Shortly thereafter Dr. Theadore and I met to discuss this head custodian situation. He would not bend. I kept pushing the issue of fairness but he retorted, "Fairness is in the eye of the beholder." He then went on to argue that there were no other head custodian positions available in the school system and seniority rights demanded that he place the outside man as our head custodian. His decision was final.

I initially chose not to respond to our meeting and accept his rotten decision. However, after a few days of agony and internal corrosion, on October 12, 1987, I again wrote to him on the matter. I knew that I would only further convince the administration that I refused to lose and that I

118

was only going to exacerbate the situation. I was also cognizant that I probably was not going to change his decision. I began my letter with my other concern, namely my fear of this man:

> I want to thank you for discussing the issue of our head custodian. You seemed to listen. I was not going to write— more out of fear than anything—but this issue dominates my thoughts. In this case I feel that our school has been treated unfairly and in fact punitively.

In this letter I once again emphasized how important Mike was to the Free School. I then pointed out that he, Dr. Theadore, had expressed irritation over my sending copies of my letters to Mike and the president of our PTSA. I explained to him that I "obviously needed protection" and that I operated "from friendships and close relationships not from impersonal bureaucratic relationships." I did write that I would "not send a copy of this letter to anyone at this time but I do want my thoughts to be a matter of record." I challenged his concept that fairness was in the eye of the beholder. I wrote, "I do not believe in this concept. I believe in fairness and justice and we should all work toward these goals. They should not so easily be dismissed. I do not believe in this case that we were treated fairly or with justice." I then dealt with his argument that there were simply no other head custodian vacancies in the school system and he simply could not create positions. I included in my letter the following: "let the record show that in the 'Superintendent's Bulletin' dated September 21, 1987, Vol. 35, No. 7, five listings for head custodian were published: NOCCA, Gordan, Audubon Montessori, Bienville, F.C. Williams." The day after we met I spoke with the principal of one of these schools and was told that this vacancy still existed.

I also pointed out that the custodian he had placed at the Free School was being removed from his previous school at the previous school principal's request. "This principal's request was obviously granted." I ended my letter by dealing with Dr. Theadore's final consideration that I had forced my head custodian to retire so that I could have Mike placed as head custodian at the Free School. I simply agreed with the area superintendent that I had, in fact, urged the man to retire. When we reported back to work for school year 1987, the head custodian had come back from a lengthy illness. He seemed to have lost many of his capabilities. As I stated in the letter, he seemed incapable of understanding my request for a doctor's note establishing that he could report back to work. He thought that one of our veteran teachers was a custodian sub. "When asked to go to the boiler room to get a light bulb, he would stand where he was for about 10 to 15 minutes trying to figure out what and where the boiler room was." I ended this part of the letter by simply writing, "He was a fine gentleman who served the school system and our school well. It was my opinion that his physical condition had deteriorated to the point that he should retire. I did urge that he retire." We lost; Dr. Theadore would not budge.

Four significant things resulted from losing this battle and our friend Mike, the janitor and chess coach. First, Dr. Theadore unblinkingly exercised his authority over the Free School. Second, despite staunchly resisting his decision, I never went above his head. Regarding personnel matters, I had fewer options. I had no bureaucratic support over the aide and knew I would have none over the janitor. Third, Mike became despondent over not getting the position, and less than two years later left the Free School. Once again, bureaucratic control proved pre-eminent over human development. Fourth, our custodial service hit skid row.

For many months, I could not get custodians to do their jobs—one even pulled a knife on me. My cries for help went on deaf ears from the area office. Finally, the health department came in and informed the system that they had the weekend to clean the school or it would not be allowed to reopen Monday morning. The school system sent in custodians, who worked around the clock for two nights to properly clean the school. The bathrooms were too filthy to describe and trash and dirt was abundant throughout the building.

A few years after this crisis, we were able to hire Ruby Smith as our head custodian and then we hired Pearl Rollins as our assistant head. They kept the building clean during their tenure at the Free School.

Our next confrontation with our area superintendent came, not over personnel, but zeroed in on our program. Apparently, the administration wanted all course grades given to students entered into the computer system. Without consulting us, seeking our input, or offering any consideration to our program, on November 30, 1987, I received from Dr. Theadore the following memorandum:

RE: Grade Reporting

Board policy mandates that academic and conduct grades must be on file for students so that transcripts may be issued. You may continue to issue a narrative report to parents at report card conferences, but students' progress must be recorded in letter grades on teacher's record card, office record card, and for data office records.

Please complete the attached data sheets and return to Data Office as soon as possible. If you have any questions, please contact my office.

We had never used teacher or office record cards nor had anyone ever requested to see one during my entire career with the OPSB. I lived in fear all the years that someone would request one of these cards and I would again end up in the doghouse, but it never happened. This was one meaningless task that we miraculously avoided. We had never seen the data sheets before and had no idea how to fill them out. At the time, I do not think we even had the proper computer equipment to complete these data sheets. More importantly, this was a new attack on the Free School.

Previously, they had tried to dismiss Jim and Jeanette, and managed to dismiss our aide and block the promotion of our assistant custodian. They had used the building to entangle us in a fight with the Montessori School and then they used the building against us by forcing us to practically double our enrollment or die. Finally, they had just tried to close us. For the first time since all of our struggles began, they were going after our instructional program.

In response, on December 9, 1987, I sent the area superintendent a letter strongly defending our non-graded instructional policy, which was initially accepted by the school board when they absorbed us into the school system back in 1973. I wrote this letter as I did all my letters mentioned in the book, but I never sent them until they had been read by many people—my secretary, Peggy Valls, who typed and edited all the letters; teachers who were present at the time a letter was written including any combination of Jeanette, Woody, Jim, Mary, Ann, Zoe, Sandra, Heidi, CherylAnn, Shelia, Logan, David, Derek, Patrice, etc.; many parent members such as Don, Kojo, Anna, Dalton, Louise, and my wife Sue. Sue was probably my harshest critic. She always felt that my letters were verbose and bordered on being preachy, but after I made some of her suggested changes, she usually supported sending them. For my part, I felt compelled to get all the issues out and present them factually and passionately. I also felt that if I left anything implied or an issue not addressed, this information or circumstance would undermine our position and probably do us harm. Here is my first letter on grades to my area superintendent.

December 9, 1987

Dr.
Associate Superintendent,
Area II,
Orleans Parish School Board,
5931 Milne Blvd.,
New Orleans, La. 70124

> "...Nobody can know for certain what the right
> steps are in particular situations. Freedom is
> possible only after we commit ourselves to
> understanding the need to accept fundamental
> diversity." The Rapids of Change, Robert
> Theobald, p. 18

Dear   ,

   I am responding to your memorandum titled "Grade Reporting" and dated
November 30, 1987.

   I need to inform you that I in no way feel that the Free School is in violation
of school board policy. When we were first adopted into the Orleans Parish School
System back in August 1973, we specifically asked and were granted permission to be
exempt from the grading policy. In fact, then Superintendent Dr. Gene Geisert
personally gave us the book of policies and requested that we go through it and
request which ones we needed to be exempt from in order to preserve our program.
We listed grading as one that we needed exemption from. We were granted this request
by Dr. Geisert and the Orleans Parish School Board. Our accepted proposal should be
a matter of record. If not, I have copies.

   To my knowledge, this exemption for the Free School from the grading policy has
never been rescinded by the board. I should also note that we have continued a no
grading policy for the past 14 years. I do not understand this sudden pressure to
alter our program. In fact, I believe that it is board policy and administrative
philosophy to offer parents more schools of choice. Schools of choice by definition
mean diversity, not uniformity. We simply cannot have both.

   Our goal to maintain a nongraded program is not only to offer a high degree of
personalization afforded at the Free School but also to provide the students a truly
noncompetitive, cooperative enriched environment. We are offering children from New
Orleans an environment which achieves academic progress without fear of traditional,
harmful social comparisons which all too often lead to low self-esteem and self-image.

   I also ask you to consider that not all students are alike or can survive under
the same school conditions. Many students need different types of school programs,
including variations in instructions, grading, enrichment, etc. I also believe
deeply that many students thrive on a different type of adult/student relationship.

Our grading practices foster, nurture and preserve this different type of relationship. Mary Ann Raywid states this point eloquently, "...Other youngsters perform better in more personalized and supportive surroundings. Only by closing our eyes to human dignity can we continue to impose on all students a single standardize school climate." (Phi Delta Kappa, June 1987, pp. 766-67)

This issue of a nongraded program is so central to the philosophy of the Free School that I included it in an article I wrote about the school which was published in the Spring/Summer 1987 issue of Changing Schools, pp. 4-5. I quote this section at length as follows:

> Peters and Waterman emphasize that the best-run companies place a strong emphasis on treating and enabling employees to be winners, not losers. They call them "champions." The best companies' attitudes toward producing winners not losers is so similar to our attitude about our students that I must include it. Again quoting Peters and Waterman: "...we like to think of ourselves as winners. The lesson that the excellent companies have to teach is that there is no reason why we can't design systems that continually reinforce this notion; most of their people are made to feel that they are winners.
>
> At the Free School we do not give grades for the same reason. In a graded system, most students walk away feeling pretty bad about the situation. In a class of 30 students about eight will feel really good about the process and then in descending order the other 22 students will progressively feel pretty rotten about themselves. This process of tearing apart many of our young people is wasteful, cruel and unnecessary. In the best-run companies they use informal evaluation procedures as opposed to paper-ridden forms. At the Free School we use a personal, anecdotal form of evaluation. We constantly celebrate and elevate excellence in all our student achievements for we are in the business of producing winners not losers.

John Goodlad summarizes this idea so well, "Schools would be markedly different if their ongoing function was to assure successful performance." (Goodlad, A Place Called School, McGraw Hill 1984, p. 242)

, I have dealt with this issue at length because it is so crucial to the essence and philosophy of the Free School. This is why we originally requested and were granted exemption from the grading policy. I hope that you will support our efforts to preserve our program. If you cannot, then I invite you to take this issue before the board once again.

Sincerely,

Robert M. Ferris, Principal,
New Orleans Free School

RMF/pv

123

I did not hear back from or discuss this grading issue with my superintendent until we met on January 13, 1988. I believe that it was during this meeting that he abruptly asked me, "How come every time we meet, the meeting is so controversial?" I replied, "Because every time you call me in to meet, it is always over something controversial."

In this meeting he went on to express displeasure with educational articles, especially a speech by David Kearns, then CEO of Xerox, that I sent to people in authority throughout our community. These articles were written by prominent educators and political leaders extolling the concept of school-site autonomy (or in educational jargon, School-Based Management). They were taken from the *Kappan, Educational Leadership,* etc. I was instigating a one-person movement to educate power people in New Orleans how to think differently about what public schools might be and how to manage them. I was subtly planting a seed in their minds that we might run public education differently than stagnant, bureaucratic education was being run. This was also a back door attempt to defend the Free School and possibly get the bureaucrats off our backs. The latter did not work. I mailed some 100 of these speeches/articles with a cover letter every month for about a year. If only I had the capacity to e-mail back then, I would have continued the practice for a longer period of time. However, if these articles and speeches irritated my boss I could simply take him off my list, which is exactly what I did. My goal was to transmit information and inspire transformation, not irritate my critics. I hoped that the recipients would examine them and discover that we had the chance to transform public education into something meaningful, responsive, and exciting.

During that meeting Dr. Theadore actually said that the Free School would be no different than any other school in the system and if I wanted a different school I should go out and start my own. That conversation on January 13, 1988, had dumbfounded me so much that it left me with a burning need to tackle these issues head on and to make this conversation a part of the public record. I sent him another lengthy letter on January 20, 1988, responding to his criticism of me, and again, staunchly defending our right to offer a different type of instructional program. Here is that letter.

January 20, 1988

Associate Superintendent
Area II
5931 Milne St.
New Orleans, La.

Dear

    I feel I must respond to our meeting concerning grades on
January 13, 1988. I believe the crux of the matter was summed up in
your statement and I quote, "Your school will be no different than
any other school." I beg to differ with you. The Free School is
different - it must be different or it is a lie to the parents who
choose it. Schools of choice, magnet schools, alternative schools
are different by definition - they must be or they are only facades.
    This past summer, I had the opportunity of hearing the
superintendent of the Parkway School District in Chesterfield,
Missouri, Dr. Len Burns, make a presentation. I share with you a
small part of his educational approach:
        The basic premise behind school-based management is that
        educational opportunities for children are improved when
        those who are most directly affected by decisions are
        involved in the decision-making process. The process assumes
        that individual schools within a school district can, and
        even should, be different from one another as a result of
        students, teachers, parents, school administrative staff, and
        the community taking primary responsibility for management of
        the school's program.

This same philosophy must apply to magnet schools and schools of
choice. They are different.
    Later in our discussion you reenforced your comment that the
Free School would not be different than any other school when you
responded to my thoughts that standardization suffocates. You
informed me that the only way I could get away from standardization
is to go out and start another school. Well, that is exactly what I
did, and the Orleans Parish School Board endorsed and supported this
school on the specific premise that it would be a non-graded, more
cooperative, open-ended approach to learning. I do not understand
this pressure to change our program. The New Orleans Public Schools
and the New Orleans community need solutions not narrow-mindedness.
    Also, if you are successful in getting rid of me and/or the Free
School, what have you gained? Too many parents, black and white,
already do not feel comfortable sending their children to public
schools. The one best system approach has not served our area. At
best, it perpetuates mediocrity and at worst, serves the perpetuation
of ignorance and poverty. Poor parents, all parents, deserve the
right of choice - real choice, significant choice - not seductive
rhetoric. People need different schools!

-1-

125

I remind you of a quote I once shared with you, "[W]e are dangerously near a time when public schools could become, like public housing or public jails, places where the poor are confined against their will." [Egerton, Education Week, September 8, 1982. I mistakenly sited this quote in my letter to you dated September 9, 1987.]

In our conversation, you criticized me for struggling to keep non-certified staff and for pushing away or making it difficult for personnel whom you claimed I did not want. I challenge you to document the claim that I pushed anyone out or made it difficult for those whom you say I did not like. Some teachers whom we wanted did not work out — they left of their own volition and sometimes their own frustration. One teacher who was assigned to us after a year saying that this place was not for him — he wanted a different structured environment. I agreed with him. One teacher who was assigned to us again without our input never showed up for the first 17 teaching days. She was replaced. It is my understanding that this lady has had a history of job-related problems. However, I do not know this for a fact.

You need to know that 8 out of 10 of our teachers are certified. The two who are not are working for certification. One has been with us for two years. She has proved to be an excellent teacher — I would be a fool and a poor educational leader not to fight for her. The other replaced the lady who did not show up at the beginning of this year. She has recently taken the NTE for the first time and passed it with flying colors. Our librarian, who is from India, has been unsuccessful in passing the NTE, probably because of cultural differences, but she is constantly taking courses and the NTE to meet state teaching requirements. She is a lovely lady — I am proud to have her on my staff and I will continue to fight for her as long as she wants to work at the Free School.

I suggest that you adopt a different perspective on this matter. I suggest that I should be congratulated for putting together such an excellent staff. I remind you that in this era when it is difficult, at best, to get highly qualified, intelligent staff, our school has a cohesive staff that we are all extremely proud of. At the present time, only one teacher is having difficulty adjusting at the Free School. I continue to hope that she will make it.

It is my understanding that the school system is putting pressure on principals not to accept inadequate teachers. Our teachers must be sufficiently engaging to attract cross-town bus riders — even some very young ones. I would be doing the parents of the school a great injustice if I accepted inadequate or mediocre teachers.

On the question of certification, I should note that there is much criticism of the certification process. I feel I should be supported in securing the best and most qualified staff I can find. I refer you to the U.S. Department of Education's document, "Schools That Work: Educating Disadvantage Children," where it clearly states the following: "...Principal may need the administrative autonomy and authority to hire unusually qualified teachers with unconvential backgrounds." I agree. I would appreciate your support.

When you say that I have forced people out, I believe that you

-2-

126

are referring to our former head custodian, as you have brought this up once before. I want it publicly stated that I did urge his retirement. Last school year, when he returned after a lengthy illness, he did not seem to have all his capacities. One day he treated a teacher who has been with us since we moved into this building around 1980 as though she were a substitute custodian. When asked to go to the boiler room to get a light bulb, he would stand where he was for about 10 to 15 minutes trying to figure out what and where the boiler room was. He left lit cigarette butts all over the school no matter how many time I asked him to stop. When I requested that he get a note from his doctor verifying that he was well and could work, he seemed completely unable to understand my request and certainly did not produce such a note. It is my understanding that Mr. Markham had requested of him that he secure his boiler's license. Every time I requested that he get this license his response was "What license?" He would stand where he was and talk to himself for 10 to 15 minutes and then go on about his chores. He was and is a fine gentleman who served the school sytem and our school well. It was my opinion that his physical condition had deteriorated to the point that he should retire. I did urge him to retire.

The fact that I struggled to have our assistant custodian replace him as head custodian is a matter of record. I believe that your actions in putting another person here as head custodian without my knowledge or without even consulting with me, and then over my protest was a punitive action toward our school and community. Not only was it punitive and cruel, but I feel that you denigrated the situation by saying that you were glad that the assistant custodian had a "fan club." (This satement was made during our earlier meeting concerning our custodial situation.) I refer you to the article, "Our Destiny, Authors of a Scientific Revolution'" by Na'im Akbar found in the book, Black Children: "...Rather than assessing people's ability to effectively manipulate objects of the outer world, one would be concerned with assessing people's adequacy in negotiating cooperative, amiable human relationships. With such criteria we might find the Western world to be a population of idoits, given their failures at effective family relationships, good human relations, transethnic relationships and cooperation, and the generally poor showing in effective interpersonal relationships..." I believe deeply in the development of human relationships; I deplore depersonalization. I feel that people should be applauded for friendship not punished.

In our conversation, you mentioned that I forced out students whom I do not want. For your information, the Free School has a long standing reputation for tolerating and usually ameliorating disruptive behavior. At the beginning of this school year we had the worst rash of fighting and disruption that our school has ever experienced. I suspended over 40 students, one of whom was expelled. (Two others were expelled but I argued on their behalf and they were sent back to the Free School.) One student left because he had been in trouble all last school year and his grandmother wanted to give him one more chance. I hated to see him leave. He was a fine intelligent young man who had trouble controlling his temper. One family left because the mother felt insulted by me. I concede that in putting an end to the rash of fighting and major disruptions we

-3-

127

were experiencing, I became much more firm and insistent on no fighting and on proper behavior. I do not feel that I insulted this parent; I know that I never intended to insult her. I apologized to her and offered to take her children back after she withdrew them. I am pleased to report that all of the other 40+ students that were suspended are still here and the fighting and disruptions have greatly diminished. I should be applauded for this success story, not criticized.

I feel the need to relate to you a story. At our next to last meeting, I mentioned to you that I had an eighth grade black girl who was new to the Free School whom I had just suspended for the third time — each time for fighting. I needed to have her transferred before her fourth suspension — I did not want and do not want to see her expelled. With tears in her eyes, she went to teachers promising to behave and begging them to plead her case. She came to me pleading not to be transferred, promising not to cause more trouble and stating that she realized the consequences of further misbehavior. This student is not academically equipped — her attendance has been poor to say the least — her behavior has been dismal. Yet there is no way that I can turn this student out. I think if you would investigate, you would find that many troubled students and students who cause serious trouble would fight, along with their parents, to remain at the Free School. I think you should ask the question, "Why?"

While our school does have a more relaxed approach to discipline (For support of this approach see Stedman, Phi Delta Kappan, November, 1987.) and simultaneously encourages an experiential, activity-based program, this does not mean that we should or must tolerate disruptive or dangerous or self destructive behavior. All of this is to say that the Free School is not for all children. I have a first grader who presently roams the building constantly — he cannot handle the activity and movement our program encourages. For his safety and our concern for him, I am about to recommend to his parent that she transfer him. I have a six grader who daily refuses to do work. We have not yet found the key to turn this student on to learning. I am giving serious consideration to the idea that the Free School may not be the best placement for this student.

I do not claim that we are miracle workers; I do claim that we are extremely good at what we do and that we should be supported. I do claim that our public schools should offer a large number of schools of choice to enable each student to find his or her niche. It is absurd and cruel to expect all students to fit into the same mold.

I feel that I have nothing to hide. I am proud of my record and am excited to make it public. Veiled threats and negative innuendoes do not dissuade me. I have never claimed that I have all the answers or that I have THE answer. I do claim that we offer one solution, one way of life, one approach to education that provides success for most of the people (students, parents and teachers) we serve. I also claim that there are many solutions which should come from a variety of people. I disclaim the one best system concept.

... you seemed agitated or irritated that I sent you a copy of David Kearns' speech. I sent this speech to you and to others to increase thought and enhance educational dialogue. I sent

-4-

128

this speech to educate, not to irritate. If you would like, I can remove your name from my mailing list.

In our conversation, you also informed me that you did not and do not appreciate me sharing your directives or my responses to these directives with others. I realize that you have explained to me that you operate from a bureaucratic mentality which is based on control and roles.. I, however, have explained that I operate from a democratic mentality which is based on inclusion and shared decision-making. I reserve the right to share information with many people. I believe deeply in the democratic principles of choice and diversity. I believe that decision-making must be in the hands of those most affected by the decisions. I believe in democracy – government of the people, by the people and for the people. It is people-involvement that I seek to enhance – active participation, empowered input. I will continue to work to achieve this type of educational system.

Sincerely,

Robert M. Ferris
Principal
New Orleans Free School

Apparently, my letter of January 20 and the area superintendent's order of January 19 crossed in the mail. While he was reading my letter, I was digesting his direct order to submit grades by 4:00 p.m., January 22, 1988:

On November 30, 1987, I sent you a memo and requested that you complete the data sheets and return them to the Data Office as soon as possible. I checked with the Data Office on January 15, 1988 and the data sheets have not been completed and turned in.

By copy of this memorandum, I am directing you to complete the data sheets and turn them in to the Data Office by 4:00 p.m., January 22, 1988.

So, now, with both our mouths wide-open, the battle line was drawn. He had my letter with information in it that I am sure he hoped would never be read by anyone else. I had his memorandum giving me a direct order that I did not want and would not comply with. When I read his memorandum I was at a loss for action. I met with our faculty and a group of our parents who all supported anecdotal feedback instead of grades. Teachers complained about the length of time required to write these reports. We constantly tried to find ways to shorten this process or give teachers more non-classroom time to work on them. However, at this time it was almost unanimous to maintain our non-graded policy. This was before the flood waters of standardized testing drowned public education. However, at this time, grades were still the be-all and end-all in almost every public school. Grades were still the critical factor in rating a student's ability and in determining the passing or failing of students. Almost all of our parents signed a petition supporting our non-graded graded policy. The petition simply read, "We, the undersigned, request that the Orleans Parish School Board continue to allow the New Orleans Free School to follow the 17 years successful policy of [being] a non-graded program." Only one parent voted against this. She wrote and signed on the petition: "I am for a graded program, in English, Math, Science, and Social studies." She signed her name. Soon thereafter, this lady caused us much grief by complaining to the area superintendent about supposed incidents at the Free School, chased away our school nurse over head lice, and abruptly withdrew her children. She claimed to be a certified witch. I did not and do not know how one gets to be a witch, but I never doubted her claim. The battle with this lady and the area superintendent would commence shortly after this discord over grades.

So, here it was, I had this direct order to turn in grades. I had been quite careful to never disobey a command. I fought vehemently over staff issues and the use of our building, never gloating when we won and never lashing out when we lost. This was a direct order. Our decision was whether to fight to the death or relinquish. We chose to fight.

I received the area superintendent's order to turn in grades by 4:00 p.m. January 22, 1988. On January 22 I turned in the data information grade sheets with just our students' names on them—no grades—by the 4:00 p.m. deadline. On January 24, 1988 I gave Dr. Theadore the following memo:

> I must inform you that I have filled out as much of the data sheets as I can without jeopardizing the integrity of the Free School. While you have chosen to ignore my letter to you, dated December 20, 1987, the issues remain. I stand by that letter and, once again, need to say that I do not feel that I am in violation of board policy as it applies to The New Orleans Free School.

I sent a copy of this memo to Dr. Everett Williams, Superintendent of the New Orleans Public School, the very man whom I feared wanted to eliminate the Free School. On January 25, 1988, I wrote to Dr. Williams soliciting his help in resolving this matter. I knew that I was now disobeying a direct order and I wanted to avoid a charge of insubordination—the guillotine of bureaucracy that is modeled on the military chain of command. I was the broken link and knew that many wanted it discarded.

I included copies of all correspondence on this matter between Dr. Theadore and me. I concluded my letter to Dr. Williams with the following protestation: "I do not understand how the system on the one hand is spending money and time struggling over the issue of black males and simultaneously trying to undermine a program that has successfully dealt with a number of black males. My goodness, all we are doing is offering students a chance at significant academic success without constant fear of, and all too often, reality of failure. Maybe something is working and is worth looking into."

With my neck firmly on the guillotine, a funny thing happened. On the same day I sent my letter to Dr. Williams, I received the following memorandum from Matthew Proctor, Jr., Deputy Superintendent of the Orleans Parish Public School, with a document titled, Resolution of Conflicts (School Site Administrators). It was dated January 21, 1988, addressed to Area Superintendents, Principals, Assistant Principals, and read as follows: "On May 10, 1983, a copy of the attached RESOLUTION OF CONFLICTS PROCEDURE was sent to administrators. If the need arises, we should follow the procedure as outlined." Here is the copy of that "Resolution of Conflicts" sheet.

RESOLUTION OF CONFLICTS

(School Site Administrators)

1.0 All members of the management team, work together
with open lines of communication. It is the purpose
of this resolution to provide each member of the management
team the opportunity/responsibility to raise concerns and
to have them expeditiously resolved.

2.0 A Principal must first discuss the conflict with his/her
Area Superintendent in an effort to reach a professional
resolution of the problem. Such conference shall be
scheduled by the Area Superintendent within 10 school days
after being notified in writing of the need for a discussion.

2.1 If the principal does not hear from the Area Superintendent
within 10 school days, or if he/she is not satisfied with
the resolution of the conflict, the Principal may contact
the Deputy Superintendent in writing.

2.2 If the Principal does not hear from the Deputy Superintendent within 10 school days or if he/she is not satisfied
with the resolution of the concern, the Principal may
contact the Superintendent in writing.

2.3 If the Principal does not hear from the Superintendent
within 15 school days or if he/she is not satisfied with
the resolution of the concern, the Principal may contact
the School Board in writing.

3.0 Assistant Principals must follow the recourse outlined
above (2.0 - 2.3) with the exception that the first person
to whom the conflict is directed shall be his/her immediate
supervisor, the Principal.

Was this manna from heaven or a bite of the forbidden apple? Dr. Williams and Dr. Proctor always seemed very close. Was this an incredible coincidence of timing or were they, the very people whom I always thought were trying to destroy us because of our non-conformist ways, throwing us a lifeline? Were they, too, having trouble with the area superintendent whom they had hired? I did not and do not know. I only know that on that same day I wrote to Dr. Proctor asking for help and sending him all correspondence on this matter.

To: Dr. Matthew Proctor, Deputy Superintendent, New Orleans Public Schools

From: Robert M. Ferris, Principal, New Orleans Free School RMF

Date: January 25, 1988

Re: Resolution of Conflicts Memorandum

I want to thank you for your "Resolution of Conflicts" memo dated January 21, 1988 which I received today.

I guess what I have is a conflict. I had already sent my letter to Dr. Williams concerning the situation, but I would like to bring this matter to your attention.

I am enclosing all correspondence that has occurred to date concerning our non grading approach. I believe that we must increase avenues of success. Too many young people are all too often caught in the downward spiral of failure and despair.

I would appreciate your help in resolving this issue in a satisfactory way for all parties.

RMF/pv
cc: Dr. Everett Williams, Superintendent
     Dr.   °.., Associate Superintendent, Area II
     Ms. Dalton Barnes, P.T.S.A. President

I received notice from Dr. Proctor on February 11, 1988, that a meeting had been scheduled in his office for 10:00 a.m. on February 23, 1988, to attempt to resolve this matter.

I went into this meeting scared to death. I believed that Dr. Proctor would support Dr. Theadore over me without any hesitation. I also feared Dr. Theadore who had pounced on me, attacked my character, and always presented a negative side of everything I did. Even though I had documented this relentless assault, he intimidated me. At this point I made one of the wisest decisions of my life. I asked the then-president of the Principals' Association, Geraldine Washington, to join me and quasi-represent me at this meeting.

Now, my first experience with a president of our Principals' Association had ended up with a knife in my back when she turned on me and wrote her scurrilous attack denigrating me and betraying any possible trust we had between us. This time was different, and for reasons I do not know, I trusted Geraldine. On the other side of the coin, I was simply too afraid to go into that meeting alone. I went into this meeting petrified. Every part of my body was shaking and all my energy went into disguising my fear. You see, I am not a hero. I am the type of person who, when you threaten to torture me, I will talk even if I do not know what you want to know. I will talk to avoid pain and punishment. In this situation, my fear shut me up. Fear oftentimes can be very debilitating. Miraculously, all of a sudden, in this oppressive, suffocating meeting, I felt myself feeling relief and a sense of calm coming over me.

Geraldine said what I could not. She did a beautiful job of explaining the Free School and articulating our non-graded policy. She was sharp in addressing the area superintendent's attacks on me. I would get a word or two in but Geraldine handled our defense. The meeting ended shortly thereafter, with Dr. Proctor stating that he would consider this issue and get back to us on it. No timeline was given.

I do not believe that I ever adequately thanked Geraldine Washington for her brilliant support of me and our program. She died some time after that meeting and to this day I have always considered her one of my guardian angels.

After not hearing from Dr. Proctor for over the 10 day grievance timeline, on March 1, 1988, I wrote him the following memorandum, because I did not want procedural issues to be used against us:

On Thursday, February 23, 1988, we met concerning grades at the New Orleans Free School. You emphasized the fairness of the grievance procedure and that you really wanted to resolve this issue favorably and without further conflict. So do I.

However, I have not heard from you on this matter and the 10 day grievance timeline is passed. If there is a problem, please do not hesitate to contact me.

I still never received a written reply from Dr. Proctor, but sometime after my March 11, 1988, memorandum our paths crossed. He verbally assured me that I was going to hear from him in the near future. He then jokingly said, "Ha ha! As long as you don't hear from me it is in your favor."

I do not think he was being demeaning or sarcastic here; he was trying to ease the tension and lighten the atmosphere. The good news was that Dr. Theadore stopped harassing us over grades. He continued his assault on me and the Free School but no longer came after us over grades.

Many more problems with Dr. Theadore that occurred during that 1987–1988 school year were equally intimidating, bordering on personal attacks and continuing to denigrate our program. On November 25, 1987, he sent me a memorandum titled, "Punctuality":

> Our Principals' Meetings are scheduled to start at 9:00 a.m. I noted that you arrived after that time at our meeting on November 19, 1987. Please take the necessary steps to make sure that you arrive at future meetings prior to the designated time. If there are questions or comments pertaining to this matter, please contact me.

I felt that this memorandum was tantamount to a negative citation. I felt it best that my response be part of the record. Thus, I sent him the following memorandum dated December, 7, 1987, and titled, "Punctuality memorandum dated November 25, 1987":

> I was a few minutes late to the principals' meeting held on November 19, 1987, because a parent requested a meeting. Before these principals' meetings I always go to school first, lead the morning assembly and then leave immediately. In this case a parent needed to meet with me urgently on a very serious matter. She requested the meeting as I was walking out of the door.
>
> The literature I read states that leaders should be trusted and respected. Also, effective principals should be visible and active in their schools.
>
> I think I should be applauded for such dedication and excellent leadership judgment. I only responded to an important parent need. I was in no way negligent.

May I suggest that our schools may be better served if you held these meetings after school hours. This would allow principals to remain in their building during school time. I should note that teachers are required to meet after hours.

I wisely, though with cowardice, did not tell him that I abhorred his boring, meaningless principals' meeting and was overjoyed by being late and wished that I had had an excuse to miss the entire meeting.

Sometime after the first of 1988, Dr. Theadore started meeting secretly with the parent who claimed to be a witch and a new teacher at our school who was having extreme difficulty with discipline and teaching at the Free School. The parent composed two lengthy handwritten letters of complaints about me and the Free School. Her first letter was six and a half pages long, dated February 24, 1988. It began with a focus on her children having head lice and what she considered our school and our school nurse's slow and inadequate response. She then went on to criticize how we served food and the quality and quantity of food served to our students. She claimed that her older daughter was "manhandled" by one of our teachers and that her younger daughter and "a black friend" were involved in a "racial incident" that "went largely unnoticed by Mr. Farris [sic]."

She attacked our Black History program by stating "my child who is Caucasian, was subjected to endless rambling about white on black racism. My child gained no meaningful insight into racism except to note its sweltering presence at the Free School. I have written the teacher in regard to this matter." She complained that her daughter's IEP contract had been "completely disregarded." She made accusations that discipline was "largely non-existent" and said there were rumors of drug use, smoking, and theft by students. This woman claimed that the teacher who was having difficulty with discipline at the Free School had had her authority undermined by me. She protested that "suspensions are given at whim, possibly for cosmetic reasons (i.e., a cover up)." She stated that our students were at risk because anyone could enter our building unnoticed and she mentioned that I had difficulty quieting people down for some of our larger gatherings.

I knew that I had to respond in a way that did not sound defensive and in no way attack the parent who wrote it. I also realized that this letter afforded me the opportunity to further explain the Free School philosophy to the area superintendent as we were still deeply in conflict over grades. I wrote two lengthy letters—the first dealt with the head lice and the second dealt with the other accusations.

My first letter dated March 7, 1988, dealing with head lice, was addressed to the area superintendent and the Administrative Supervisor of

School Nurses. I began by discussing our school nurse's umbrage over being labeled incompetent. I stated the fact that the parent had one of her daughters go to the nurse and tell the nurse that her mother said she, the nurse, was incompetent. I found this situation to be unbelievable, but the little girl told me directly that her mother sent her to the nurse to deliver this message. I wrote that I called the administrative nurse directly over our school nurse (not the administrative supervisor of school nurses), on or about January 26, 1988. She expressed disapproval over a nurse's competency being questioned but agreed to send a group of nurses within five days to our school to conduct a thorough examination of our students and school for head lice.

The nurses never came within that week. However, during this week, the complaining parent came to me to speak about the problem. Though she was angry, she was also calm. In discussing this situation with her, I found out that she was willing to let our school nurse examine the students for head lice. I told her that I would have the nurse perform the head lice check on her next working day. She was only with us a day and a half a week.

My recording of the end of that meeting in my letter reads as follows: "In the conversation, as I often do when talking about head lice, I found myself scratching away. She (the parent) said she could tell if I had head lice. She checked my hair and stated that she found none. I felt we had ended this meeting on friendly and favorable terms." I need to say that this parent and I usually were on very good terms. Several faculty members, my wife, and I, had only recently attended her birthday party and all had a great time. For me the problem with this lady was not that she claimed to be a certified witch but that she was more a Dr. Jekyll and Mr. Hyde character. When she was on her good behavior she was a charmer and a pleasure to be around; when she was on her bad behavior she was a terror to encounter. I never expressed these thoughts in my letters, but I certainly kept them in the front of my mind. My letter continued with the following information:

> The nurse did not show up for her next full day at our school. This only left a half day for her to check for lice for that week. Begrudgingly and slowly, she began a thorough check for head lice. She only got to one or two classes that week, which left the rest to examine the next week. However, during this week, the complaining parent came storming into my office around 4:00 p.m. she screamed at me for what seemed like an eternity but was probably more like five minutes. She was angry because she said her younger daughter "had lice again." She threatened to go to the school board, to

go to my supervisor, to charge me with the bill, and so on. She never stopped screaming at me. She screamed at me for not responding to her right then and there. She walked out of the building still screaming at me.

In the letter I documented that I made sure that the nurse, upon her next work day, completed her ordered inspection for head lice. Some children were checked over and over again. Almost simultaneously to her completion of this head lice inspection, I received a phone call from the nurse's supervisor that she had been ordered by the deputy superintendent to send in a team of nurses to conduct a check for head lice. I informed her that I was not pleased that she had not already sent in a team of nurses as she had promised but I was thankful that they were coming.

I concluded my letter by taking a firm position: "I want to say that seldom have I been so rudely and abusively treated." I also stated that I had responded to the complaining parent's concern about the head lice problem and never did I take her complaint lightly. A number of students have been removed from school because of the problem.

> I want to go on record that I feel our school nurse has also been harassed and insulted by the complaining parent. I believe complaints should be made in a humane and respectful way—not in the demeaning way this was handled.

> I know parents get upset over head lice, but to use threats and insulting character smears does not deal with the problem. It only creates hard, unhealthy feelings and directs our attention away from the problem. I believe in spite of the complaining parent's behavior, I have made every effort to respond to the problem.

On this same day, March 7, 1988, that I gave my area superintendent the above described letter, I gave him a second lengthy letter addressing the other accusations raised by this complaining parent in her February 24, 1988 letter. As far as the cafeteria situation was concerned I let my cafeteria manager deal in writing with this accusation. As to assertion that "discipline is largely non-existent at the Free School or inconsistent at best," that her daughter "was on one occasion manhandled by a teacher," and that "a racial incident involving my (her) daughter & a black girl went largely unnoticed by Mr. Farris," (sic) I gave the following lengthy responses:

> Discipline – Discipline is a complex problem for any humanitarian approach to education. Too often students inter-

pret our personalness and care as weakness. They become abusive, rude or attempt to be king of the mountain through continuous fighting.

Our program has been compounded since we have had to double in size in the past two school years—one out of every two students and faculty members are new to the system. This has had a shock effect to say the least.

Our program is based on an experiential, activity-based approach to education. The literature argues that there must be more dialogue, increased activity and thinking skills in our schools. What the literature doesn't tell us is the other side of the coin. Increased dialogue can easily become disruption, increased activity can turn into chaos and thinking skills can become disrespect. I do not deny that we walk an extremely difficult line offering our type of program. It is far easier to secure quiet, passivity and rigid order than it is to encourage thinking, talking and activity, but it is not good education.

Discipline is alive and well at the Free School and most students are very well behaved. At the same time there are some students whose behavior is out of line. These are very difficult students to deal with but the Free School has always tried not to think in terms of discarding difficult students. We try to deal with individuals and individual situations in as fair and humane a manner as possible. Our program is designed to build up the students not to concentrate on punishing their failures. This effort may at times appear to some as inconsistency but it is oftentimes necessary to deal with individuals fairly.

(The complaining parent) states that her daughter was manhandled on one occasion. This incident was brought to my attention in talking to (her daughter) about something else. While it did not seem like a serious accusation, I did talk to the teacher about it. He explained to me that he was monitoring the halls. He was making sure that students went directly to class and not to the restroom or to get water. Her daughter insisted on trying to get around him. He said there was really nothing much to the incident.

As far as racial tension, almost every fight has been white on white or black on black. If a fight has been between a white and a black student, it has been rare and almost always between friends. In fact, one of the ugliest scenes between a white and a black student involved (the complaining parent's) daughter and a black student. They were both in tears, calling names and shouting at one another. I managed to separate the two before violence occurred. Neither girl was pleasant to deal with but the separation worked and there has not been another altercation between them since to my knowledge. I did not attribute this incident to racial tension; I attributed it to neighborly hassles as the two girls live next door or near one another... (the complaining parent) refers to a racial incident between her 'daughter and a black friend' which 'went largely unnoticed by' me. I remember no such incident unless she is referring to the incident above which I dealt with. Unknown to the two girls, I observed their behavior for several days after the incident to make sure that it did not continue. I certainly never heard anything further about it.

As to her condemnation that our Black History program was "endless rambling about white on black racism' and that there was a "sweltering presence" of "racism" at the Free School, I simply offered the following reply:

Black History Month – I really do not have any information about the letter which (the parent) says she wrote to her child's teacher. I asked the teacher if she kept the letter and she said no. What did bother me about this accusation was the comment that there is "sweltering presence" of racism at the Free School. I just simply want to deny this. We may have our arguments or disagreements but our closeness has always superseded the issue of race.

In her multiple accusations the parent alleged that that the teacher who was having trouble

...had her authority undermined from the onset of her tenure at the Free School. Mr. Farris has made his intention to rid himself of her presence apparent to even the children, who often speak to (the teacher) of her job instability. I wonder how she was expected to teach in an environment where she was subjected to open ridicule & a complete lack of disciplinary support. My children have a saying—'I went to Bob—he laughed'...or 'he did nothing.'

I responded at length to these charges while, again, trying to explain practices and procedures at the Free School:

> I must say that I have had nothing but complaints about (this teacher) from parents, students, and teachers. Her classroom is extremely chaotic and void of meaningful lessons. I believe she came with the attitude that the responsibility for student behavior was on the shoulders of the students and that she has not adequately dealt with the reality that students are not always capable of dealing with that responsibility. The most difficult problem facing the Free School is this: How to find adults who have the ability to present a humanistic and activity-based program while still maintaining excellent classroom management. (This teacher) has demonstrated an inability to do this.
>
> While I have been extremely frustrated in dealing with this situation, I resent being told that I have given up. I have repeatedly said that (this teacher) cares about our students and that she is working very hard. What she is doing has not been effective but that does not mean she is not trying.
>
> I offered (her) time to visit other classrooms. I tried to help her develop a plan of peer coaching but she rejected this idea, which was her right. I suggested that she work with (an instructor) from the teacher center (run by the teachers' union) to work out her problems which she has been doing.
>
> To help (her) get better control of her classroom situation and to improve the overall atmosphere of the school the faculty voted on March 1st to institute an after-school detention center. (She) was absent from school Monday through Thursday of this past week and was unaware of this plan.
>
> When she returned on Friday, I met with her to discuss it but she stated that she wasn't sure that she will be staying with the school. She had hoped to hear from (the head of personnel) this past Friday about an available position.
>
> In discussing her staying or leaving, I urged her to weigh her decision carefully. I suggested that if she got a good of-

fer, she should go for it. But if she was only offered positions that may be extremely difficult, she should remain here.

I know that this teacher has felt a lack of support. This is one reason why I suggested the detention hour. I also know that I sent an extremely large number of disciplinary letters home to parents of students sent to me by (this teacher). I also know I suspended a large number of students from (the teacher's) room for disruptive, disrespectful and/or fighting.

On the one hand (this parent) criticizes me for not supporting (this teacher's) efforts at discipline and on the hand she criticizes me for suspending students too casually—on a whim for cosmetics and as a cover-up. I'm damned if I do and I'm damned if I don't. Regardless, I do realize that everything we have tried so far to help (this teacher) has failed—the situation has not improved. The detention idea is one more effort to help (this teacher) control her class and to improve the overall atmosphere of the school.

As to (the parent's) accusation that her children say that I laugh or do nothing when they are sent to me, I really cannot remember them being sent to me for major disciplinary reasons. I remember seeing them on a few occasions and I have found that getting them to smile and then giving them a brief time out period usually takes care of their frustrations. I never remember having to take disciplinary action against either of them. (The older girl) gets upset sometimes as she did in the incident mentioned above; but cooling off always seems to take care of the problem.

Addressing her accusation that her daughter's IEP had been "completely unnoticed," I pointed out that the school system had had difficulty securing a gifted teacher for our students but had finally sent us a teacher on March 1, 1988. By then the complaining parent had "withdrawn her children from the Free School and this issue may be moot."

I also dealt with a couple of the parent's criticisms that I simply agreed with. It was difficult to get the group to be quiet when we had large gatherings because we had a very poor P.A. system. Further we, too, feared that someone unauthorized walking into our building potentially could do harm. We had repeatedly asked for bars on our ground level basement windows and a lock with a buzzer on our front door.

On the day after the parent hand-wrote the above six and a half page letter of complaints, on February 25, 1988, she hand-wrote a second four-page letter complaining about how students behaved on a particular field trip and how she was treated as a trip chaperone. I responded with a third letter. I now felt that the area superintendent was attempting to build a case to have me removed. It was evident that this case was built on claims by a very angry parent and a distraught and unhappy teacher.

I still appreciated the gravity of the situation and realized that I must carefully, truthfully, and thoroughly place all the information on the table and in the record so that no accusation against me or the Free School by these protesting parties would go unanswered and potentially come back to destroy us. I include both the parent's and my entire letters to tell this chapter of the story. With my response letter I included to Dr. Theadore letters written by students and faculty that collaborated my version of what happened that day, though I do not include them here. I begin with the parent's letter.

Feb. 25, 1988

Dear Dr. _____;

Today I + a friend accompanied
_____ + 30 Free School students
to the Pittsburgh Science Exposition at
the Convention Center.

At 9 AM I pulled a student
from the bus line for displaying
a condom-like balloon to a
snickering crowd. I brought
both to the office + stated that
due to the sensation the boy
was creating, that I would
like him pulled from the
field trip.

Upon entering the bus,
I observed a young man (7th grade)
eating candy. The children
had been given a blanket order
of not eating or having food

on the trip. This was stated by ②
Mr. Farris, Ms. _____ & myself to
a quieted classroom.

The child told me another
teacher said he could eat.
What she had in fact stated was
that he should swallow the
mouthful he had. She was
unaware of the bag of candy. I
asked the child for the candy
& he responded in a rude,
disrespectful fashion. I asked
him to leave the bus & escorted
him to the office. I explained
what had occurred to the secretary,
seated the child & returned to the bus.

When we arrived at the
Convention site & were being
directed to the viewing area,
Mr. Farris appears, in his own
vehicle = the child. He asked
the student & teacher involved
what had happened. I intervened
stating that I was responsible for

146

the child's removal, as he was in ③
direct conflict c̄ Mr. Faris orders.
Mr. Faris informed Me that there
are exceptions.
          I told Mr. Faris that if the
child was allowed to remain +
if he continued to reprimand ME
in front of 29 elementary children,
that I would see him at your
office. He replied "Stop threatening me with that." I stated
that he was out of line, that
I was an adult volunteer,
and that I had witnessed
EVERYThing + made a prudent
decision. Mr. Faris, upon leaving
the teacher concur c̄ me,
returned the child to the
Free School. The remaining
morning was wonderful. The
other children had a positive

experience. Three thanked me &
two gave me silk Roses acquired
at the exposition.

Back at the Free School,
I witnessed a very tall (6 ft.)
student attempt to physically
intimidate Ms. ___ & my male
companion interceded on her
behalf. Obscene language was
used throughout by the student, in
fact cursing appeared to be common-
place.

I am appalled that I was
reprimanded by Mr. Fanis in
front of 30 students, if at all.
I was, afterall, a parent volunteer
at 5 PM this evening, I go to work &
remain until 1 AM. I could have
used extra sleep. This behavior
by Mr. Fanis will not encourage others
to volunteer for anything.
— Thank you.

I responded to these frustrating and unfortunate clashes as follows.

To: Dr.   , Associate Superintendent, Area II

From: Robert M. Ferris, Principal, New Orleans Free School RMF

Re: Field Trip To Pittsburgh Science Conference

Date: March 7, 1988

In response to yet another letter of complaint from Ms. ¦   dated February 25, 1988 regarding the seventh grade class' field trip to the Pittsburgh Science Conference, I offer the following:

The New Orleans Free School was offered an opportunity to take a field trip through the school system to attend the Pittsburgh Science Conference at the Convention Center. The program was being planned through Barbara MacPhee's office. She requested that all students be well supervised.

When   and I first discussed the trip it was to include her class and the 3rd grade class.   is the science teacher for the upper grade children. I wanted her to be involved since I knew she was having trouble and the trip could enchance her science program. I also felt that since the 3rd grade teacher, Ms. Ann White, was going the students would be well behaved as she can manage the students.

However, about a week before the trip we found out that only one class could go. Since I had placed   in charge of this program, I felt I had to let her go. I worried about the trip for a solid week. I asked   two or three times if she thought she could really control her students. She always said yes. I told her I was going to send Robin, a new teacher, with her to make sure the students behaved well. When I noticed that   was the parent volunteer, I began to worry more. This trip was to take place after the ugly scene over lice and I did not feel that   was the person to trust with our students. She had already exhibited too much nastiness and anger.

The night before the trip, I decided I had to do something different. I had to send someone who could control the students.

I knew that   was having extreme difficulty controlling the students, that Robin was too new to be depended upon, and that   was too angry at me to handle conflictual situations. The morning of the trip I asked two faculty members if they would attend. Neither wanted to attend because they both felt   could not control the students.

They both reluctantly agreed to go. I felt relieved; I thought everyting would go smoothly. All of a sudden   comes storming into the office, barking orders and verbally attacking a student whom she claimed had a condom-like object.   did not request that he be pulled from the trip; she demanded it. She was not calm at all; she was abusive.

I examined the object - it was like a rubber glove only it just covered one finger. It looked somewhat like a condom but the situation could have been dealt with so much more humanely. I granted   demands that the student not be allowed to go on the trip in order to avo   a confrontation with her. I felt that the anger she expressed at the student was really anger meant for me but there was nothing at the moment I could do about it. Subsequently, I heard from the student that she had grabbed him and pushed him toward the office.

I stepped out of the office for just a couple of minutes. When I returned, my secretary said that   just stormed in and out of the office again, this time not letting a second student go on the trip because he had candy. He was saying that another faculty member had allowed him to eat it. By the time I got to the office both Ms.   and the student had left the office: Ms. ,   returned to the bus; the student went to find me. I went looking for this second student but could not find him immediately. I saw the bus leave; I hoped he was on it. About a minute later I saw him in the hall fighting to hold back tears.

I do not know this student very well. He has only been with us a couple of months. But his story was believable. He said that Jeanette had seen him with the candy in his mouth and told him to finish it. He felt that he was obeying, not disobeying. His side of the story is that Ms.   rudely and roughly grabbed him by the arm digging her fingernails into his arm and pushing him.

I felt that Ms.   was again venting her anger at me and taking it out on the students. I knew that even if she was correct on the issues she was treating our students in an unacceptable manner.

This second student was very upset and felt that he had been extremely mistreated. I felt after witnessing how she had treated the first student, that this situation needed to be diffused immediately. I took him down to the convention center to try to clear it up. If his side of the story was substantiated, then I was going to let him go on the trip. If there was more to it than he expressed, then I would not let him go. I was hoping that there had been a misunderstanding and that this would clear up the problem and that he would be allowed to go on the trip. He certainly felt that he had been misunderstood and that he had been physically abused. It turned out that there was more candy involved and that I did not let him go with the group.

Ms.   did come up firing statements at me and threatening to go to the school board if I let the student continue on the trip. I did tell her to stop threatening me and I did manage to keep the discussion on the facts of what happened.

In her letter Ms.   , related another incident which occurred after returning from the field trip. She claimed a 6 ft. tall student was physically intimidating the classroom teacher,   The student did come to the office but he claimed that Ms.   male companion who had accompanied the class on the field trip was shouting at him, grabbing him and pushing him. The student definitely came

151

to the office very upset and angry. I kept him in the office. I chose not to pursue this issue for fear of things getting more out of control and uglier.

In one day I had three students complaining of being physically handled by either Ms. ＿＿ and/or her male companion. Previously, Ms. ＿＿ had verbally and vicisously attacked our school nurse and myself. She has withdrawn her children. I think her anger and hatred had reached such a peak that this was by far the best action that could be taken. I really believe that if she had remained at the Free School, she was going to seriously hurt someone.

I am enclosing statements by students and teachers concerning the events of that day.

I should note that around March 7, 1988, the day I submitted my letters to the area superintendent, two things happened that actually helped us. The complaining parent withdrew her children from the Free School, and Dr. Theadore facilitated the transfer of this troubled teacher without ever conferring with me on this matter. While I was pleased with this transfer, I was also frustrated by it only because no one from central office or the area office had had the decency or professionalism to inform or consult me on this matter. I wanted this fact to be part of the public record. I was sure now that the area superintendent was building a case against me; I needed to carefully rebut all charges against us. I wrote and sent the following memorandum to him on March 11, 1988:

> It has been brought to my attention that (the teacher in question) was in consultation with you concerning her teaching position here at the New Orleans Free School. I find it hard to believe that neither you nor anyone from the personnel department conferred with me concerning this matter nor informed me of her transfer. However, I think everyone is best served by her transfer.

While I realize that these letters and those I wrote throughout our history of struggles with the school system's administrations were self-serving and somewhat preachy, they helped the Free School tremendously. These documents, along with parental, faculty and community support and leadership, enabled us to tell our side of the story and to make it part of the record. We let no issue remain unchallenged. While I was scared to death to send them, and I never lost that fear, I knew they must be having some effect. Numerous administrators told me not to send them, to quit sending copies to everyone, and to stop running to our parents. I discerned that they hated internal administrative conflicts being shared with outsiders. They desperately wanted correspondence and conversations to be kept in-house and even carefully limited there. Of course, I was not privy whom they were sharing their information with although I had a good idea. Also, if I let them control the information, I was giving them all the power and retaining nothing. In spite shaking inside and losing much sleep, I kept sending the letters over the years and never stopped going to the parents. These tactics kept us alive; however, they never ended the attempts to crush us.

We would not have had such time-consuming conflicts like those we experienced with this unhappy parent, frustrated teacher, and vindictive bureaucrat had we been a charter school. Charter schools operate outside the governance of the local school board, which frees them of many of the rules, regulations, and interference of the local boards with their top-heavy administrations. This includes but is not limited to the hiring and firing of personnel, scheduling, class size, and so on. Charters for school are obtained in a number of ways. Some are state chartered, some university chartered, others are local association chartered, and many are chartered by local school boards.

Had we charter status, we simply could have required the parent to withdraw her children when she treated our nurse so rudely and screamed and hollered at me. We could have dismissed the teacher without enduring a bureaucratic circus, and we would not have experienced a harassing supervisor breathing down our necks. I could have focused on education instead of writing twelve-plus single-spaced pages responding to these endless allegations. I am not suggesting that charter schools will be free of conflicts; they simply should not be encumbered by a bureaucratic structure. However, for me the value of charter schools rest not with just their freedom from bureaucratic control but also on their ability to provide high quality, fair and equitable education for all children, especially children of the poor who have been consistently provided an inferior education.

Charter schools are a golden opportunity to reinvent and redesign public education with innovation, responsiveness, and a passion for teaching and learning. At the same time, I fear that this freedom to be creative and innovative will be greatly curtailed by the newest form of noose-fitting, pervasive high-stakes testing, the forced weapon of choice under the rubric of "accountability." Since I intend to end this book with a critique of the pervasive testing smothering our educational landscape along with a more in-depth discussion of charter schools, let me continue with this story.

Dr. Theadore did not let up for the rest of school year 1987–1988. During the conflict when the parent complained about head lice, lack of discipline at the Free School, her daughter's IEP not being dealt with, a teacher's authority being undermined by me, and improper behavior on a field trip, the area superintendent received a lengthy letter of complaint from another parent who was upset that her son had hit his head (as he went to dunk a basketball the goal came loose and fell, striking him on the head) and no one notified her. I noticed two things about this parent's letter of complaint. The first thing was that her laundry list of complaints was incredibly similar to the initial complaining parent's charges. This seemed too well orchestrated to be just a coincidence. The second thing I noticed—which reinforced my initial reaction—was that her anger level matched that of the first parent. Even knowing that the two ladies were acquaintances, if not friends, this rage surprised me. This latest parent and I had always had a very cordial relationship, even though at times it had been give and take. Responding to her letter, I focused almost exclusively on the incident. This fifteen-year-old eighth-grade boy had not complained to a teacher about the incident, nor had he reported it to the office. At least three adults, including me, saw him with his head down in class. Each time someone asked why he had his head down, he replied that he had hit his head during recess and was just resting. Nothing more; nothing less. He exhibited no signs of serious injury and definitely left school as though nothing happened. I also sent the area superintendent documentation by students and faculty members who witnessed or participated in this incident.

The harassment of our program did not stop here. Dr. Theadore questioned my evaluation of the janitor whom he had placed at our school over my objection at the beginning of the school year. The irony of this situation was that only a couple of weeks before I completed the evaluation, Dr. Theadore's administrative assistant conferred with the janitor about his excessive absences and threatened him with dismissal. He, the area superintendent, had also recently visited the school and complained to me about the mess throughout the school. Finally, he tried to block our school's annual three-day, two-night camping trip. I had to go to the deputy superintendent to get permission for this trip.

During that spring, I tried to make amends with the man. On April 20, 1988, I sent him a letter hoping to improve our relationship. I suggested that we start over in our dealings with one another since the school system had just won a citywide millage election, creating a very positive and supportive atmosphere in the city. I explained that in the past, area superintendents had instructed principals to take problems to department heads first and then, if unresolved, to bring the problems to them. I told him that from that point on I would bring all problems to him directly. I then listed all problems we were having at that time and invited him to attend our student performance at the New Orleans Jazz and Heritage Festival. I even asked if he would join a meeting with neighbors and our city council representative to discuss the possibility of having our building declared an historic landmark, making us eligible for federal funds to renovate and preserve it.

I am not sure this reconciliation letter had much effect on Dr. Theadore unless he perceived it to be weakness on my part. On May 6, 1988, he wrote me a letter of reprimand and chastised me for my poor judgment and leadership concerning the complaining parent's accusations over the field trip incidents, inconsistent and absent discipline, the parent's daughter supposedly being manhandled by a teacher, lack of action on her daughter's IEP and, of course, our handling of the head lice situation. His reprimand read as follows.

EVERETT J. WILLIAMS
Superintendent

Associate Superintendent
Area II
(504) 483-6361

May 6, 1988

Mr. Robert Ferris, Principal
New Orleans Free School
3601 Camp Street
New Orleans, LA 70115

Dear Mr. Ferris:

As you recall, a conference was held on April 11, 1988 to address complaints by Ms. _____ _____ _____ Persons present at the conference were:

        Ms. _____ _____, Parent
        Mr. Robert Ferris, Principal
        Dr. _____ _____ _____ Area Superintendent

We reviewed Ms. _____ _____ concerns about the incidents related to the field trip to the Pittsburg Science Exposition at the Convention Center. Two (2) students were behaving in a manner unacceptable to her and she brought both to the office. The latter boy had a bag of candy and was eating it after being informed by you, his teacher, and the parent volunteer that there would be no eating or carrying food on the trip. The student refused Ms. _____ request for the candy and responded in a rude manner. Ms. _____ _____ escorted the student to the office, explained what had happened to the secretary, and returned to the bus.

Subsequently, you took the student to the Convention Center in an effort to clear the matter. The student's version of what had happened differed from Ms. _____ _____ version and he accused Ms. _____ of treating him rudely, grabbing him by the arm, and digging her fingernails into his arm. These discussions took place in front of the students. Ms. _____ _____ informed you that if the student was allowed to remain and if you continued to reprimand her in front of the children, that she would leave the field trip and report the matter to the Area Superintendent. The student returned to school with you. A review of this matter reveals that no disciplinary action was taken on this student; nor was an investigation made on the student's complaint that Ms. _____ _____ had treated him rudely, grabbed his arm, and dug her fingernails into his arm.

After the field trip a student came to the office and complained that a male who had accompanied the class on the field trip was shouting at him, grabbing him, and pushing him. You chose not to investigate the matter.

Taking the student to the Convention Center and attempting to resolve the matter at the site was not the wisest thing to do. The confrontation with the parent did not reflect good judgement. This matter would have been better resolved at the school, not in public.

Ms.   claimed that discipline is non-existent at the New Orleans Free School. Moreover, she claims that disciplinary measures are inconsistent when applied. Her daughter,   , was manhandled by a teacher at New Orleans Free School. Ms.   believes there was an over-use of force in this situation and there are other situations where no action is taken.

You did not consider Ms.   statement about her daughter being manhandled as serious, but you talked to the teacher. There was no indication that you followed up on the matter and investigated it throughly to ascertain there was no wrong-doing on the part of the teacher or the student. There was no indication that you reported your findings to the parent.

Ms.   reported that her daughter,   ., is a gifted student. Ms.   stated that she signed her daughter's IEP on October 5, 1987. On February 24, 1988, the IEP had not been implemented, nor had the parent been informed as to the reason the IEP had not been implemented.

Ms.   was dissatisfied with the lack of action on the head lice matter. She went to Dr. Proctor and asked for assistance because there was a lack of attention given to the matter at the New Orleans Free School by you and the school nurse. Based on the narrative you provided, more than two (2) weeks passed without the students' heads being checked for lice. Moreover, a month elapsed after Nurse LeBlanc contacted you relative to head checks and there was no indication that you took steps to bring resolution to the problem. At no time from January 25, 1988 to March 7, 1988 did you bring this matter to the attention of the Area Superintendent or his staff.

Ms.   requested grades on her daughters and received them in a relatively short period after her request. You are to be commended for the prompt response. However, Ms.   was dissatisfied that   received an F in mathematics and Ms.   received nothing from the school that the child was failing. I realize that the New Orleans Free School is non-graded, but it is unacceptable that any child be allowed to fail and no attempt is made to inform the parents of the child's lack of performance.

It appears that you have a personal problem with Ms.   and you have failed to resolve the problem. So far, you have refused to discuss the problem with Ms.   and waged a personal battle with her. You frequently talk of empowering parents and teachers, but your actions fail to demonstrate acceptance of the concept. If parents and teachers disagree with you, you tend to take it personally, withdraw, and suggest they are angry with you.

I am not pleased with the behaviors that have been demonstrated in these complaints by an employee of the New Orleans Public Schools. The actions have demonstrated a lack of concern for others. I am not proud of your lack of response to this parent's concern. While you might not have agreed with what she had to say, you could have responded as one individual to another and attempted to resolve the problem. Clearly, there has been a lack of leadership on your part. Thus, I am placing this letter of reprimand in your personnel file and providing you an opportunity to improve your skills in working with people and resolving conflict in an amicable manner. I hope this has been a learning situation for you and you will accept the challenge to address the needs of your students and parents. If I can be of assistance, please contact me.

Sincerely yours,

Associate Superintendent
Area II Schools

WT:lr

pc: Ms.
    Dr. Frank Fudesco
    Miss Ella Voelkel

Attachments: 5

I noticed four things about this letter of reprimand. First, there was no mention of the other parent who complained about most of the above, along with her son's basketball injury. I guess Dr. Theadore figured out that this new complaining parent made too much of this incident and realized her litany of complaints was too similar to those of the first parent's complaints, and might send up a red flag that this was conspiracy rather than accuracy. Second, I noticed that he ignored my responses to these indictments and all supporting documentation—letters from the school nurse, secretary, cafeteria manager, teachers, and students. Third, I was astonished that he tried to lay the blame of the parent's frustration over her child not receiving contractual IEP requirements; i.e., her child did not have a gifted teacher. He certainly should have refrained from chastising me for not being the good bureaucrat in this situation. On October 23, 1997, the Interim Program Specialist, Special Education Area II (my superintendent's area), wrote directly to the area superintendent: "We are requesting Itinerant Gifted teachers to service Abrams and New Orleans Free School. There are four students at each site who are in need of service."

My area superintendent required principals to not only attend monthly meetings but to also attend monthly cluster meetings. It was at these cluster meetings that we were to bring our concerns and problems. I made certain that our lack of a gifted teacher was included in the meeting minutes of November 5, 1987, January 7, 1988, and February 4, 1988. How my area superintendent missed this information and tried to lay the blame for this situation on me only confirmed my belief that he was simply out to get me. Finally, the issue of the child's "F" grade caught me by surprise, not because the parent was upset over the grade, because this is what I expected. I was stunned by the area superintendent simply taking the parent's version of this situation as gospel and never looking into the matter. He simply used the issue to attack me.

While I realized that I could not ignore this reprimand, I decided to take the matter to the deputy superintendent. I felt Dr. Theadore was strangling me and I needed air. Even though the deputy superintendent, Dr. Proctor, had yet to rule on the grading issue, I felt he was my only hope of receiving a fair hearing. On May 16, 1988, I sent the deputy superintendent four letters.

The first was a grievance against the area superintendent concerning how I handled the parent and her complaints. I included copies of all written letters along with all documentation written by all parties. I also included a copy of the letter my teacher wrote to the area superintendent at my request also dated May 16, 1988, concerning the letter "F" grade she gave to the daughter of the complaining parent. A copy of that letter follows, with my grievance concerning this reprimand, along with copies of two other grievances: the area superintendent preventing us from going on our camping trip and blocking us from using a half-time teaching position as a full-time position for half a year instead of as a half-time position for a full year. I concluded this packet with a letter of complaint about how I was being treated by the area superintendent regarding the evaluation I had given to our head custodian.

NEW ORLEANS FREE SCHOOL
3601 Camp Street
New Orleans, LA 70115
899-0452

May 16, 1988

Dr. Matthew Proctor
Deputy Superintendent
New Orleans Public Schools
4100 Touro Street
New Orleans, La. 70122

Dear Dr. Proctor,

When I met with you earlier this schoolyear, 1987-88, you made a very passionate and convincing plea that you are a fair person and that the administrative grievance procedure is a fair process. I am writing to you today because I feel that I and the Free School community have consistently and constantly been treated in a very unfair manner all schoolyear by Dr. 	 , Associate Superintendent, Area II, Orleans Parish School Board.

Specifically, I am grieving the official reprimand 	 gave me dated May 6, 1988. At this time I am asking for several things. First, I would like to know what the school board procedures, guidelines, etc. are for issuing a reprimand. I would like to ask if a reprimand should depend on one parent's word against a principal or should it instead be issued after a thorough investigation of the matter questioning all parties involved. Second, I am requesting that an impartial investigation of this matter be conducted immediately. My actions in this matter were proper and not deserving of a reprimand. I want an opportunity to clear my name and have this reprimand removed from my record. Third, I would like an official clarification as to Orleans Parish School Board policy on making an official reprimand a public document.

Your immediate attention to this matter would be most appreciated.

Sincerely,

Robert M. Ferris
Principal

RMF/pv

5/16/88

Dear Dr. _____,

This letter is written at the request of Mr. Bob Ferris, concerning the grades given to _____, a former 5th grade student. I had previously wanted to write and inform you of my position but I did not think it appropriate to interfere in a matter concerning my principal and his supervisor.

_____ transfered into my class subsequent to the beginning of the school year. She was moved up from the fourth grade because of her demonstrated superior academic ability. From the very first day of her arrival in the fifth grade she made it known to myself and the other students that she was very displeased with the change. She stated on numerious occasions that it was her intention to fail in order to be reuinited with her friends in the fourth grade.

During the first couple of weeks after arrival in my class, I tested her in order to ascertain her true academic level. I was tremendously impressed with her extraodinary ability in the verbal realm. Her reading, writing, vocabulary, spelling, etc., were all well above fifth grade level. Her creative abilities were

also quite impressive. In math, . . . refused
to be tested. It soon became quite apparent that
. . . attitude was creating a problem for everyone
If we were writing on a topic which she enjoyed she
would participate; otherwise she would try to spenc
the entire class time reading. From the beginning,
it seemed as if all my efforts to induce . . . to
participate were futile. Taking her books away did
not help as she would sneak others. Using readin
as a reward for doing other work also did not
matter to . . . Punishment did not work becaus
in her own words she did not care.

. . . lack of participation became
one of my primary concerns. I discussed it on
personal basis with other teachers in order to enli
their ideas in solving the problem. I spoke to my
principal for any suggestions he might have. .
was also a topic of discussion at no less than 3
of our faculty meetings. All of the suggestions wer
tried and all failed. . . . would only stare a
me and sit in her desk in do nothing. After a
while I simply let her read.

I met with her mother on 4 occasions
(2 official, 2 impromptu). I made it exceedingly
clear to . . . that . . . was refusing to
cooperate in every area (a rare story once in a
while). Our first meeting was when . . . came

to pick up the Nov. 11, report. The report mainly related ▓▓▓ strengths and her abilities that were demonstrated in my earlier testing of her. & the report & praised her obvious talents and potential. For my comments & noted my over-whelming concern about her lack of participation in class. When I met with ▓▓▓ the same concerns were more forcefully voiced. I noted to ▓▓▓ that that each student was responsible for a social studies project that they had worked on in class and I told ▓▓▓ that ▓▓▓ had done nothing towards making project. I also told her that since ▓▓▓ had been in my room that she had done no math and very little in any of the other subjects. The exception being reading.

▓▓▓ was very pleasant and obviously concern she assured me that she would speak to ▓▓▓ and that the situation would change. Two days later ▓▓▓ brought to class a project on an Indian village. It was detailed and extremly well done and I was very pleased. I thought her mother had indeed brought about a change in ▓▓▓ attitude. That was ▓▓▓ first and last project. She immediately returned to doing nothing. I tried to meet ▓▓▓ where she was. I came up with special topics that she could read and write about that somehow incorporated other areas of our study. If she felt like doing the assignment she would participate

She usually did not.

I sent messages home with _____ sister which stated that _____ was not doing her work. I requested th_ _____ come to see me. I did not hear from _____ until the weeks before the Christmas hollidays. She sent me a note about an assignment that I had given the class. I was very surprised by the negative tone of th_ letter. We were studying the wars of the United States. each child picked a war and had to read and answe_ a list of questions. _____ stated that such an assignment was unsuitable for fifth grade (I was encouraged because _____ went home and talked about the assignment).

I replied to _____ and explained how the assignment was appropriate and sent her a copy_ the questions. The next day _____ arrived with a book on Viet Nam. I again thought there would be a change in _____ attitude. She never did the assignm___

After Christmas things seemed to improve with _____ as she became close to another student in the class. She began to take out the proper books for wha_ we were studying and I heard no more excuses, such a_ "I can not see and hear; I lost my books; I hurt my hands and can't write". She began to minimally participate for a couple of weeks I was encouraged and tried to involve her with work that she had earlier refused to do, especially math. As I started to work_

165

more with her she stopped working. I again asked that _____ come to school. Mid-year reports were due out soon and I was sure that _____ would come to school. I heard nothing until a few weeks after the reports were out. _____ had not picked up _____'s report. One day _____ remarked that her mother was at school. I immediately asked for her to come to my room. I met _____ in the hallway and asked her to observe _____ behavior. She saw the other children actively engaged in their work while _____ read a book. I explained that it was same old problem. She ( ) said that she believe _____ had been working more in class. _____ asked _____ from the room and discussed the rudeness, and the negative effects of _____'s behavior. I was greatly impressed with the way _____ communicate with _____ apologized for her attitude and for not doing her work. _____ and I agreed to meet 3 days later to discuss a course of action that would enable _____ to catch up on missed work.

During the next couple of days _____ was a new child. She was animated and excited about school, she expressed a desire to do all that was necessary in order to catch-up, _____ came to school and we focused on _____'s most problem subject, math. I had _____ work some problems and found that she was at best 150 pages behind the class. _____ said that her boyfriend had agreed to tutor ____ and asked that I send home special math assignments. I agreed to help in any manner that I was able to help. ____ came to school the next day with all of her homework done an a partial chapter 3 completed in math. I was exceptionally pleased with the progress ____ was showing. I had no way of knowing that that was ____ final day at school. I could hardly believe it when she was withdrawn from school. ____, I do not understand why ____ says that she had no knowledge of ____ difficulties or the problems that I had to deal with because of ____. She was informed exactly as I explained. When ____ withdrew and grades were requested I had no choice but to give her a failing grade in math. The other grades were based more on ability that actual work done. If there are any questions I will be glad to answer them at your convenience.

Sincerely,

P.S. please excuse the lengthiness of this letter but I felt the situation needed to be explained in detail.

NEW ORLEANS FREE SCHOOL
3601 Camp Street
New Orleans, LA 70115
899-0452

May 16, 1988

Dr. Matthew Proctor
Deputy Superintendent
New Orleans Public Schools
4100 Touro Street
New Orleans, La. 70122

Dear Dr. Proctor,

I want to grieve   decision not to let us go on our annual end of the year camping trip as planned. He sent our initial request back asking that we review Board Policy Number 6153.

I subsequently met with him and explained that in the past we have always been allowed to take this trip. I received his May 9, 1988 memorandum which in essence denies our trip as planned.

Two years ago this issue came up with Dr.   It was decided that we could continue taking this trip since we do not take the ½ days of school at reporting time as do other schools. Our reporting sessions have always been held in the evening after school hours.

We are arguing not for less instructional time but for more. In addition the camping trip in our view enhances not replaces the instructional program. Too many of our students exist in a poverty of experiences. The camping trip is one small gesture toward eliminating this deficit.

Your immediate attention to this matter would be appreciated. Our time is running out.

Sincerely,

Robert M. Ferris
Principal

RMF/pv

168

NEW ORLEANS FREE SCHOOL
3601 Camp Street
New Orleans, LA 70115
899-0452

May 16, 1988

Dr. Matthew Proctor
Deputy Superintendent
New Orleans Public Schools
4100 Touro Street
New Orleans, La. 70122

Dear Dr. Proctor,

I would like to grieve Dr. decision not to allow us to use our .5 teaching position next school year in the manner we used it this year. This year we held up the .5 position until the second half of the school year enabling us to have a full-time teacher for half the school year.

This use of our .5 position utilizes the same amount of employment time and results in the same expense to the system. Service to students is the same.

Next year we have an opportunity to hire noted educator, Herb Kohl, for a full-time half year position. I have spoken with many people about this idea. They all think it is a great idea and agree that it would be a big plus for the Free School, Orleans Parish School System and the city as well. I need support in this matter. This is really too good an opportunity to pass up.

, at staffing, said no. Since then I have written him and talked personally with him about this. I have had no response and I noted in the vacancy list just released that the position has been advertised as a half time position for the year.

I can wait no longer. I need to appeal this decision.

Sincerely,

Robert M. Ferris
Principal

RMF/pv

NEW ORLEANS FREE SCHOOL
3601 Camp Street
New Orleans, LA 70115
899-0452

May 16, 1988

Dr. Matthew Proctor
Deputy Superintendent
New Orleans Public Schools
4100 Touro Street
New Orleans, La. 70122

Dear Dr. Proctor,

I recently received this handwritten memorandum from Dr. _____ (Copy attached.) Dr. _____ placed this custodian at the Free School without consulting me and against my subsequent objections. I have felt all along that no matter what I did in this situation Dr. _____ would try to use it against me.

Ironically, Dr. _____, through Kate Scully, had a hearing on May 2, 1988 concerning Mr. _____ excessive absences. He informed Mr. _____, in writing, that his job is in jeopardy over this issue alone.

I feel justified in giving him the rating I did.

Sincerely,

Robert M. Ferris
Principal

RMF/pv
Encl.

The issue over the custodian was puzzling. One would think that the area superintendent would not let this man perform poorly or would come down hard on him if he did. After all, this was one of the men I had vehemently protested being placed at the Free School over the selection of our own well-liked custodian. This argument started before the grading conflict and the letters from the two complaining parents.

In spite of this head custodian leaving our building in a constant state of filth and disarray, in spite of the administrative assistant for our area citing and threatening the custodian with dismissal over his excessive absences, and in spite of Dr. Theadore's sole visit to our school resulting in him complaining about how dirty the school was, his only response to the negative rating I gave to the head custodian was the following hand written comment:

> I note that (the head custodian) is rated Average on 11 items
> and Below average on 2 items. Yet his overall evaluation is
> below average. This seems hard to believe.

I included this issue to substantiate my claim that the area superintendent was more focused on attacking me than he was on handling any of these issues fairly and responsibly.

The second issue in my grievance was the area superintendent's refusal to allow us to go on our whole school camping trip. This adventure was traditionally a three-day, two-night trip ending our academic year. Denying this trip on such short notice was debilitating to the morale of students and staff. Thankfully, his superiors overruled him.

The last issue in my grievance concerned a part-time teaching position allotted to the Free School. We were presently using that position as a full-time teaching position for half a year instead of a half-time teacher for a full year. I simply wanted to continue that practice for the upcoming year because I was trying to convince noted educatoral author Herb Kohl, to take the position. We had spoken by phone and he stated that he would consider the possibility.

When I proposed the idea to Dr. Theadore, he rejected it saying simply that he thought kids would be better served by having a half-time teacher for a full year rather than a full-time teacher for half a year. The opportunity to bring in Herb Kohl made no difference to him. He would not allow it.

One of the beauties of charter schools is that they would never have to face this type of absurdity. I have to admit, I am jealous but pleased for the charter autonomy they presently experience from such nonsensical and unnecessary meddling. Shortly after I had written this grievance letter, however, Herb informed me that after careful consideration of the idea, it was too difficult at that time to uproot his life for just four and a half months. The issue became moot but the angst and enmity I had toward the area superintendent remained.

While I never heard back from Dr. Proctor concerning my latest grievances, I received a phone call on June 5, 1988, informing me that I should go before the Pupil Progression Plan Committee to defend our policy of not giving grades. The full committee met the following day to finalize an already-written proposal. I was given a one-day notice to be involved in a process that was almost finished. I do not remember and have nothing in my notes about going before this committee, but I assume I went. We never heard back anything official from this committee, but I had heard through the grapevine that our request to continue our narrative evaluation process had been denied. Grades would be required.

Around June 12, 1988, I again called Dr. Proctor and asked what to do next on this grading issue. He informed me that he was going to talk to another administrator and that he would get back to me immediately. He did not. From about June 15, 1988, to June 22, 1988, I tried to reach Dr. Proctor by phone and two personal visits. I was not successful nor did he return my calls. On Friday, June 24, 1988, one work day before the school board meeting, I received a call from him informing me that the grade question was going before the board the following Monday night. I was convinced that the board had already decided it would require us to give grades. Nevertheless, I felt it was imperative to make our case. From that Friday through Monday, I prepared my rebuttal.

In my prepared presentation, I argued for the preservation of a successful school culture—it should not be whittled away or destroyed; it should be studied. I argued vehemently for a school program that supports deviation from the norm, maximizes school-site decision making, and establishes an environment that has a passion for innovation and a destiny for creation. I suggested that the school system needed a view of the innovator as lawmaker, not lawbreaker. We no longer needed a system focused on convergent thinking, pushing the one best concept; we needed a system dedicated to divergent thinking coming up with many solutions, even contradictory ones.

The Free School focused on process not product, cooperation not competition, and success in lieu of failure. I pleaded that our emphasis on an open-ended, cooperative, inquiry-based approach to learning necessitated a more personalized approach to evaluations. I clearly and forcefully stated that a graded program depended on failures, and proudly proclaimed that our non-graded program afforded students the opportunity of academic success without the constant and, all too often, reality of failure.

I never made the presentation.

Only a few of us went to the board meeting that summer night in 1988. We arrived on time at 6:00 or 6:30 p.m. and sat until well past midnight before the issue was presented to the board. Late though it was, we were prepared to make one last pitch to preserve our non-graded policy, even in our fatigued state. We were completely caught off guard. The administration proposed that the New Orleans Free School, and two other school programs, be exempted from using letter or number grades, but instead when a student exits, or graduates, from the school, that student would be issued grades. We were tired and frustrated having been kept there for over five hours to fully appreciate this two-minute victory, but once it sunk in, we were elated. One board member encouraged me to speak because, as she stated, board members always had to listen to people who did not get what they wanted, so she wanted to hear from someone who did. I gladly responded to her request, thanking the administration and board members, but I think the excitement of our little entourage spoke more forcefully than my words.

School year 1988–1989 began with the controversy about grades behind us, but with the problem of the custodians continuing. Now both of our custodians were frequently absent from the first day of school forward, and classrooms were again not cleaned. In the charter school world, those custodians would be dismissed. I now had to resort to my only means of addressing this situation: to write my area superintendent forcing our war of words and letters to start anew.

As a result of this ongoing problem, I contacted Deputy Superintendent Proctor to get a hearing on my grievances I sent him in a letter dated May 16, 1988. The grievances covered the issues of the camping trip, which was resolved favorably back in May, the half-time teaching position, made moot by Herb Kohl's withdrawal from consideration for the half-year teaching position, the letter of reprimand I had received from Dr. Theadore dated May 6, 1988, and all that it entailed, and the issue concerning our head custodian (though not written as a grievance but as a complaint). A meeting was granted for September 28, 1988. Dr. Proctor stated in his September 21, 1988, letter inviting me to "bring a representative of your choice to accompany you at the conference."

I recall only one conference with Dr. Proctor, my area superintendent, Geraldine Washington (the president of the Principals' Association of New Orleans Public Schools, Inc.) and me. That single conference covered grades and all of the above issues. Obviously, my memory is incorrect. The grades issues had been settled by this time. So, I do not know if Geraldine Washington attended this meeting or if someone else accompanied me.

I do know that in this second conference (if there were two conferences) all the issues did get articulated and at some point Dr. Theadore pointedly asked me, "Well, Bob, what are you trying to say?" While the words "You are trying to destroy me!" were screaming from my mind, I could not get them out of my mouth. Fear of this man and my apprehension that I would appear irrational, hostile or out of control (actually all of the above) stopped my words from coming out of my mouth. There was only deafening silence. After what seemed like an eternity, which was probably only a couple of seconds, I heard Dr. Proctor say to my utter surprise, "Why, that's easy, man. He says that you are trying to get him." I did not know that calm could flow so easily and quickly from such anguish and tension.

The meeting ended after that statement from Dr. Proctor and I never heard any more about any of the grievances. It was like they never happened. The area superintendent and I coexisted for the rest of that school year until his departure sometime in the summer or very early fall of 1989. However, the issue over the custodians did not disappear. After what seemed an excessive amount of documentation, the assistant head custodian, Michael Smith, who had not forgiven administration's overlooking him for promotion around the time of his chess team's championship, was transferred in February 1989, almost two years after his chess group's victory. On March 20, 1989, the area superintendent finally had the head custodian demoted to the position of custodian and transferred to another school.

However, even in his demotion letter to the now former head custodian, the area superintendent included, whether intentionally or not, information that questioned my handling of the matter. He wrote, "Also, you stated that you did not have adequate supplies to clean the building. In some instances, you purchased supplies with your money and you were not reimbursed." Again, always fearing that the area superintendent's sole purpose in his handling of Free School matters was to destroy me, I immediately sent him a reply trying to keep the matter pleasant but not letting him get away with any negative suggestion concerning my actions.

On March 30, 1989, I sent the area superintendent the following memorandum:

> I want to thank you for finally reconciling our custodial problem. Our new custodian...so far has been excellent. Our substitute custodian...also seems to be a hard worker.
>
> In your letter to (our now former head custodian) dated March 20, 1989, you wrote that (he) stated the he did not have adequate supplies to clean the building and that he purchased supplies with his own money and was not reimbursed. I have no recollection of (the former head custodian) making such statements at the March 17 conference. However, let the record show that only once did (the former

head custodian) present me with a receipt for supplies he purchased. While I had not authorized this purchase, I reimbursed him with check #1626 for $6.13 on February 20, 1989. Every time (the former head custodian) requested supplies, I obtained them for him. The problem was not lack of supplies, but (former head custodian) repeatedly waited until we were out of something before requesting more of that item.

I agree with (former head custodian's) conclusion that he was not ready to be a head custodian.

Again, thank you for assisting us with this awkward problem. Our building is finally getting cleaned.

I received the following memorandum from the area superintendent dated April 7, 1989:

(The former head custodian's) comments relative to the lack of adequate cleaning supplies were not made in your presence, but in his conference with me after you left.

The area superintendent and I only had one last discord. It concerned a burglary in our building on March 26, 1989. The security report read as follows:

At approximately 5:30 p.m... S/C (security counselor) discovered one (1) window located by the front entrance doors open, the apparent point of entry. S/C entered the building through the open window and proceeded to search the building. On the third floor in Room #4, S/C apprehended three (3) female juveniles with various miscellaneous items in their possession.

The area superintendent sent me the following memorandum concerning this matter on May 31, 1989:

Please note the attached security report. A security counselor found your building unsecured. Incidents of this nature cause losses to the district that we are never able to reclaim. Please provide me with a written report on steps you have taken to insure that an incident of this nature does not occur again. Your report is due in the Area Office within seven (7) working days of the above date.

I sent the area superintendent the following reply dated June 12, 1989:

Please be advised that our acting head custodian had only recently started working at the Free School at the time of this incident. Nevertheless, he claimed he had locked all windows. As I previously have reported to you, our windows to the basement are ground level and easily accessible. Many are easy to jimmy. Once opened, it is impossible to tell if the window was locked or not. However, since this incident, I have once again had zone maintenance put new locks on these windows making it more difficult to break in. I have also, in conference with the acting head custodian, emphasized the necessity of securing the building each night upon departure.

I once again request iron screens be placed on all basement level windows to further prevent breaking into our building.

I must reply to the tone of your request. While I feel it is easy to blame the victim, I can assure you that it does not engender support. The implication of negligence on my part once again radiates from your memo.

The area superintendent replied on June 19, 1989:

A piece of paper does not have a tone. A reader may add any tone he wants. It is a fact that Security found New Orleans Free School in an unsecured condition. It is a fact that you are Principal of the New Orleans Free School. As the person charged with the responsibility for overseeing New Orleans Free School, I expect the building to be secured properly when it is not occupied.

If I felt you were negligent, I would have stated that and would have taken corrective action to see that condition did not exist in the future.

We had such a loving relationship! However, something good may have come out of this cantankerous struggle. Award winning filmmaker Dorothy Fadiman, created an acclaimed documentary film, "Why Do These Kids Love School?" available to be viewed on the internet. In this film, in which the New Orleans Free School was one of eight schools featured, the area superintendent made the following statement:

> As I assess myself personally to alternative achievement, I feel that I have grown tremendously. It hasn't been easy. Uh. I guess it's the working of staff members who feel very committed and I think I have to attribute much of my growth as an educator to those people because they opened my eyes and I found out that we don't have to do the exact same thing, teach the same way or have it at the same time for boys and girls to learn.

10

Another Attempt to Close the Free School

The school year 1989–1990 saw no conflicts between the Free School and the administration. Dr. Theadore left the system, I believe, to become superintendent for a small rural Mississippi county. In August 1989, I received my doctorate from Vanderbilt University and all seemed well. We were now placed under the area superintendent, Dr. Bill Macey, who was our area superintendent when we dealt with our dismissed aide in 1985, the requirement to double our enrollment or die in the spring of 1986, and the proposed closing of the Free School in the summer of 1986. So, two years later, we were not prepared for what was to come. The 1990–1991 school year ended horrendously. It was as though a battleship smashed into our sailboat. Our tranquil swim in calm waters during the months between September 1990 and March 1991 ended in shark-infested waters. Here's what happened.

On April 2, 1991, I was informed that the school administration was again going to propose closing the Free School. I immediately went to work informing staff, parents, and community friends of this news. The entire process was again set in motion to save our little school. On Thursday, April 4, 1991, the area superintendent, Dr. Macey, called me at 2:30 p.m. My secretary informed him that I was in the building teaching a class, but she could get me if necessary. He told her that it was not necessary and that I could call him later that day or in the morning the next day.

I returned his call at approximately 3:20 p.m. that day. He began the conversation by informing me that a group called the Committee of the Whole had proposed closing our school. He contended that he was defending us but asked me not to go to the faculty or parents over this matter. He then requested information about what parts of town our students came from. I felt I had to tell him that I had already informed the faculty and the parents about the possible closure. I had not disobeyed a command. Bureaucracies characteristically treat underlings like children—they could try and send me to my room, but they were too late in shutting me up.

The area superintendent became upset and frustrated. He demanded to know the source of my information. When I would not give it to him, he pointed out that I was under his supervision and that he held loyalty to him to be very important. Bureaucracies also often treat employees like prisoners of war: "Do as I say or die!"

Upper-echelon bureaucrats will often pretend to be on your side, to be cooperative and supportive, but when they give an order, the message is clear: "Do as I say, not as I pretend." This man was a good guy; he was not an evil human being. But his message was pure bureaucrat: Be a team player, follow orders and always be loyal to the chain of command. This decent man, albeit a good bureaucrat, was not upset that our little school was being bullied by this fat giant and he was not angry that we were walking a plank. In fact he wanted us to walk that plank with our hands tied behind our back by ordering me not to go to our faculty and parents. He was bent out of shape because the cat was already out of the bag and he had lost the ability to control us. He was public education's version of a military commander who feared that he would look inept because some of his troops had gone AWOL.

This area superintendent pointed out that he had defended us to the Committee of the Whole and that he was calling me in good faith two days after the meeting. He asserted that he valued trust and loyalty, and that I was not living up to these qualities. I replied that my source informed me that this issue was to go before the board on April 8. Thus, his two days later, non-emergency phone call, allowed me only two days to deal with this matter. I told him that I believe in trust, but trust must be a two way street. I pleaded that I, too, valued loyalty, but that loyalty must be based on principles, not blind obedience.

No matter what I said, his frustration did not wane. He ended the conversation by stating that he had supported us, but, if I refused to divulge my source, I was choosing to go it alone. He suggested that I think about it for the night and call him the next morning with my reply. If I did not call him, he knew where I stood.

I went home that evening on April 4 or 5, 1991, and wrote the area superintendent a letter detailing the above conversation. At the end of the letter I wrote, "I will make the call" meaning that I would tell him who gave me this information. However, in the letter, I continued arguing that in a true site-based school system, loyalty would reside at the school house, not the central office. I also stated that I wanted his loyalty and support, but would always involve parents and faculty in all matters.

Here, things get a little muddled for me. On my only copy of this letter to the area superintendent I used white-out on one paragraph and two lines and wrote a hand-written sentence over the covered section. I do not remember if I sent the original letter or a corrected copy to the area superintendent, or if I even sent any letter. From that letter, it appears that I was going to make the call though I have nothing in my notes or in my memory as to who told me of the decision to close the Free School. For me, the issue was never about who told me, nor was it just that we were never consulted. The urgency for us was to reverse this decision. Nevertheless, if I made that call, I am ashamed of myself. Fortunately, old age has its advantage in this case. I simply do not remember if I made that call or who told me of the plan to close the Free School.

This issue did not come up before the board on April 8, 1991, as we were initially led to believe. It did not reach the board until June of that year, affording us two months to better mobilize and garnish wide support to keep the Free School open. Mobilize we did: mailings, petitions, phone calls, and letters to the editors of *The Times-Picayune* and *The Louisiana Weekly*. We targeted our response to board members, Superintendent Everett Williams, community, educational and political leaders, and all local news venues.

Our first line of attack was a six-page open letter extolling the merits of the Free School and countering claims that our school was not cost effective and our building was structurally unsound. The administration was trying to justify closing the Free School based on needs to cut cost and on the poor condition of our building.

Two things occurred that significantly strengthened our position. With this letter I did what I did with most every letter I ever wrote defending the Free School—I let many people read it and make comments and/or suggestions for changes, additions, or deletions. My good friend, Lou Miron, a professor at Loyola University at the time, read the letter and told me that he really liked it, but asked me these questions, "Isn't it the school administration, and not the school board, who is trying to close you? Are you not asking the school board to vote to keep you open?" This was an 'aha' moment for me. I was guilty of treating them as one entity and not two. I immediately changed the letter and referred only to the administration's arguments for proposing to close the Free School. Wherever the letter stated "the school board wants" I changed to "the administration wants… desires…etc."

The other pertinent fact that augmented my letter was a document penned by an educator named Terri Bush, from New York, who visited our school on March 19–20, 1991. She submitted a lengthy, single-spaced typewritten report recording and analyzing her visit. This happened just prior to our discovering that the administration was once again targeting us for closure. I began my reply with Ms. Bush's written conclusion. Below is a copy of the letter we sent out to over a hundred people to share our story and make a plea for their support of the Free School.

NEW ORLEANS FREE SCHOOL
3601 Camp Street
New Orleans, LA 70115
899-0452

An Open Letter to the Orleans Parish School Board Members, Superintendent Everett J. Williams, and Citizens of the New Orleans Community:

CONCLUSIONS

The New Orleans Free School has few material resources compared to other schools we have visited. Its building is badly in need of repair, its budget barely adequate, there are scant materials and little advanced technology available to children and teachers. Ninety percent of the children take free lunch. The Board does not provide for teaching art or music.[1] Children must provide their own paper and pencils and some of their books.

The school's material resources, limited though they are, are made adequate by careful and creative management. The use of community resources such as the Arts Connection, the drug education services, the collaboration with the University of New Orleans, greatly enriches the school's program and connects it to the larger community in which it lives. Further, the personal resources that parents can bring are welcomed. Teachers all do some other job for the school in addition to the classroom work. It is an extraordinary set of arrangements which results in a maximum use of available resources in the service of common goals.

Resources are scarce, but it is not a poor school. On the contrary, it is rich in the resources that matter most in the shaping of young lives: caring adults, respect for young learners, high expectations, and a determination to make things work. The community of teachers, parents, and children who are the Free School recreate their world every day, harkening to a vision of what can be. They do not feel for what they lack, but rejoice in what they have. And, while each day brings its problems along with its joys, there is great strength here, developed over twenty years of continuing commitment. It is indeed a heartening example for anyone who works on behalf of children.

---

[1] The Board does supply our school with a vocal music teacher for one and a half days per week.

This passage is not another of Bob Ferris' efforts to create an image of quality education happening at the New Orleans Free School. I must point out to you that this passage was written by Ms. Terri Bush, a New York educator and Associate Director of the Center For At Risk Students, LaGuardia Community College. Ms. Bush spent 2 days this past April at the Free School as part of her ongoing research on educational models for "at risk students" throughout the United States.

I am writing to you to address the situation in which the New Orleans Free School finds itself. For the 4th time since 1980, the New Orleans Free School is once again target of efforts to close the school. For the 4th time our community is once again disrupted and must fear annihilation.

In this letter I will make the following points:

1. The New Orleans Free School's standardized tests scores increased last year.
2. The New Orleans Free School has received and is receiving national recognition as a model school with model programs. We have achieved excellent national publicity for the city of New Orleans and the Orleans Parish School System.
3. The New Orleans Free School serves as a model of school/community relations.
4. The New Orleans Free School is a school of choice serving mostly, but not exclusively, low income families. Our school program offers a unique educational experience which survives only on the merit of its program.
5. The New Orleans Free School is unfairly being targeted for closure.
6. The New Orleans Free School is cost effective.

What we are requesting is that the administration keep the Free School open and that The Orleans Parish School Board vote not only to keep the Free School open but to provide needed and deserved resources to enhance our model school program.

The administration wants increased achievement as recorded in high standardized test scores. Yet last school year California Achievement Test scores in Orleans Parish only stayed the same in reading and dropped in mathematics while the New Orleans Free School increased their test scores 11% in reading and 4% in mathematics. And this was accomplished in a school with a student population of over 90% of its student body on free lunch. Such success should be awarded with support. We should not be facing closure.

The administration desires a positive image for public schools. Our school was featured on a national documentary

2

titled, "Why Do These Kids Love School?" which was aired by PBS last September. The New Orleans Free School name and educational and community practices may also be part of a chapter in an upcoming revision of Carl Rogers' book, Freedom To Learn. Such national recognition should be locally acknowledged and applauded. Our school should not be facing closure.

The administration wants community involvement in our schools. The New Orleans Free School recently recruited its own 2nd business partner, the law firm of Middleberg Riddle and Gianna. They are going to help finance and support a law curriculum program for one of the 6th grade classes. This program is designed to respond to the horrible statistic that there are possibly more college-age black males in our prisons than in our colleges. We want to afford our students the educational opportunity of experiencing the positive and supportive side of the law.

Our school is a professional development school. The UNO Portal School Program is housed and operated at the New Orleans Free School. Professional development schools are genuine collaborations between a university and a school where university education majors take course work and implement teaching strategies at a school site. Teachers at the school site benefit because they are exposed to the latest in teaching research and they participate in teacher training. The portal school program came to us two years ago because of their discontent in another public school setting. The program has been so successful that they have just received from the State of Louisiana a sizeable grant to do a three year study of the portal program at the Free School. I am also pleased to announce that Dr. Joan Gipe, Dr. Janet Richards and Dr. Robert Ferris will receive the Presidents' Salute for Exemplary Partnerships for Minority Achievement. This comes from the American Association of Higher Education. We have been invited to be in Atlanta, Georgia to receive this award, but it is on the date the school board is scheduled to vote on whether or not to close the Free School. What irony! I hope and pray that I will be able to be in Atlanta to receive this award.

Not only do we intricately involve the community in the education of our students, we also involve our students with the community. We have a student internship program where many of our 7th/8th grade students are placed in the world of work for an hour and a half each week. The purpose of this program is to help adolescents enter into adulthood in a very positive and meaningful way and to afford many in the community the opportunity to participate in the education of our young people.

We just had approximately 100 of our students do an hour long performance at the Louisiana Jazz and Heritage Festival. Our students performed folk dances, choir, band, sign language, Cajun dancing, rap and tap. The band was financed by a grant from the Louisiana Jazz and Heritage Foundation. We also had

3

100+ of our students from grades K-8 dramatically perform original pieces or pieces from literature at our annual Literature Reading Night at the Chateau LeMoyne. This is a most impressive evening. The Chateau LeMoyne is our first business partner whom we got through the school system. We are most grateful.

We furnish our students with all of these opportunities because we deeply believe that all children must experience success and the meaningfulness of learning. Our program is based on activity, inquiry, depth and experiences. We have shunned isolated skill development, narrow test focused curriculum, surface coverage of material and rigid lockstep behavior in favor of student engagement in learning. Community involvement is a mainstay at the Free School, as our business partners, the UNO Portal Program, our internship program, our yearly Jazz Festival performance and annual Literature Reading Night attest. The New Orleans Free School should not be facing closure.

The administration strongly urges that parents have a voice in their child/ren's education. Well, every parent who has a child in the Free School has chosen to put their child there. Why take this choice away from them? The Free School exists only because of parental choice - we have no guaranteed audience - we have no district - we survive only on the merit of our program. And many, many low income parents elect to send their children to the New Orleans Free School. Choices for this community's less economically advantaged should be encouraged. After all, there is no question that magnet schools which attract mostly middle and upper income students will remain open. But schools of choice for all students should be a goal for this school system. I agree with the administration's claim that we must serve the poor and meet their needs. Our school models this philosophy and practice.

The administration states that they can close our school because of the availability of space in surrounding schools. Does not some of this space exist because parents in our school have rejected those schools in favor of our more active and enriched educational practices? Does not this tell us something? Our school is not in want of students. Need I say more?

The administration claims that they are not targeting the Free School or that closing the Free School is not personal. Yet this is the 4th time in the past 10 years that the Free School has been put in this position. Below is a quote by Herbert Kohl, progressive educator and author of 36 Children, Open Classroom, and Basic Skills. The quote is taken from an interview printed in this May's issue of the Phi Delta Kappan, the leading educational journal in the United States today. It is as follows:

4

Other Ways, our school in Berkeley, was considered a model for a while. But the school district would not leave it alone. It refused to provide us with facilities, turned money intended for our programs into support for central administration and evaluation, tried to assign antagonistic teachers to the school, and put us in a position of having to fight every year for even a line on the next year's budget. That same thing happened to many well-designed schools around the country. Open education did not fail in the 1970's. It was hounded, harassed, and starved into retreat.

Unfortunately, this same situation has existed and exists for the Free School. Yet our principles, our ideas, our educational practices are on the front burner of education today throughout the United States. We do not purport to have the answer; but we do rightfully claim to have an answer as to how to educate our youth today. Our answer challenges standardization, bureaucratic control, isolated skill development and mediocrity. Our answer includes autonomy, choice and voice, smallness, personalism, engaging and challenging academic and artistic endeavors. We concentrate not on what children do not know; rather, we concentrate on using their strengths, intelligences, and artistic abilities to aid in their further development. Our philosophy and practice is a true celebration in the beauty and potential of the child.

The administration claims that the reason for closing the Free School is money, but the Free School does not receive more money per pupil than any other public school. If anything, we are on the bottom of the Orleans Parish financial ladder. We do not receive any federal Title I monies nor, to my knowledge, do we receive any of the magnet school monies. The irony of this issue is that it may cost the school system more money to educate our students if the Free School is closed. Our students would probably end up in a school offering Title I services or in better financed magnet schools. In both cases the per pupil expenditure would be greater.

Five years ago, the New Orleans Free School was targeted for closure because it was not cost effective. In response to that claim, the Free School was required to double its enrollment. We complied. The demand for our program continues to grow. We should not be facing closure.

The administration claims that they must close the Free School because our school building is structurally unsound. However, it is my understanding that it will only take $250,000 to make our building safe. Money dedicated to capital improvements was already appropriated and work was to begin this June. In fact, a considerable amount of money has already been

5

spent to make our building structurally safe. Engineers and architects have also been paid to evaluate this work. And, to my understanding, plans have already been drawn for the work contemplated. In other words, the school system has already spent a considerable amount of money on the planned renovations which were to be completed this summer. The information provided to us is that our building has been given a structural bill of health. The $250,000.00 is to replace the roof, fill in cracks, and replace the falling front structure. Another $500,000.00 was in the capital budget to renovate the school. This would give us a modern, very pleasant teaching and learning facility. We can wait on the decorative aspect of our building.

In this letter I have extolled the merits and significance of the Free School. However, in no way do I want to imply that the Free School is flawless. There are students whom we do not reach educationally; there are students whom we must suspend or threaten with suspension if we are to keep them in line; there are inner squabbles which are part of any family; and, even though our standardized test scores are rising, they are still not where we would like them to be. I do not believe that any school which serves many children trapped in the crises of poverty in America today can be flawless or without struggle and turmoil. But I also believe that poor children, all children, can learn in a very creative, energetic, caring and vital environment - a school where people at the school site are the decision makers. At the Free School we have successfully demonstrated this rhetoric with action.

I appreciate that the tone of this letter is a little harsh. But the position that our school is being put in is rather uncompromising - death through closure. I believe strongly that if we are to solve the myriad of problems facing urban life, especially education, we must abandon our traditional convergent approaches and seek and implement divergent answers. Complex problems require complex answers, even contradictory answers. The irony in this situation is that the New Orleans Free School models exactly what the school system strives for.

Can you not find a solution that serves to move parents, teachers and students out of this quagmire?

Sincerely,

Robert M. Ferris, Ed.D
Principal

6

This letter reiterated the six arguments to save the Free School. The goal was to always solidify support and to get our story out to as many people, politicians, leaders, and news organizations as possible.

Both our business partners, Sid Siddigi, CEO of the Chateau Le-Moyne Hotel, and Ira Middleberg, of the prominent law firm of Middleberg, Riddle, and Gianna, wrote letters to each board member pleading our case. Educators throughout the community and nation wrote letters to the superintendent and board members supporting our school. This happened with the assistance of Jerry Mintz, who has spearheaded the alternative school movement in the United States (and the world for that matter) and is the founder/director of the Alternative Education Resource Organization (AERO).

Our parents again sought after and secured a city council resolution demanding to keep the Free School open. I include a copy of the resolution because it so publicly and powerfully stated our case. Following the resolution are three letters printed in *The Times-Picayune*. One letter was written by an elderly neighbor volunteer who taught a literature class at our school. One was from parents who felt strongly about keeping the Free School open and one was from the combined faculty of the Free School. I retain copies of many letters sent to the superintendent and board members along with others published in *The Times-Picayune* lauding the Free School but feel that the City Council Resolution and the three letters below adequately capture the intense spirit of keeping us alive.

RESOLUTION

R-91-110

CITY HALL: _____ June 6, 1891 _____

BY: COUNCILMEMBER SINGLETON
SECONDED BY: COUNCILMEMBER TAYLOR

WHEREAS, the New Orleans Free School is unique in its personal approach to education, believing that the educational needs of children should not be separated from all other parts of their lives; and

WHEREAS, the school offers an alternative to the traditional classroom and provides a nurturing atmosphere for all students, from the "gifted" to the "slow" learners, without making obvious distinctions between them; it encourages active participants instead of passive recipients in the learning process; and

WHEREAS, the New Orleans Free School has been recognized on the national documentary, "Why Do These Kids Love School?", and the American Association of Higher Education will award to the New Orleans Free School later this month, the Presidents' Salute for Exemplary Partnerships for Minority Achievement; and

WHEREAS, the New Orleans Free School has accomplished rising test scores in a district struggling for higher achievement; and

WHEREAS, the New Orleans Free School is a school of choice serving mostly, but not exclusively, low income families; and

WHEREAS, the New Orleans Free School serves as a model of school community relationships as exemplified with its business partners, UNO, Chateau LeMoyne, and Middleberg Riddle and Gianna; and

WHEREAS, all teachers assigned to this facility are there by choice, and are dedicated to the Free School's philosophy of teaching; and

WHEREAS, the school building has been given a structural bill of health, and it is in fact in writing that work was to begin this June; and

WHEREAS, the **New Orleans Free School** does not cost more per pupil to educate that other public schools and, in fact, may cost less since it does not receive federal chapter 1 monies, nor magnet school monies; and

WHEREAS, this City Council joins the Parent Teacher Association in asking New Orleans Public Schools, "why get rid of something that works?", based on the merits that this school possesses, every effort should be made to keep this school open and utilize it as a model for other schools in the Orleans Parish School System; now, there

BE IT RESOLVED BY THE COUNCIL OF THE CITY OF NEW ORLEANS, That this Council does hereby urge and request the Orleans Parish School Board to reevaluate its position regarding the **New Orleans Free School** and take the appropriate steps to keep this institution open.

BE IT FURTHER RESOLVED, That the Clerk of Council is hereby requested to transmit a certified copy of this resolution to the members of the Orleans Parish School Board, the Superintendent of New Orleans Public Schools, the Director of Planning New Orleans Public Schools and the Parent Teacher Association of the New Orleans Free School.

THE FOREGOING RESOLUTION WAS READ IN FULL, THE ROLL WAS CALLED ON THE ADOPTION THEREOF AND RESULTED AS FOLLOWS:

YEAS: Clarkson, Giarrusso, Jackson, Singleton, Taylor, Wilson - 6

NAYS: 0

ABSENT: Boissiere (temporarily absent) - 1.

AND THE RESOLUTION WAS ADOPTED.

CRS 91-

THE FOREGOING IS CERTIFIED
TO BE A TRUE AND CORRECT COPY

Emma J. Williams

CLERK OF COUNCIL

The Times-Picayune

ASHTON PHELPS
Chairman of the Board 1967-1983

Issued daily by The Times-Picayune Publishing Corp. at
3800 Howard Ave., New Orleans, La. 70140

ASHTON PHELF
President and Pub

JIM AMOSS
Editor

TOM GREGOI
Associate Editor, .

MALCOLM FORS
Associate Editor, Ea

YOUR OPINIONS | Letters

Don't close the Free School

TIMES-PICAYUNE 5/18/91

New Orleans

The Orleans Parish School Board must be out of its collective mind to be considering closing Howard School No. 2, known as the Free School, or to think of closing any schools at this time when the student population is growing and the classrooms are already overcrowded.

The Free School is the only magnet school for poor children, and the experts agree that the only answer to our social problems is to educate those below the poverty line. And the School Board plans to close the underprivileged kids' magnet school!!

Further, the Howard School building itself is historic, having been built at the beginning of this century, and it is a magnificent example of the architecture of that period.

Additionally, the School Board cannot sell the Howard building and put the proceeds of the sale into its general fund. Under a court judgment entered into a few years ago between the board and the Howard family, any money from a sale of the school must be put toward the construction of another school. Everyone knows it is cheaper to restore a fine old building than to erect a new one.

The School Board has already spent quite a lot of money having a firm of local engineers monitor the Howard building to be certain that it is capable of being reno-vated, and the public has voted for a bond issue to restore the building.

The School Board has already budgeted $750,000 for the complete renovation of the Free School, a project that was scheduled to begin this summer. It is senseless to abandon a project so carefully conceived — and wasteful, too.

Finally, the Free School is a wonderful educational institution, and its principal, Robert Ferris, is outstanding, the type of dedicated educator President Bush has in mind when he speaks of rewarding exceptional teachers.

I speak from personal experience because for the past six years I have, as a volunteer, taught a literature class at the school one morning every week. The proof of the Free School's worth is that every year some of its graduating students are accepted at Franklin.

Anyone who is knowledgeable on the subject can only conclude that the Free School should remain open under Robert Ferris to continue its excellent work in giving a good education to poor children, and that the School Board, instead of closing it down, should adhere to its plan of several years to restore and renovate this beautiful building.

Louise Korns

190

Closing New Orleans Free School is absurd

TIMES PICAYUNE   6/12/91

New Orleans

New Orleans Free School is one of the few bright spots in the New Orleans Parish Public School System and should not be facing closure.

The New Orleans Free School receives national recognition for its active, enriched and unique educational program and philosophy. It is a school with 20 years of positive accomplishments, merits, achievements and success. It would be totally absurd to close it down.

The New Orleans Free School is a school of choice. The parents elect to send their children there. We chose the school for our children because it promotes quality education through a non-bureaucratic approach and allows us the choice of where we want our children to go to school.

To close the school would take this choice away and force us to send our children to a school in our district that cannot be com-pared to it in any way.

We are proud of the positive academic achievement our children have made while at the Free School. Rather than diminish their attitude toward education and send them to our district school, which uses the standard, run-of-the-mill education approach, we would resort to home schooling.

Timothy Moore Sr.
Joycelyn Moore

The Times-Picayune

ASHTON PHELPS JR.
President and Publisher

JIM AMOSS
Editor

ASHTON PHELPS
Chairman of the Board 1967-1983

TOM GREGORY
Associate Editor, News

Issued daily by The Times-Picayune Publishing Corp. at
3800 Howard Ave., New Orleans, La. 70140

MALCOLM FORSYTH
Associate Editor, Editorials

YOUR OPINIONS | Letters

Do not close down the New Orleans Free School

New Orleans

Being fortunate enough to work on the committed faculty of the New Orleans Free School, we are dismayed and discouraged that our school is once again being threatened with closure.

We are dismayed because we realize how beneficial our close-knit, caring community is to our students. We are discouraged that the school system is making its fourth attempt in ten years to eradicate our unique program.

This attempt represents the second violation of our own verbal agreement to leave our program intact as long as we maintain the agreed enrollment level.

The New Orleans Free School is one of the few alternative schools that cater primarily to the needs of low-income students. It exists only because parents choose to send their children here, and we believe these children and their parents have a right to this choice.

Why should a school where students choose to attend and teachers choose to teach be subject to closure? We offer an experiential program based on respect for children as active, inquiring learners. We are dedicated to seeking new ways to meet the needs of these learners. Through the use of these ideas, we contribute to the intellectual, emotional, creative and moral growth of our students.

Our school is rich in creative ideas and use of community resources. The University of New Orleans Portal School Program offers all our students and teachers the opportunity to learn and implement with education majors the latest theories and practices in the teaching of language arts.

This program has earned for its two designing professors, Dr. Joan Gipe and Dr. Janet Richards, and also our own principal, Dr. Robert Ferris, the American Association of Higher Education's Presidents' Salute for Exemplary Partnerships for Minority Achievement.

A dedicated neighbor of ours has come in for years to teach a weekly literature class. Nearly one-third of our class participated in sign-language, band, choral, rap, tap, folk and/or Cajun dance productions at the Louisiana Jazz and Heritage Festival.

All our students are offered weekly elective classes ranging from gardening to chess to arts and crafts. All our students also have the opportunity to participate in our annual out-of-town camping trip the last three days of school.

Perhaps this partial list of learning opportunities provides an idea why our school was one of the schools featured in a nationally televised PBS documentary, "Why Do These Kids Love School?"

While we are rightly proud of our efforts, we do not claim to offer a cure-all for today's educational problems. We do believe that today's complex social and educational problems require many different solutions and that ours should be among them. Money does not equal quality; ideas and commitment do.

It is disheartening to once again be in the position of having to fight and plead for our survival. We have always survived on minimal resources and are willing to continue to do so if we must; but we deeply believe that survive we must.

Our faculty members seek and receive grant funding on their own to implement programs that are not funded through the school system. We ask only what has been promised and budgeted in writing for us. We appeal to the school system to support our program as a creative search for new educational alternatives.

We believe this need is obvious and that we deserve to be one among many different paths to the shared goal of quality education.

Jeanette St. Etienne
and 15 other faculty
and staff members,
New Orleans Free School

During the months of April and May 1991, while we were making our case and seemingly gaining ground, the administration was subtly changing its attack and was now more openly stating that I was too uncooperative, a nuisance, and not supportive of the administration. They also heightened their claim that our building was structurally unsound, unhealthy, and too expensive to repair. Simultaneously, the school administration attempted to control the flow of information; i.e., they wanted to stop me from sending information to board members.

The new Deputy Superintendent (who I will call Bill Jones) sent board members, department heads and principals a memorandum with the subject line "Communication Process for Requesting Information and Assistance from School District Personnel" dated May 13, 1991.

To: AREA I PRINCIPALS SAC

TO: Board Members

FROM: Deputy Superintendent

RE: COMMUNICATION PROCESS FOR REQUESTING INFORMATION AND
           ASSISTANCE FROM SCHOOL DISTRICT PERSONNEL

DATE: May 13, 1991

A fundamental belief of this administration is that well informed Board Members make better decisions and thus are better able to articulate the position of the district on various issues. In order to improve the communication process for providing information and assistance to Board Members and to assure the accuracy of information disseminated, the Superintendent and the Deputy Superintendent are responsible for reviewing information prior to that information being transmitted to the Board or to individual Board Members.

To facilitate this process of quality control, improve accountability among district personnel, assure the equitable distribution of labor, improve employee morale, and to avoid putting district personnel in an untenable position between Board Members and their superiors, I am requesting that Board Members limit their request for information and assistance to the following administrators: (1) Superintendent; (2) Deputy Superintendent; (3) Appropriate Division Head.

By copy of this memorandum, I am directing all Division Heads to give full cooperation to Board Members whenever there is a request for information or assistance. Each Division Head MUST inform the members of his/her division of this procedure and require them to refer all requests for information and/or assistance to him/her for assignment to appropriate personnel.

Thank you for your cooperation in our attempt to improve the efficiency of our communication process. Should you have any questions, please advise.

JLS/wvd

cc: Dr. Everett J. Williams
      Dr. Frank Fudesco
      Miss Ella Voelkel
      Area Superintendents
      Mrs. Brenda Hatfield
      Mr. Jim Henderson
      Mrs. Linda Stelly

This was a cleverly crafted document shrouded in democratic terms that attempted to muzzle just about everyone in the district. I do not know if it ever achieved its intended effect. It had none on me.

Sometime in late May or early June Deputy Superintendent Jones spoke at a principal's meeting. He argued sternly and forcefully, articulating the administration's need to close schools and that as members of "the administrative team," we should not fight the decision but must, in fact, support it. When he finished the speech, there was silence. He asked if there were any questions. I gingerly raised my hand, never expecting to be called upon, but I was.

Although I did not want to speak, I could not let his message go unchallenged. He was a tall, strong looking, deep-voiced, authoritative person. He was not the type of person one would want to challenge, especially in such a public arena where he was the obvious authority. I had already sent one open letter to board members and citizens of the community; I knew I was prepared to send more. I knew that if I left his message unchallenged, I was placing myself on the defensive and possibly violating his directive.

Fear sometimes gives one strength to do or say something one would never do under normal circumstances. I spoke with my knees shaking and my voice cracking. These are the words I spoke as I best can remember them: "Sir, I must respectfully disagree. While I know and understand that there are those who strongly advocate and insist on a hierarchy with those us on the bottom following and implementing orders from those on the top, there is also a movement in this country that believes in a much different model. This movement, this idea, this practice, believes that loyalty resides at the local school, not the central office, and that we have an obligation to support, defend, and develop these schools."

As I sat down, silence never became louder. Even seated, my knees never quit shaking. After what seemed like an eternity, this deputy superintendent finally said, "That's what I get for asking if there are any questions."

After the meeting, several principals thanked me for making the statement and many told me "what you said needed to be said." Even today as I run into principals from that era, they bring up that collision. Not long after this meeting, I sent out my second letter to board members, primarily to respond to the accusation that I was uncooperative and a nuisance who did not support the administration. I included another copy of my six-page letter and an article I wrote in 1987 explaining the practices at the Free School. Here is a copy of my letter.

NEW ORLEANS FREE SCHOOL
3601 Camp Street
New Orleans, LA 70115
899-0452

May 28, 1991

Dr. Jefferson and members of the board,

It has been brought to my attention that some of you may not know what the New Orleans Free School is all about. I am giving you three pieces of literature. One is an open letter addressed to you, the superintendent and members of the New Orleans community. This letter states our position as to why we should remain open. We do offer a unique educational option and our school is receiving national recognition for our successful practices. The second piece I am sending you I wrote back in 1987. This piece explains the many unique practices employed at the Free School. I am also enclosing our brochure about the Free School.

The one issue not covered in these three pieces, and which may be the main reason why the Free School is so often targeted for closure, is that we represent a different conceptualization of public education. I have been an outspoken critic of the bureaucratization of urban public schools and a strong advocate of schools of choice with school-site autonomy. I believe in a public school framework that has schools entering into partnerships with school systems. The principal is no longer a middle person in a chain of command. He or she becomes an educational leader serving a community. Teachers are no longer responsible for carrying out the prescriptions of others. They become and function as professionals. Allegiance, loyalty and resources shift from the system to the school-site - the only place where teaching and learning actually happens.

This professional model of public schooling is strongly being endorsed in educational literature today:

> The traditional bureaucratic model of school
> organization, based on the assumption that most
> teachers are minimally competent and therefore
> require close inspection and supervision, is not
> only outmoded but harmful. Real reform and high-
> quality schools require putting teachers and site
> administrators at the center of the educational
> process with their students. This necessitates the
> creation of a true profession and the implementation
> of a professional model in our schools. (Watts and
> McClure, "Expanding the Contract to Revolutionize
> School Renewal," Phi Delta Kappan, June 1990, p. 767.)

I hope that this wealth of material helps familarize you with the Free School and that you can appreciate the value of such an important learning environment.

We, of course, believe that the Free School should be exposed not closed. We believe that model quality education should be supported and expanded.

Please help us resolve this problem in a way that is favorable to all.

Sincerely,

Robert M. Ferris, Ed.D
Principal

By June 1, 1991, it came to our attention frequently that school officials were telling people that they had to close the school because our building was structurally unsound, in violation of fire code laws, and uninhabitable. Our building was old, certainly in need of updating and aesthetics, and desperately in need of air conditioning. However, these accusations were certainly a stretch of information to the point of being deliberately deceptive. Who the source of this fabrication was, I do not know. I have always suspected the Director of Facility Planning, Dr. John McCarty (again, a fictitious name). His name came up in every conversation about the attempted school closure, and he certainly had information to dispel these accusations before the board, which to my knowledge he never did.

I immediately sent the board members a letter refuting these claims with documentation clearly showing that we complied with regulations of the fire department, the health department, and our planning department. The irony of this situation was that our planning department had declared the building structurally sound after previously doing structural work in the attic and monitoring the situation for about two years. They authorized renovation to begin in the summer of 1991, the very summer in which we now faced closure. It is worth repeating that Dr. McCarty never came to our defense even though it was he who had declared our building to be structurally sound after observing it for two years. He always told me that he had good news concerning our building.

Here is my rebuttal letter to the attack on our building and supporting documentation.

NEW ORLEANS FREE SCHOOL
3601 Camp Street
New Orleans, LA 70115
899-0452

June 11, 1991

Dear School Board Members,

I am told that the reasons for closing the Free School are because our building is structurally unsound, is in violation of fire code laws and is uninhabitable. I would like to address each of these issues because the information I have does not substantiate these accusations.

It is true that our building had structural damage but this was corrected two years ago by the school system at considerable expense. We were then told that our building was to be evaluated for one year, again at expense to the school system, to see if the work was successful or if there were continuing structural problems. At the end of the year's evaluation I was told by Dr. ____ that he had nothing but good news for me. Our building was evaluated to be structurally sound and the first phase of a planned renovation would soon occur. In March of this year (see enclosed) I received in writing that work was to finally begin on our building. It is my understanding that Verges Associates Architects, 4640 South Carrollton Avenue, phone number 488-7739, has already drawn up plans for this first phase and is just waiting for the go ahead.

I have also heard that our building is in major violation of fire code laws. I am enclosing a copy of the latest fire inspection of our facility which was conducted on February 28, 1991. As you can see the first six violations are extremely minor and almost cost non-existent. Number 7 presents a problem in other old school buildings. However, if we are required to comply we could move our first grade to an already existing space on our ground level. The kindergarten class is already on the ground level. No expense would be required.

Our building was also given a clean bill of health by the Board of Health last school year once we were able to get rid of a head custodian who refused to do his job. I am enclosing a copy of the health report dated May 24, 1990. Last summer Mr. Brannon did send someone who patched the holes in our building. The light fixtures have been fixed and the rugs were, of course, thrown away. The head custodian we hired this school year has done a superior job and there are absolutely no health problems that I am aware of.

I believe that our building is worth saving. It is a beautiful, sound old structure worth preserving. It definitely needs work. But the money was there and plans have been drawn up to do the first of two phases to renovate our building. Three months ago we were celebrating the notification that work was to begin this June - now. Now we are facing closure. We do not understand why this is happening.

Thank you for your attention. Again, I hope we can reconcile this issue in a favorable manner for all.

Sincerely,

Robert M. Ferris, Ed.D, Principal

RMF/pv

198

```
┌─────────────────────────────────────────────────┐
│           M E M O R A N D U M                     │
├─────────────────────────────────────────────────┤
│              Facility Planning                    │
└─────────────────────────────────────────────────┘
```

TO: DR.
        DR.
        MR.
        MS. LINDA J. STELLY

FROM: Director
        Facility Planning

SUBJECT: MAJOR RENOVATIONS UNDER CONSTRUCTION THIS SUMMER
         (REVISED LIST)

DATE: MARCH 05, 1991

Please be advised that we anticipate the following schools
to be greatly affected by major renovations beginning as
soon as school closes in June.

Renovations:	Dunbar Frantz Kennedy (gym only) Meyer McMain	Bell (Library) Live Oak N.O. Free School Woodson (gym only)
Asbestos Abatement:	Beauregard Chester Crocker	Edison Lafayette

No summer programs should be planned. Also, schools will be
asked to prepare for interior disruption during construction.

If you have any questions, please let me know.

FJD:bee
pc: Dr. Frank D. Fudesco
    Dr. Samuel A. Scarnato
    Ms. Barbara MacPhee
    Mr. Mike Brannan
    Ms. Doris Riley
    Ms. Rosalynne Dennis
    Facility Planning Staff

C.C. Schools

199

FIRE PREVENTION DIVISION
NEW ORLEANS FIRE DEPT.
317 DECATUR ST.
TELEPHONE # 581-5457
NEW ORLEANS, LA. 70130

INSPECTION REPORT

FIRE DISTRICT: 6 ⊕.
TIME OF INSP: 2:25
CONTACT: NATHAN JONES

NUMBER OF STORIES: 3
TYPE OF CONSTRUCTION: III
TYPE OF OCCUPANCY: EDUCATIONAL
C OF C DUE DATE _____ TO _____

℅ MIKE BRANNAN
OWNER: ORLEANS PARISH SCHOOL BOARD
OWNER'S ADDRESS: 4300 ALMONASTER
OWNER'S TEL. NUMBER: 942-3400

NUMBER OF PERSONS: VARIOUS (300)
SQUARE FEET: 40,500
ISSUE C OF C UPON PAYMENT OF $_____
INSPECTED BY: C. Udro

IN COMPLIANCE WITH ORDINANCE 4912 M.C.S. YOU ARE HEREBY ORDERED TO CORRECT THE
FOLLOWING VIOLATIONS:

1. SPACE BENEATH EXIT STAIRS CANNOT BE USED FOR THE STORAGE OF COMBUSTIBLE MATERIALS. (4912 M.C.S. SECTION F-121(.0)

2. DISCONTINUE STORAGE IN EXIT WAY AND EXIT STAIRWELLS (4912 M.C.S. SECTION F-284(.0)

3. DISCONTINUE THE PRACTICE OF BLOCKING FIRE EXIT DOORS IN THE OPEN POSITION (4912 M.C.S. SECTION F-123(.0

4. PROPERLY MAINTAIN ILLUMINATED EXIT SIGNS THROUGH BUILDING. (S.B.C. 118)

5. HAVE FIRE EXTINGUISHERS CHECKED AND TAGGED SHOWING LAST CURRENT RECHARGE DATE. (4912 M.C.S. SECTION F-151(

THE ABOVE VIOLATIONS IF ANY MUST BE CORRECTED WITHIN 30 CALENDER DAYS FROM THE
DATE OF THIS INSPECTION. IF ANY OF THESE VIOLATIONS EXIST AFTER __3-28-91__
A $50.00 RE-INSPECTION FEE WILL BE ASSESSED AND MUNICIPAL CHARGES WILL BE FILED

Inspector: TEG
Number: 910245
Date Received: 03/01/91
Address: 3601 CAMP ST
Name of firm: N O FREE SCHOOL
Compl/CONTACT: NATHAN JONES
Telephone: 899-5311
Viol Code: P
Violation: INSPECTION
Disposition: PD V/P
Date Inspected: 2/28/91

RECEIVED BY:_____

DATE RECEIVED:_____

CC: MR. BOB FARRIS, PRINCIPAL
Y/o. N.O. FREE SCHOOL
3601 CAMP ST
N.O., LA

200

6. CLOSE ALL OPENINGS BETWEEN FLOORS (MISSING CEILING TILES) TO PREVENT SMOKE AND FIRE PASSAGE. (N.F.P.A. 101-85, SECTION 6-2)

7. DISCONTINUE THE USE OF ALL CLASSROOMS USED FOR PRE-SCHOOL, KINDERGARTEN OR FIRST (1ST) GRADE LOCATED ABOVE THE FLOOR OF EXIT DISCHARGE (GROUND LEVEL NFPA 101-85, SECTION 11-1.1.1)

2:20 pm

DHHR
OFFICE OF HEALTH SERVICES & ENVIRONMENTAL QUALITY
DIVISION OF HEALTH
DIVISION OF EDUCATION

CHOOL PLANT HEALTH
HECK LIST
HE 19 A (R 7/77)   X5

Reinspection done with Mr. Brannon + Principal

chool: N. O. Free School
ncipal: Mr. Robert Ferris
ddress: 3601 Camp Street

rish: Orleans
perintendent: Dr. E. Williams
Address: 4100 Touro St.

PUPIL REGISTRATION   Boys 150   Girls 150

uilding (type and use)		GOOD	NEEDS ATTEN-TION	COMMENTS
I. Site and Play Area	a. Size and Shape	☐	☐	
	b. Drainage	☑	☐	
	c. Clean and Free from Hazards	☑	☐	
	d. Walks and Driveways	☑	☐	
	e. Trees, Flowers, and Shrubs	☑	☐	
	f. Fenced from Traffic Hazards	☑	☐	
II. Building	a. Location	☐	☐	
	b. Entrance and Safety Exits	☑	☐	
	c. Appearance (repair and paint)	☑	☑	
	d. Housekeeping, Floors, Walls, Etc. (clean, well kept)	☐	☑	Several classrooms need painting
	e. Heat and Ventilation	☐	☐	
	f. Light (natural and electric)	☑	☐	
III. Toilet Facilities	a. Rooms (clean floors, walls, fixtures, etc.)	☐	☐	
	b. Light and Ventilation	☑	☐	Classrooms need adequate lighting
	c. Toilets (type, number, condition)	☑	☐	
	d. Lavatories (sufficient soap, individual towels)	☑	☐	
	e. Toilet Paper (ample stock)	☑	☐	
	f. Sewage Disposal (STATE METHOD)	☑	☐	
Solid Wastes	a. Storage	☑	☐	
	b. Disposal (STATE METHOD)	☐	☐	
V. Water Supply	a. Approved Source (potable)	☑	☐	
	b. Drinking Fountains (angle stream)	☑	☐	
	c. Cooler with Individual Cups	☑	☐	

SAMPLE COLLECTED   Date   ☐ Negative ☐ Positive

ADDITIONAL COMMENTS

Rugs in class rooms on second floor are unclean and unsanitary. Remove rugs and clean dusty debris.

X Robert M Ferris

Date May 24 / 1990   Inspector Ms. Joy G. Freeman R.S.

STATE SUPERVISOR OF SCHOOL PLANTS

Mfd. by The TM Corporation

On May 31, 1991, *The Times-Picayune* ran a story exclusively on the Free School closing titled, "Parents rally to preserve Free School." In the article, the author declared that the end of the school appears in sight. However, the article also included a picture that proved the old adage, that a picture is worth a thousand words. The picture was of a mock trial at our school with a female student playing a prosecutor in the trial of a student accused of stealing a library book. The New Orleans Public School System was considered one of the worst school systems in the country. Here was a school conducting a mock trial, yet it was facing closure. This was not the image of Bob Ferris or myriad advocates defending the school; it was simply a picture of a good school educating children. This may have been the rock that cracked a hole in the battleship.

Even with the positive press and the voluminous letters of support, we feared the worst. I had been required and complied with all administrative requests for necessary information to close the school: student addresses, textbook counts, furniture inventory, school bank reconciliation, etc. On June 19, 1991, I wrote the parents and faculty a letter trying to prepare them for what seemed like the inevitable. Below is that disheartening letter:

June 19, 1991

Dear Parents and Faculty,

Win, lose or draw we are going to the board meeting on Monday, June 24, 1991, 7:00 p.m. at McDonogh #35, 1331 Kerlerec Street. Please wear Free School T-shirts. Again, we will meet at the Free School at 6:00 p.m. - dinner again at Ruby Red's after the meeting. A vote should be taken at this meeting. It is now do or die.

Thank you for a very impressive and highly professional showing at the June 13th meeting. I believe that our message got across and that the evening helped our cause. Thank you for your support - we need it one more time. If you have been unable to participate and want to help support the Free School, Monday night is the time. Monday night!! Monday night!! Monday night!!

Please remember, if we lose the vote, we die with dignity.

If we lose the vote, I will do everything I can to assist you in transferring your child/ren. This process cannot begin until August 15, 1991. However, if you are able to make individual arrangements beforehand, please do so.

If we win the vote, please make sure your friends and relatives contact us on August 15, 1991 for enrollment. Because of all this closure talk, we may have a few openings in classes that are now full. Even though we have more applications on file than we have graduates or other students known to be leaving, we still may end up with a couple of openings. We do have openings in kindergarten.

Thank you for your continued support. You have made me proud to serve you. I hope we win. But, if we don't, I will remember you forever.

Remember A

Remember B

But C that you remember me!

Yours educationally,

Dr. Bob

Actually the final vote came on June 27, not June 24, 1991, as my letter states. On June 27, 1991, a number of us went to the meeting, expecting a vote on closing the seven schools, including the New Orleans Free School. I went into the auditorium bathroom and ended up at a urinal next to my area superintendent, Bill Macey, who half glanced my way as he said, "Well, it looks like you dodged the bullet again." I do not know how long he had known we were not going to be closed or who else knew. I only knew I was breathing easier as I entered the auditorium. Our group quickly began to look at the agenda, only to find our school removed from the hit list.

If my memory serves me right, about a year after escaping closure in June of 1991, Dr. Williams took ill and was absent for a considerable amount of time. He did recover, but he retired shortly afterwards. The system hired one superintendent after another who continually led the system downhill. It seemed to me that we had entered the arena of "dumb and dumber" floating in and out of "mean and meaner." The next decade was not a good time for the Orleans Parish School System.

11

One New Superintendent After Another: The Sesquipedalian Superintendent, the Military Man, and the Con Artist

The first superintendent to oversee Orleans Parish schools was Dr. Morris Holmes, superintendent from 1993 to 1999. He had a propensity for using big words incorrectly and sounding furious but signifying ignorance. Standardized test scores rose significantly in many schools during his administration, leading to a series of articles with a *Times-Picayune* front page headline, "Too Good to Be True." The articles documented highly questionable test practices in Orleans Parish public schools and labeled the effects of these practices as "spikes"—dramatic fluctuations in test scores from year to year that seemed unreasonable. As reported in one of the articles, "Holmes objected to the use of the word 'spike.'" The article went on to quote Holmes, "That is one lexicon that has not been part of my vocabulary. I don't know what that is." He may not have known what "spike" meant in this situation—spike is testing jargon for unusual rise and fall of test scores—but he left the system not long thereafter.

As I was no fan of Morris Holmes, I decided to have some fun with the issue. That year at our annual faculty/parent Christmas party, I gave everyone a special Christmas gift—a spiking nail. Now most did not know that this six to eight-inch nail that attaches gutters to houses was called a spiking nail. Thus, initially, many missed the humor of the gift. My friend Lee, who is a contractor, immediately thought it was hilarious. Once the rest of the group caught the connection between spiking test scores and the spiking nail, most had a good laugh. Anyway, Morris Holmes abruptly left his helm but only after securing a $50,000 lifetime annual pension, compliments of our school board.

The next man the board hired was a retired colonel in the United States Marine Corps, Colonel Alphonse Davis. He served as superintendent from 1999 to 2002. The board was excited that it had broken the mold and hired a non-educator to run the system. However, he too, proved just as disastrous. He did not like being called superintendent, so he gave himself the title CEO and changed the titles of area superintendents to "cluster leaders." He put in new people as cluster leaders, but nothing changed. The boat kept sinking.

Then came along Tony Amato, a huckster for the reading programs, "Success for All" and, to a lesser degree, "Direct Instruction." He smothered the school system with these programs by removing any attempts at meaningful education and replaced them with scripted teaching, ever more tests, and paperwork piled on paperwork. Peddling these programs at great expense, he left with the school system in great debt. Another faux pas was sending school board contractors to board up his house to protect it from a pending hurricane. The press had a field day with this issue. He lasted only two years, from 2003 to 2005.

Since Dr. Morris Holmes left no lasting impressions on the school system other to make it look corrupt and inept (all three superintendents with others in the system helped make the school system look corrupt and inept—no one had a monopoly on these actions), I will pass over Holmes and concentrate on Davis and Amato.

When Colonel Davis first spoke to principals, he surprised me. He gave each of us two books to read, *Developing the Leader within You* by John C. Maxwell (I believe this was one of the books, though I am not sure. This book was about leadership.) and *Standards for Our Schools* by Marc S. Tucker and Judy B. Codding. I quickly read both books, but enjoyed the latter more because it focused on education rather than leadership. Yes, I have my doctorate in Educational Bureaucracy (i.e., Doctorate of Education), but my love is for the school house and the learning journey, not the bureaucratic leadership role.

Both Morris Holmes and Colonel Alphonse Davis were imposing figures who led more by intimidation than educational strategy. Morris Holmes failed because of his sham vocabulary, his highly suspect tests practices, and his lack of vision. Colonel Davis, also visionless, fell because his father, a head custodian in one of the Orleans Parish public schools, was paid approximately $100,000 one year, accumulated through working overtime hours, a feat impossible to achieve. Both leaders clearly illustrated the proverb quoted by John Maxwell in his book *Developing the Leadership Within You*: "He who thinketh he leadeth and hath no one following is only taking a walk" (1). Unfortunately, Colonel Davis wreaked havoc on the Free School before he departed. He embroiled us in one of the bitterest fights for survival we had yet to encounter. The year was 2002, the Free School was 31 years old, and he proposed to close us. This caught us completely by surprise. Most of our old adversaries had left the system, so we assumed we would no longer be targeted for closure. We were wrong—our naiveté again impeded our understanding.

12

The Firing Squad Once Again Raises the Rifles

I chose the above title for this chapter because, after all, we were dealing with an ex-military man supervising the public school system. In March of 2002, I was called to a meeting with CEO Al Davis and the top administrator from facility planning, Dr. John McCarty, our old nemesis, plus one or two top men from the firm Alvarez & Marsal, brought in to clean up the financial mess the system was currently engulfed in. I, of course, smelled a rat when I was told to report to a meeting with both the CEO and the director of facility planning. I hoped that I was being summoned to be informed that work to upgrade our building was finally to begin, but I sensed the worst.

Four or five other school principals attended or were represented at the meeting as well. The news for them was just as disheartening. We were quickly told that they were proposing to close our schools so that they could "right-size" schools based on enrollment and utilization. This meant that schools with low enrollment not filling all the desks and schools with high enrollment but not using all of the building, needed to be closed and/ or merged. They said they would lease or sell the empty buildings. This is the old "consolidate and save" concept, which contributed to the morass of urban public schools.

Anyway, the bureaucrats were quick to emphasize that teachers would follow students and we, the principals, did not have to fear being displaced—there were plenty of principalships available. They argued that closing schools was the best use of the funding, was best for the children, and that the faculty would be taken care of. After reassuring us that principals would have a job, they carefully stated that we could help or hurt this process. Without a pause they kept right on talking, reiterating that this closure was simply a proposal: it was "in process and not a done deal."

Note that this was more than a proposal to consider closing these schools; it was a proposal to close these schools. Nevertheless, someone in the meeting did say not to let it ruin our Easter—it was not a done deal. For me, Easter was no longer a chance to relax; it was an opportunity to mobilize.

Nothing they said seemed a reason to close the Free School. In fact, we were right-sized for our building and had maintained our mandated enrollment for the past fifteen years or so. We were filled to capacity and using every inch of our building. I had to ask, "Why the Free School?"

I got my chance, and I did. I was told by Dr. John McCarty, who had been director of facilities planning through all of our struggles over our building, that our enrollment was too small. He did not mention that it was right sized for our building, the very term he used to justify the proposed closing of other schools. He mentioned that our building was old, but he did not reveal that funds, almost one million dollars, had been approved by the board to implement the already-completed architectural plans for the renovation. He concluded his justification for closing the Free School by saying the system was pushing a middle school initiative with plans to eliminate all K-8 schools by either closing them or making them K-6 schools. I asked him about the Audubon Montessori and Lusher schools, both of which had K-8 enrollment. He simply said that they would get to them. We both knew that they would never touch those two elite magnet schools.

I then directly addressed CEO Al Davis. I reminded him that when he first came to the system, he gave every principal two books to read. I told him that in one of these books (the one with two authors though I do not remember if I mentioned this fact) one of the authors' main recommendations for reforming urban public education was to establish and maintain small K-8 schools. I will never forget his reply: "Well, that is just one person's opinion." I so desperately wanted to retort: "You gave us the book and it wasn't one person, it was two people's opinion." I kept my mouth shut.

Back in 1999 shortly after Colonel Davis first came to lead the school system, I wrote a paper titled, "No More LEAP." Louisiana Educational Assessment Program (LEAP) is the high-stakes testing program implemented in Louisiana. I sent a copy of this paper to CEO Colonel Davis requesting that he read it, and I offered not to seek immediate publication if he thought it would do harm to the system. I never expected a reply and never dreamed for a second that he would personally call me and say not to publish it. I should have had that dream. He did call me to ask I not publish the paper—because he wanted his principals focused on raising test scores. I felt then and I knew now that Colonel Davis was not an educator.

I left the building in a sullen state, drowning again in the waters of bureaucratic evilness. The waves against our little school were virtual tsunamis. These people did not have one good reason for shutting down the Free School. I believe to this day that the director of facility planning had once again sold the superintendent (in this case the CEO) a bill of goods. I do not know why the CEO went along with the plan, but he did. The school system's auditing firm had closed schools in Saint Louis and I felt confident that they assured Colonel Davis that they could pull off closures in New Orleans with a minimum of resistance. I think the auditing firm also used the consolidation argument in St. Louis.

Even before the system announced the schools targeted for closure, they appealed to the media with a plan they called Agenda for Excellence. According to *The Times-Picayune* article by Natalie Pompillio appearing

March 28, 2002, the thrust of this plan was based on declining Orleans Parish School enrollment from 82,000 students in 1996 to 71,500 in 2001. It was also based upon Orleans Parish's poor LEAP (Louisiana Educational Assessment Program) scores. The LEAP test is a statewide, high-stakes assessment program that includes failing forth and eighth graders who do not pass the test. High school students are kept from graduating if they do not pass the high school LEAP test. During the 2000–2001 school year, the system had a retention rate of 47 percent in fourth grade and 64 percent in the eighth grade. Pompillio wrote that the director of facility planning presented the Facility Utilization Plan to the school board by stating that the "district is seeking to 'right-size' schools. That means determining a school's capacity and then making sure the space is being used to its maximum potential."

Not only did the school system attempt to use the media to gain support for their agenda, but they also carefully orchestrated how each school was to respond to the proposed closures. Up until now, the top bureaucrats had simply told me to shut up, follow the leader, and don't run to your parents. This time they were firmly telling all of the schools how and when to respond.

They required each school to set up a school facility committee implementing the following procedures as listed on the revised memorandum from Cluster Executive Directors dated April 23, 2002:

1. Identify the Facility Utilization Committee which shall be composed of three parents (PTA President, Vice President, parent volunteer), three community persons (business partners, community partners), one teacher, the principal, and the Cluster Executive Director.

2. Cluster Executive Directors shall chair the committee.

3. Parent and staff surveys will be distributed on April 23, 2002, and returned no later than April 26, 2002.

4. The principal shall be responsible for providing the Cluster Executive Director within district and out of district data as well as compiling the results of the parent and staff surveys.

5. The Cluster Executive Director shall be responsible for collecting other pertinent data.

6. One meeting shall be held with committee for the purpose of reviewing all data and making a recommendation.

7. One meeting shall be held with parents for the purpose of presenting the committee findings.

8. A final copy of the report shall be submitted to the School Board for a final decision.

The system was attempting to control our every move and even have as our spokesperson to the CEO our Cluster Executive Director, who was to chair our meeting. It did not work out exactly as they had planned.

Immediately upon learning that our school was targeted for closure, I met with all faculty members and a number of key parents. We started assembling a packet to send to parents, community members, school board members, and the CEO. We also planned meetings, started phone calls, and began a letter writing campaign.

Our PTSO president was Kojo Livingston, an extremely capable community activist who spearheaded our attack. He was intelligent, likable, a very good speaker, and an excellent organizer. He always ended our meetings by forming a human circle of unity, hope, and good cheer. I admired this tactic so much that I ended my Aunt Mimi's funeral with just such an activity as we all circled around her casket proclaiming, "My Aunt Mimi, your Aunt Mimi, our Aunt Mimi!"

Kojo called for a PTSO meeting on the afternoon of April 10, 2002, where we put together a 28-page packet. We knew the system held the power. We had working against us the high-priced auditing firm of Alvarez & Marsal, the head of the facility planning department, and the CEO with the bureaucratic school structure, but we also knew that we had information on our side. Goliath wanted to ram our little boat with his great big ship while we were dropping leaflets of information protesting such brutality and proclaiming our purpose. Information was the wind beneath our sail. In early April, we sent out over 100 copies of our lengthy packet.

The packet began with a PTSO fact sheet describing ways the Free School had proven academically successful with inner-city black students, that we were already a right-sized school, that money was in the bank to complete our renovations, that we were a school of choice, and that we were properly configured as a K-8 school. The sheet also noted the K-8 schools had the highest eighth grade LEAP scores in the city, ours included.

This first page was followed by a letter to Orleans Parish School Board members, CEO Alphonse Davis, and citizens of the New Orleans community. It was signed by three parents, four teachers, and me. In the letter, we made a plea that our story be told, shared, and listened to. We were seeking a fair and proper hearing. It listed the other items in the packet: a three-page document addressing the reasons against closing the Free School, an article by me explaining the Free School written several years previous, excerpts from our Citywide Access Schools proposal, the open letter I had sent to then-Superintendent Everett Williams and board members written to help prevent the closing of the Free School back in 1986, the documentation sent to board members in 1991 affirming that the Free School building was structurally sound and other repairs to the building that had already occurred, and finally, an article by famed educator Deborah Meier titled, "Just Let Us Be: The Genesis of a Small Public School."

I do not include the entire packet here, but present the document titled, "Why the Free School?" because it most poignantly established our case that the Free School should not be closed.

NEW ORLEANS FREE SCHOOL
3601 Camp Street
New Orleans, La 70115
896-4065
Spring 2002

WHY THE FREE SCHOOL?

The administration of the Orleans Parish School System has announced plans to recommend closing the New Orleans Free School at the end of the 2001-2002 school year in June. This is the fifth time in the past twenty-two years that the top administration of our school system has proposed closing the New Orleans Free School.

Of course the immediate question that comes to our mind is "Why the Free School?" Does the Free School have a long-standing opponent in the upper echelon of the school system who is bound and determined to end the Free School? After all, this is the fifth time we are experiencing this nightmare. Or, is this simply an attempt by someone within the school system to make the top administration look bad? Anyone with knowledge of a school system knows that closing schools has the potential for arousing passion and stirring up controversy. What better way to undermine the administration than to embroil the school system in an unwise educational decision.

We do not have the answers to the questions, but we feel compelled to closely examine the primary question: "Why the Free School?" To answer that question certainly a close examination of this situation seems appropriate and sensible. Surely in this age of what is being called "high-stakes testing", which now determines school closings/take-overs, teacher and principal jobs, students' failing grades, this is the first and primary reason for a decision to close a school. However, this criteria does not work with the New Orleans Free School. The Orleans Parish School System administrators and BESE just awarded the New Orleans Free School with a combined total of over Ten Thousand ($10,000) Dollars for the Free School's achievement of Exemplary status with the Louisiana Accountability Program. One month we are being rewarded and given gifts and praise and the next month we are facing closure! This is not to say that the New Orleans Free School is leading the pack on test scores, but it does mean that our school is one of the many guiding lights leading the Orleans Parish School System out of the current educational morass Orleans Parish has been in for so long. Certainly our administrative leaders looked at this information before they decided to recommend closing the New Orleans Free School. The decision does not appear to be one made based on academic achievement. So, we are back to the question, "Why the Free School?"

The Times-Picayune on Thursday March 28, 2002 had a headline in the Metro Section of the paper which read: "Board May Close Underused Schools". Is this the reason for the recommendation to close the New Orleans Free School? No. The Free School has maintained student enrollment at or near the 300 student goal mandate by the Orleans Parish School Board in 1986 to avoid closing at that time. The Free School student population of at or near 300 has been maintained and is the right size for the building and space available. In fact, every available space is fully utilized but the building is not over-crowded. Even Mr. _____, Chief Operating Officer, concedes this point in his April 2, 2002 letter to Parents of Free School Students when he stated about our building "...and has no room for expansion." This is absolutely correct. We are the right size for our building and do not want to expand. We offer Orleans Parish a unique, small school and have lived within our mandated enrollment for well over a decade. We should be rewarded not punished for consistently achieving this goal. So if space and enrollment are not the issues, "Why the Free School?"

Mr. ⸱   ⸱, Chief Operating Officer, recently stated in a meeting with principals of the recommended closing schools that the closing of the Free School is because of the age of the building. In the above mentioned letter to the parents he also stated, "The building is in very poor condition..." Lots of public school buildings in New Orleans are old and in poor condition, but they have not been recommended for closure. Additionally, many of these "old" buildings have recently had tax money used to renovate and preserve buildings and add air conditioning. The voters approved the $175 million bond issue in 1995 for just this purpose. For at least the past four years the New Orleans Free School has been on the list of schools approved for the allocated update for air conditioning, heating, bathroom modernization and other renovations for a budget of $950,850. The plans have been drawn and the money for the work allocated and approved, but no work has begun. The renovation has been planned and approved. This is not an argument for closure but a cry to get the job done.

It should also be noted that back in 1991 when our school was up for closure for the fourth time, one of the primary reasons given was that the building was structurally unsound. As things turned out, the building was evaluated by Dr. ⸱   ⸱, Director of Facility Planning, as being structurally sound. The school remained opened and work on the roof began shortly thereafter.

The New Orleans Free School community was surprised when the headline appeared in the Time-Picayune on Saturday, March 30, 2002 which read "Students Working In Cool Comfort". It seems that once again the Free School got left out. This article and the statement by the same Dr.   ⸱ mentioned above are not completely accurate. The money allocated for air conditioning the New Orleans Free School has not yet been spent.

It is true that thanks to the efforts of Councilman Oliver Thomas and Mr. Hans Wandfluh, CEO of the Royal Sonesta Hotel, the New Orleans Free School has one window unit for air conditioning each classroom. About four years ago these two gentlemen spearheaded the effort to obtain private donations to have the building wired and a window unit installed in each classroom. No school system funds were used for this project. However, the single window unit in each large classroom can hardly be called having the classrooms air conditioned. These single units certainly help but on many repeated hot days, especially in the late spring, early and late summer, and early fall these classrooms are quickly returned to the oven-like stage.

Remember, funds to provide central air and heat and to build two new student bathroom facilities have been appropriated and plans for the work have been drawn and in place for over three years. So, if the building proved not to be the issue 11 years ago and if the building was not the issue three or four years ago when the money was allocated and the plans and money were and are available and waiting, why is the age of the building now the excuse for the recommendation to close the Free School? The question may no longer be, "Why the Free School?"; it may now be, "What's going on here?"

For the sake of argument, let's assume that the building is beyond repair, which it is not. In fact, someone would certainly love to buy this building and fix it as condominiums or offices. The location is mere blocks from the Touro Infirmary complex. The old McDonogh 6 building which is nearby has been converted to lovely apartments. But if the building was beyond repair and unusable, why not move the Free School. There are obviously other buildings which the school system is proposing to vacate. The New Orleans Free School is not a building; it is a community. Space is obviously available. The Free School community just keeps coming back to the same question: "Why the Free School"?

The administration of the New Orleans Public Schools in developing plans for schools in corrective action recently approached BESE and asserted that school choice could not be allowed in New Orleans because there was no place for the students to choose to go. Does it make sense for these same administrators to now recommend closure of a school which survives on parent choice? The Free School has no district. Every child attending the school is there because a parent chose and chooses to put their child at the Free School. Should not our school system be providing more choice, not taking parent choice away. In Brian Thevenot's recent Times-Picayune article dated 3/27/02, he stated that... "(Leslie) Jacobs and BESE President Paul Pastorek urge New Orleans officials to consider more revolutionary reforms..." One sensible interpretation of this exhort would be to create more small and unique schools of choice.

What about the issue of "choice"? The New Orleans Free School is a Citywide Access School (CWAS) and a school without in-city district boundaries. No student is placed at the Free School. No student is required to be at the Free School. The New Orleans Free School survives on its ability to attract and retain its clientele. Have the Free School parents gone through the bureaucratic and cumbersome CWAS process to place their children at the New Orleans Free School only to have their right of choice withdrawn? Does this seem fair, logical, legal, reasonable, or just? "Why the Free School?"

One rationale given for the recommendation to close the Free School has been the "Middle School Initiative". The claim has been made that all middle school classes will be moved to middle schools. The Free School is presently instructing students in grades kindergarten through eighth grade. It was pointed out to Dr. ___ ___ that there are a number of schools with the kindergarten through eighth grade configuration, including Lusher and Audubon Montessori. His reply was that this "was in the future." Again, "Why the Free School?"

If changing grade configuration of a school helps that school, then change the configuration. If it hurts the school, leave the school alone. It is interesting to note that almost every school in Orleans Parish including the Free School with the kindergarten through eighth grade configuration had some of the highest scores on the 8th grade LEAP test for Orleans Parish. It goes without saying that the eighth grade LEAP scores in Orleans Parish are at the bottom of the barrel. Making a change in schools that are working and bringing up the Orleans Parish tests scores makes no sense at all. "Why the Free School?"

The Free School community does not purport to have all the answers to education nor is the school a miracle worker. The Free School has its problems, just as does every other school. Fortunately, the successes at the Free School far outnumber the failures. The Free School simply provides parents an educational option for them and their children alike. The Free School community wants the right to exist. The community would like to have the building upgraded from the existing allocation of funds that have been available for the past several years. If this is not possible then assistance is requested in finding a suitable alternative location. The Free School community requests that this administration act as an advocate and work with us in overcoming the obstacles identified. Our community hopes that you will agree that the final question is not "Why the Free School?", but "Why not the Free School?"

Along with this packet I wrote a special letter to parents and friends of the Free School to give them the names and addresses of news media and school board members, pleading with them to write letters of support. In this letter to parents and friends, I again expressed my belief that I felt the issue was more personal with a desire to shut me up than it had to do with any educational issue. I wrote the following:

> At this point I cannot help but think that the top administration simply wants to silence me. I have been, and am, an outspoken critic of the bureaucratization of urban public schools and a strong advocate of schools of choice with school-site autonomy. I believe in a different conceptual framework for public education—one that poses the school-site as the focal point of the school system. The principal's role becomes one of educational leader with teachers as professionals and schools entering into partnerships with school systems. Schools would no longer be controlled institutions. They would become professional organizations.

In early April the school system sent letters to parents and staff members of the six schools telling them of the proposed closure. Principals were directed to send out these letters by no later than April 5, 2002. I complied because I did not want disobeying an order to become the issue. I knew these letters were part of the strategy by the administration to control information sent to parents and faculty, but there was also nothing in them that countered our arguments to keep the Free School open.

Kojo and I called for a meeting of parents and faculty on the evening of Wednesday, April 10, 2002, immediately following our students' presentations of their "Great Brain Projects" presented to parents as they received their child(ren)'s third quarter report. Kojo invited CEO Al Davis to attend our meeting, but he never showed. Much action was planned at the meeting, including going to the school board forum planned for the next night, April 11, 2002, and the faculty agreed to again write a letter, as one, to the editor of *The Times-Picayune*. With everyone so solidly behind keeping the Free School open and with our plan of attack in operation, we ended the meeting feeling optimistic. It was just a feeling with no concrete facts but the spirit in the air was certainly on our side.

A disorienting event occurred immediately following the meeting, around 6:00 p.m., as I was saying goodbyes to parents and faculty while standing in the front yard of the school. I remember it like it was yesterday. It was still daylight. I felt like I was being mugged and was certainly being overpowered. I received a phone call and no sooner said, "Hello," than she started screaming at me. The statements came at me something like this:

"How dare you have a meeting and not tell me about it or invite me? The CEO was invited, but I wasn't! How come?"

My problem was not so much the attack, the anger, or the message; I simply did not know who was on the other end of the phone. As I tried hopelessly though politely to respond, I was racking my brain trying to figure out who was screaming at me. And then it dawned on me. The person on the other end of the phone was my Executive Cluster Director (equivalent of Area Superintendent), Dr. Alice Hatler (fictitious name).

She was livid, rude, and extremely demanding. I remember thinking, while nervously and cautiously responding to her accusations, that she would be the last person I would ever want to come to one of our Save Our School meetings. She had never expressed an interest in our school and this anger only solidified my feeling that she would never be helpful in our struggle. Little did I realize that she would be appointed chair of our mandated school committee to consider closing the Free School. That point had not yet sunk in. It did now.

We got through the phone conversation by my explaining that I did not invite CEO Al Davis. Kojo Livingston had done so. Dr. Hatler ended the abrupt conversation by directing me not to attend any more meetings at our school concerning closure without her permission and/or attendance. She hung up without ever identifying herself. I had never before received such an angry affront from someone so high up on the ladder of power. To say that it was unnerving would be an understatement.

The next night, Kojo lead a group of faculty, parents, and me to a school board forum to discuss the closing of the school. In the April 12, 2002, *The Times-Picayune* article titled, "Heat Turned Up at School Forum," author Sandra Barbler described the event:

> One of the most passionate speeches was by New Orleans Free School Parent-Teacher-Student Organization President Kojo Livingston. The quality of a building does not reflect the quality of the education inside, he noted. At the Free School, he said, the bathrooms are deplorable because the board has never followed through with promised repairs. He then pointed to an elementary school-aged child in the front row, said 'That's my daughter. She has to go to a restroom everyday that's worse than Angola.' [Kojo was referring to the Louisiana state men's prison.]
>
> But, Livingston said, his daughter and the other Free School students are getting a top-notch education. When he asked its supporters to stand, about two-thirds of the audience did so and cheered. The district's plan calls for closing the Free School and dispersing its students. (A-7)

Shortly after that school board meeting, the faculty did get together and wrote a letter to the editor, published on Thursday April 18, 2002.

YOUR OPINIONS

Faculty protests plan to dissolve Free School

Recently, the Orleans Parish School System proposed a series of cost-cutting measures. Several schools must close at the end of this school year ("Thousands of students may have to get moving," April 6).

The School Board says it will consider declining student attendance and substandard physical conditions in its decision. This is understandable. But imagine the astonishment we at the New Orleans Free School felt upon realizing that our school was expected to quietly dissolve in accordance with this formula.

We do not deny that our building needs improvements. However, these conditions exist because renovations and improvements budgeted and promised to us by the school system over the past few years have never materialized.

In fact, recent improvements to our building, including air-conditioning, were not funded by the school system but by our staff, parents, business partners and friends.

In any case, neither our students nor our faculty have ever allowed missing amenities to affect our performance.

We accept students from all over the city. We are mandated to accommodate 300 students and we have always exceeded that number.

The Free School's academic performance is above reproach. Our test scores have consistently demonstrated the growth mandated by the state.

Just this year we were awarded in excess of $10,000 for meeting academic expectations.

If our school is closed now that the deadline for admission to Citywide Access Schools has expired, our parents, who are strong advocates for choice, will be left with no choice.

Please, repair our building or allow us to move.

Don't extinguish the Free School — it is more than just a building!

Jeannette St. Etienne
David Clarke
Teachers
and 30 others
New Orleans Free School
New Orleans

Kojo continued leading our efforts to save the Free School. He had a meeting at the Free School of faculty and parents that I could not attend because I was ordered to attend no more such meetings without permission from the cluster director. At that meeting, they decided to attend a school board meeting, that was scheduled to discuss closures.

On April 22, 2002, the day of the school board meeting, Kojo was informed that neither he, nor anyone else from the Free School, would be allowed to speak because closure had been taken off the agenda. He and the parent group decided to attend anyway. I met them there. One of our parents, an elderly gentleman, managed to speak on another topic, but quickly brought up the Free School. He was treated rudely by the president of the board, Ms. Brooks-Simms, who chastised him for speaking out of turn and did not allow him to continue.

She looked menacingly at Al Davis and said something like, "You need to get your principals under control." I was livid but never said a word. This board president had been just as arrogant as a principal as she had been that evening as a board president. Since that event, she has been convicted of taking a bribe of $100,000 for endorsing and pushing through a school system contract and is serving an 18-month sentence. She got a sweetheart deal from the judge because she cooperated with the FBI to catch an even bigger crook. I still thought that she should have received several years in prison for such theft, but at least they caught her.

That evening, not long after the public rebuke by Ms. Brooks-Simms, our entourage quietly left the meeting. Kojo went home and wrote a blistering letter to Ms. Brooks-Simms detailing her rude conduct at the meeting and reminding her that she worked for us. I will let the letter speak for itself since it so clearly documents the harsh treatment inflicted on our community by her, the board, and the administration, while also clearly articulating the need for accountability to parents by school officials.

4/22/02

Ms. Simms:

As President of the Parent-Teacher-Student Organization for New Orleans Free School I must express my shock and concern at both the attitude and demeanor you displayed toward the parents who attended the school board meeting tonight.

Like the rest of the city, we were misled to believe that the delegation night process was designed to be a forum for the people to address any of their concerns to the full board.

We filled out the appropriate forms. I personally left work to deliver the forms to the school board office. We don't even believe that people should have to go through all of that to address a board that we elected, but we still complied. We did everything we were supposed to do to address "our" school board.

Finally, on Friday, after 4:30 PM we were told that we definitely would not be able to speak at the meeting. We informed your representative that we would be there anyway.

After what had to be an embarrassing start for the meeting (a rather lengthy discussion as to whether or not the board had voted on a matter) it was time for presentations. When one of the grandparents asked that the rules be relaxed to recognize the parents who had come you seemed to really lose it, asking him who told him to come here, as if he did not belong. You were rude, hostile and disrespectful to him and us as a group. (We have our own video of the meeting.)

What you failed to mention tonight was that myself and other parents of the Free School followed the process you laid out for participating. The parents have been planning to attend this meeting since before the forum at Walker High School. We felt that it was important for the board to know that the parents were actively committed to keeping the Free School open.

For your information, it was not Bob that asked the parents to come. It was I. So if Ms. Tyler needs to confront someone about inviting unwanted parents to school board meetings she can come to me. I welcome it.

But how can it be a bad thing for parents of NOPS children to be asked to come to a public meeting that is supposedly held for the purpose of them speaking their minds?

Unless I am mistaken, the clause that allows you to decide who can speak on what topics is only relates to situations where a disruption is in progress. We have never been disruptive or abusive towards the board or administration. In fact we have shown you a great deal more respect, courtesy and consideration that you have shown us...and we're supposed to be YOUR boss.

All of the rhetoric about the need for parental involvement sounds false when parents do take the time to show up, only to be met with hostility and regulations that minimize or eliminate their right to speak.

Why do we insist on addressing the board? Because the process is *terminally flawed*. The entire board must vote on this matter, but only part of the board is at the forums and other meetings that lead up to this.

The only time the entire board will hear our views is on the night of the final vote. They will be expected to digest all the information about all of the schools and make an intelligent decision on the spot. What's worse is that, even then, you will only hear your staff's interpretation of our views. For obvious reasons this is not a comforting thought. You have placed your Executive Directors in charge of the parent participation process. The one for our school insists that parents and business partners must meet at her convenience. There is not even a pretense of a belief that any of you work for us.

Everything about this process minimizes the ability of the parents (the people directly affected) to address the board (the people who make the final decision). The facilities utilization process has been going on for over a year, yet you only include parent and community participation on the tail end, after telling us you plan to close the school in two months! We have a few weeks to develop a response to year long process. It's not right. It's not fair and it's unacceptable.

If you won't hear us and won't respect us, we will find other ways to be heard and respected.

We are determined to keep the Free School open. It's a stupid idea to shut down a program that is working for children in a system that has so many failures. It's evil to do this just to silence a principal or sell a building. We are determined to change the way parents are treated and minimized. We are probably a lot more resourceful than you realize.

We have been civil to a fault, but we do have limits. We are developing our own process for addressing this matter. We will apprise you of it at the appropriate time.

And yes, we will continue to have representatives at board meetings until this matter is resolved.

For the Children,
J. Kojo Livingston
President

Kojo also wrote a similar letter to *The Louisiana Weekly*, a local African American newspaper, published May 6, 2002. In spite of the school system's efforts, our story was reaching the public. Kojo wrote the parents concerning the meeting.

Your showing up was important for two reasons.

First, the board needed to see that our parents take this matter seriously and will not stop coming after one meeting. Most times they wear parents down by dragging things out. They have to know that you will not lose interest or get discouraged. Secondly, it was important that you see how these people operate. If you saw how hostile and confused the board is, then you know we must stick together!!! We can win this! We just have to stay serious about it. It won't be long before it's time to vote for a school board again.

Things happened the next couple of days that I now feel greatly enhanced our case for keeping the Free School open. The first occurred on April 24, 2002. I received a phone call from Colonel Davis himself, telling me not to bring "forty to fifty" people to a public school board meeting, not to talk to BESE (Board of Elementary and Secondary Education—the Louisiana State Board of Education) board members, and to follow the School Facility Committee procedures. Well, my heart must have dropped a thousand feet, but I managed to remain civil and simply uttered, "OK" to each dictate.

For me, this was just an acknowledgement that I heard him, not agreement. I strongly believed that if I was personally having a major conflict with high-up public officials, I must keep the conflict in an open, public arena. The phone call was not the place to do battle. I also knew I could better express myself in writing, which allowed for reflection, than in any spontaneous verbal controversy.

Thus, I proceeded to write a letter to Colonel Davis with a copy sent to each board member, Leslie Jacobs, the state board member with whom I had had a conference, Ollie Tyler, the Assistant Superintendent of Orleans Parish Public Schools (actually not sure of her title, but she was second in command), and each member of The Free School Committee to Save Our School (We even changed the name of our mandated committee). In my letter I defended my actions, attacked his process for closing schools, and argued for higher ground for the both of us. I include the letter here.

April 29, 2002

A. G. Davis (Colonel. USMC, Retired)
Chief Executive Officer
New Orleans Public Schools
3510 DeGaulle Drive
New Orleans, LA 70114

      RE: The New Orleans Free School

Dear Colonel Davis:

This will confirm our phone conversation of April 24, 2002 in which you instructed me not to bring "forty to fifty people" to a public School Board meeting, not to talk to BESE Board members, and to follow the School Facility Committee Procedures.

It is my understanding that School Board meetings are open to the public. Neither am I aware of anything which prohibits speaking to a BESE Board member. I came and left the School Board meeting on April 22, 2002 alone. I did participate in discussions encouraging people to attend the School Board meeting on April 22, 2002 in favor of keeping the New Orleans Free School open. The New Orleans Free School community made the decision to attend the School Board meeting even knowing that we may not be allowed to speak at that meeting. The New Orleans Free School community did not come to attack anyone; we came simply to tell our story and to make our case before the School Board, the people who will ultimately make the decision as to whether the New Orleans Free School will be closed or remain open. We were naturally disappointed that we were not permitted to speak at the meeting but left peacefully and orderly.

Your phone call reinforced the impression that the administration is attempting to stifle an open presentation of the issues surrounding the recommended school closings. It appears that you are trying to restrict schools from presenting a fair and open argument against the recommended school closings.

As to your dictate that I follow the School Facility Committee Procedures, my reply is simple and two-fold: First, the New Orleans Free School community is following the procedures. We hope and pray that you and every School Board member read every survey and every piece of information we supply you with **before** making a decision to close our school. Second, we feel that the process is rigged and unfair. It appears that an effort is underway to control debate and discussion of the issues and to muzzle our collective voice. The New Orleans Free School community has a story to tell and we wish to tell it in as many places and in as many ways as we possibly can.

We find the School Facility Committee Procedures unfair and flawed. The School Facility Committee Procedures appear to be a method for allowing the administration to dictate how our school community should attempt to counter the administration's stated goal of having the New Orleans Free School closed.

We have been dictated the time and place of our meetings and the type of people we must have on our committee. We cannot even choose our own chair. The Cluster Executive Director has been mandated as the chair. We feel that we are administratively being blocked out of the process that is suppose to be our process to respond to the recommended closing of the Free School.

In the meeting with the cluster leaders and the principals of the schools targeted for closing, Ms. Ollie Tyler emphatically stated that the schools targeted for closing could have only one community representative on each committee. The reason given for this dictatorial position was that the "policy" said "a community representative" and "a" means one.

At that same meeting I informed Ms. Tyler that the New Orleans Free School had already invited three people to be on our committee since that was the initial instruction given as to the number of community representatives on the committee. Ms. Tyler's response was "Then you will just have to uninvite them. Bob, we go by Board policy." However, minutes later someone else read the policy. The policy clearly stated that the committee must be made up of "parents and community members". No number was given. Only then did Ms. Tyler say: "Okay, you can have your three." Since no numbers were given in the policy, there was no reason for Ms. Tyler to limit community committee membership to only three people.

It seems that the School Facility Committee Procedures are being used by the administration to exercise absolute control. At the same meeting, one of the principals raised the issue that no faculty members were on the committees. The response was that it was not in the policy. But later that evening when Board President Ellenese Brooks-Simms raised the issue of faculty participation, the administration simply nodded in agreement.

I do need to add and to express thanks to Ms Tyler for her remarks that evening concerning the role of the principal in school closings. One principal was not at this meeting because she was attending a conference. Ms. Tyler emphatically expressed that if someone was trying to close her school, she would not be at any conference. Ms. Tyler then caught me off guard when she asked me if I had talked to my board member, Ms Carolyn Ford. When I said, "No", she again emphatically stated, "You need to talk to Ms. Ford." My opinion of Ms. Tyler skyrocketed.

I would like to add that I am not being insubordinate in pursuing the goal of keeping the New Orleans Free School open. I will agree that I am having difficulty with the many dictates coming from the administration concerning the proposed school closings and the process. In the recently released New Orleans School Board's "Agenda for Excellence" (Times Picayune, April 2, 2002 article by Brian Thevenot), Goal Three was identified as "Maximize resources to instruction, rather than administration". I have long been a critic of the bureaucratic model of education administration which views the school principal serving as a middle person in a chain of command. Rather, I have advocated the professional model of public education administration with the principal serving as the education leader for the school community. I have made every effort to practice this method at the New Orleans Free School. I am also an advocate for small schools of choice with school-site autonomy. I see my role as principal as the school community leader. This school community is struggling to keep our school open.

I am a devoted advocate of the New Orleans Public Schools. I am committed to your leadership. I attend many functions sponsored by the school system. I have worked hard to promote all the millage campaigns. But, at the same time, I believe passionately in this concept:

> My School System, right or wrong.
> When its right, to keep it right.
> When its wrong, to make it right.

I think your recommendation to close the New Orleans Free School, and the process required by the administration to implement that decision, are both bad and wrong educational decisions. Open this process up to let the New Orleans Free School tell our story in any and every way we can. To close the New Orleans Free School makes no sense. In my opinion, it opens up the New Orleans School System to criticism to close a small school that is working for our children. On Friday, April 26, 2002, I listened to Ollie Tyler raise the spectrum of the Orleans Parish Public Schools being labeled as a "failed system". With that possibility staring us in the face, it makes no sense to allow the New Orleans Public Schools to become the laughing stock of the nation by closing small schools that work.

The New Orleans Free School is not a "failed" school. It is working for the Free School community, those parents and children who chose to be a part. The rating The New Orleans Free School has received from the State of Louisiana is EXEMPLARY. The educational research shows that small schools (those much smaller than what is recommended by · · ·) are having a very positive impact for improving children's academic performance, particularly children of poverty. Instead of closing small schools, this administration should be supporting and expanding small school programs with demonstrated success such as the program at the New Orleans Free School. This is the soundest approach for the children of New Orleans.

In closing I would like to tell you that I spoke to Leslie Jacobs with the BESE Board to obtain her advice and input as to the best way to present our case for keeping the New Orleans Free School open so that people would listen. She had nothing but praise for you and Ms. Tyler and your efforts with the New Orleans Public Schools. She shared her belief with me that you really want to improve the New Orleans Public Schools. I would like to think that we are on the same team in this regard.

I am enclosing five pages of material which makes our case for keeping the New Orleans Free School open. One is a two page document titled, "New Orleans Free School - Save Our School"; the other is a three page document titled, "The New Orleans Free School and the 'Agenda For Excellence.'" I hope that you will agree with us. I hope you will decide to keep the New

Orleans Free School open and help us facilitate educational growth in our program as well as that of all public schools in New Orleans.

Thank you for your attention. I look forward to working with you towards that goal.

Sincerely,

Robert M. Ferris, Ed.D
Principal
The New Orleans Free School

cc: School Board members
        Leslie Jacobs
        Ollie Tyler
        Members of The Free School Committee to Save Our School

In addition, I included a short document to Colonel Davis that concisely and powerfully made the case for keeping the Free School open, while defending it regarding size, choice, money, and concept. On the second page we compared our school's 2001 LEAP test scores with Orleans Parish 2001 LEAP test scores. The results were shockingly in our favor. You see, even we were surprised by the comparisons. Again, this document was sent to well over a hundred people throughout the New Orleans community.

NEW ORLEANS FREE SCHOOL - SAVE OUR SCHOOL

The New Orleans Free School is a unique public school of choice. We have no in-city district. Parents choose to put their children in our school. We provide a very progressive and personal approach to education that affords students from around the city an educational curriculum enriched with a multitude of hands-on activities, cooperative learning endeavors and field trips.

Performance: Our test scores speak for themselves. We are consistently above average for the Orleans Parish Public School system and have recently achieved EXEMPLARY status with the Louisiana State Accountability Plan.

Size: We are a small school serving 300 students grades K-8. We are right sized for our building meaning we are full but not overcrowded.

Size: Again, we are a small school. In the document "Smaller. Safe. Saner. Successful Schools" by Joe Nathan and Karen Febey, Center for School Change, Humphrey Institute of the University of Minnesota, 2001, it states the research on smaller schools as follows:

> Smaller schools, on average, can provide
> .a safer place for students
> .a more positive, challenging environment
> .higher achievement
> .higher graduation rates
> .fewer discipline problems
> .much greater satisfaction for families, students and teachers.

Certainly our test scores, lack of many serious problems and strong parental, student and faculty support substantiate these findings.

Building: Our building is old, but beautiful and is in need of repairs. The sum of $950,850.00 has been budgeted and approved since before 1999 in order to fix up our building. Plans were drawn up in 1999 to make these needed repairs. Please, spend the money; make the repairs.

Building: If in their wisdom the OPSB decides to sell our building, then simply move us to an acceptable site that protects the integrity of our program. The Free School is not a building. It is a progressive educational program. It is an idea that has been working for the children, parents and the New Orleans community for the past 32 years.

NEW ORLEANS FREE SCHOOL

FACTS SHEET

1. How N. O. Free School's LEAP scores compare with OPSB LEAP test scores for last school year, 2000-01. (Sour Times-Picayune, August 7, 2001)

	LEAP for Free School			LEAP for OPSB	
	% of Passing	% of failures		% of Passing	% of failures
	Grade 4	Grade 4		Grade 4	Grade 4
Language Arts	81	19	Language Arts	66	34
Math	59	41	Math	55	45
	Grade 8	Grade 8		Grade 8	Grade 8
Language Arts	88	12	Language Arts	59	41
Math	78	22	Math	35	65

2. How N. O. Free School compares with the rest of Orleans Parish schools with middle school grades on the School Performances Score for the Louisiana Accountability Program. (Source: Times-Picayune, November 7, 2001)

Name of School	Performance Score	'99-'00 Growth Level	% on Free or Reduced Lunch
1. Lusher	131.3	Recognized	29%
2. Audubon Montessori	113.4	No Label	32%
3. Thurgood Marshall Middle	70.5	Minimal	80%
4. N. O. Charter Middle	60.4	Declining	85%
5. NEW ORLEANS FREE SCHOOL	52.5	EXEMPLARY	90%
6. Benjamin Banneker	46.4	Exemplary	91%
7. Francis Gregory Jr. High	41.7	Minimal	78%
8. O. Perry Walker	34.0	Minimal	75%
9. Charles Colton Middle	28.5	Minimal	83%
10. S. J. Green Learning Academy	27.9	Minimal	80%
11. Livingston Middle	27.4	Minimal	80%
12. S. B. Wright Learning Academy	26.9	Minimal	92%
13. McDonogh #28 Learning Academy	26.4	Minimal	79%
14. P. A. Capdau Learning Academy	24.2	Minimal	83%
15. I. M. Augustine Learning Academy	20.4	Minimal	87%
16. E. H. Phillips Learning Academy	19.7	Recognized	89%
17. Andrew Bell Learning Academy	19.4	Minimal	80%
18. C. G. Woodson Learning Academy	16.3	No Growth	80%
19. Live Oak Learning Academy	13.3	Minimal	76%

We never let up. We kept hammering away, telling our story to anyone and everyone in any way we could.

Sheila Stroup, a columnist for *The Times-Picayune*, visited the Free School to research an article on the closing of our school. Ms. Stroup is what I would call the grandmother columnist of *The Times-Picayune*. She writes about her kids, grandkids, dogs, grand-dogs, etc. She creates feel-good columns based on common sense and goodness. She wrote an article about St. Augustine High School's famous black band, the Marching 100, playing in Slidell, Louisiana where, only a few years ago, the band refused to play out of concern for the safety of their members. In short, she focuses on the hope and goodness of the present time. She presents good things as they are and other things as they should be. Her column is popular and loved by many members of the New Orleans and surrounding communities.

Shelia Stroup's article captured the feelings of all in our community and every citizen who was puzzled by the proposed closing of the Free School. The first line of her May 9, 2002, article, "Why Close a School that Works?" clearly stated what everyone was thinking: "When I saw New Orleans Free School on the list of schools that the Orleans Parish School Board wants to close, I wondered why" (B-1). This article certainly buoyed our spirits and enabled us to believe that we might continue on our educational journey. Sheila Stroup certainly proved that the pen was as mighty as the sword.

An interesting side story was related to me by Kojo. The Colonel had complained to him that I had sent him thirty-five pages defending and resisting closing the Free School. According to Kojo, his response went something like this: "Come on Colonel. You're a military man. You have the wagons circled with the only opening a cliff. Bob can quietly surrender, jump, or come at you with all he's got. We're coming after you!"

The bureaucracy's main line of attack centered on forcing us to narrowly follow the School Facility Committee procedure. The date, place, and time of our school committee meeting was dictated by the cluster leader, Dr. Hatler, to accommodate her schedule. This was the woman who had harangued me over the phone for not inviting her to a meeting at our school to discuss the school closing proposal. She had also forbidden me to attend any more meetings in our building over the closing issue without her permission and/or presence. She even insisted that we not hold the committee meeting at the Royal Sonesta Hotel, one of our business partners, and that we conduct the meeting at the Free School during school hours. Since we had no meeting room at the school we had to hold the meeting in one of our classrooms, forcing the students in that classroom to miss class and remain in the basement until the meeting concluded.

I kept getting abrupt, unpleasant phone calls from this cluster director making sure that I was adhering to her demands. I even received a phone call from her the night before the meeting assuring I had the mandated parent and faculty surveys done properly and was told by her to get to school before the 8:00 a.m. meeting and make sure everything was done correctly.

The parent and faculty surveys were drawn up by the system and we were told when to distribute them and when to collect them. We were also told how to tabulate the results. I gave this task to my secretary, Peggy Valls, because I knew that she would accomplish this task flawlessly, which she did. However, the area superintendent's evening call did unnerve me and I was not able to calm down until I arrived "early" the next morning only to find everything in order.

Two things about the surveys fascinate me to this day. The first thing, which solidified my belief that this whole committee process was just for harassment and not for an educational purpose, was that Dr. Hatler, who ran the meeting, did not even ask for, look at, receive, or take the surveys with her when she left. If decency or professionalism permitted, I would have kicked her in her behind as she was leaving.

The second profound aspect of the surveys, which filled my heart with joy, was the overwhelming support we received, not only from the faculty, but most importantly, from the parents. One after another emphatically stated that they disagreed with closing the Free School, and most expressed beautiful, short comments praising the school.

One particular response captured our soul, gave us strength, and best articulated how we felt about the bureaucracy. This survey was unsigned: "I've been a cheerleader for the Free School now for some many years. I am very upset to think you can uproot an organization and system that is working and has worked for not only this family, but a generation of families. Shame on you… Go to time out & Stay There!"

On Tuesday, May 7, 2002, we had our school committee meeting at 8:00 a.m. Our school board member, Betty Ford, attended the meeting conducted by the cluster director. All went well. Kojo volunteered to write the Free School recommendation to the CEO concerning closing the Free School. I believe the cluster director agreed to this because the board member, our three community representatives, and faculty members were present at this meeting. As a result, cordiality, not sparks, prevailed. We got our point across and Kojo was going to deliver this message. Below is the message as drafted by Kojo.

NEW ORLEANS FREE SCHOOL
3601 CAMP STREET
NEW ORLEANS, LA 70115
896-4065

NEW ORLEANS FREE SCHOOL COMMITTEE TO SAVE OUR SCHOOL

RECOMMENDATIONS TO THE BOARD

1. New Orleans Free School remain open whether in present building or alternate site. The concept here is that closure is not an issue. The only question being addressed is where the school will operate.

    A. Size of school be preserved
    B. Integrity of program be preserved

2. Leave the Free School where it is and fix our building

    A. Spend the $950,850 already budgeted
    B. Implement the plans that have already been drawn up

3. Find an agreeable alternate site

    A. Maintain enrollment at present level
    B. Maintain integrity of program
    C. Maintain present area if at all possible
    D. Involve the Free School community in the process from the beginning

The School Facility Committee procedures then required each school to have a meeting "with parents for the purpose of presenting the committee findings." Our area superintendent demanded that we have this meeting at 4:00 p.m. on Thursday, May 9, 2002. Having no choice, we scheduled the meeting for this date and time, finding out just a day later that the school board also had a meeting at this time on the same date precluding any board member from attending ours. While frustrated that no board member could witness this gathering, we scheduled the meeting as directed and also scheduled a rally to coincide with it. This helped gather a larger crowd for the meeting.

Our fifth-grade teacher, CherylAnn Jones, moderated the event. Emile, the husband of our head custodian, Ruby Smith, provided us with an elaborate sound system, enabling all to hear, probably within a block radius. The students performed at the rally with wonderful enthusiasm. Cheers were abundant, emotions were high, and joy was truly in the air. Speaker after speaker condemned the closing of the Free School, sang the praises of the Free School, and cheered us on.

It was during the speaker segment that our cluster director arrived—she was tardy. She instantly, by talking loudly into my ear over the sound system, demanded to see our program, which was just a single page, handwritten sheet held by our moderator. I got the piece of paper and handed it to the director. She commanded me to interrupt the meeting to introduce her and two other bigwigs, our nemesis, Dr. John McCarty, the director of facility planning, and someone from the Marcel & Alvarez team. She then told me to read the recommendations to the audience. I dutifully stopped the meeting and introduced the three who spoke for a combined fifteen minutes. Everyone listened politely and attentively. I should note that in this meeting Dr. McCarty specifically stated that plans were drawn up to put central air in our building and to renovate our boys and girls basement bathrooms. He stated that money was in the bank for these designed repairs and the only thing needed was board approval. I never heard him offer this information to the board.

When I went up to read the committee recommendations, Kojo said that he was coming too. I said, "Oh good, you can read the recommendation." After all, he had drafted the document stating our school's recommendation concerning the proposed closing of the Free School. I never saw the cluster director again that evening. Kojo took over the meeting. He first allowed a couple of other speakers to address the audience, who again fired up the crowd with their speeches of support (they had been waiting to speak since the moment I was ordered to stop the meeting and introduce the cluster director and her cohorts). Then he read our committee's recommendation to keep the school open, which brought the applause to a crescendo. He ended the meeting with one of his unifying circles—this time a

VERY large one with everyone holding hands and loudly professing unity, support, and victory. This ending was like being in a movie with all of us leaving in a euphoric state, believing we were involved with something important, beautiful, just, and right. We believed we could win! Again, I should note here that I never saw the cluster director after she told me to introduce her and the two other administrators and then read our school's recommendation concerning closing the Free School. I do not know when she left.

We felt that we were down to attending the board meeting for the vote on closure and presenting our case as best we could under the narrow guidelines provided to us by the board. But the bureaucracy was not through with us yet. To my utter and complete surprise—I mean I never saw it coming—I received a memorandum of "Willful Neglect of Duty and Insubordination" signed by Dr. Hatler May 10, 2002, the day after the Parent Forum. I quote the reprimand verbatim; it still amazes me every time I read it:

> Upon arriving to your school Thursday, May 9, 2002, for the Parent Forum, I directed you to conduct the meeting, I also informed you of the format of the meeting. I specifically instructed you to deliver the committee's recommendation to the audience. However, when it was time for you to address the audience, you announced that you were turning the meeting over to Mr. Livingston, the PTA President. You did this without any discussion with me. As a result, the forum strayed from its purpose.
>
> Your actions demonstrated a lack of leadership. By copy of this letter, you are officially being notified that any future occurrences of insubordination or willful neglect of duty will result in disciplinary action.

When I first read this I felt as though I had had the wind knocked out of me. I knew from experience that some bureaucrats often times play dirty, blindside you and stab you in the back, but this frontal assault caught me off guard. I could stay there struggling for air, remain under water, let them close the school, and be content with just resurfacing, or I could pop out of the water with more air than I knew I could breathe and confront this lady over her ill-conceived charges.

I had been careful to avoid ever being accused of insubordination. At the same time I quickly grasped that this situation afforded me the opportunity to further expose just how poorly we had been treated through this whole struggle to save our school, while all the time complying with the mandated School Reconfiguration Committee process. I also felt it might be interpreted as an admission of guilt not to reply. I knew that I could not let this charge be just between the cluster director and me because in her memorandum no one was copied. I addressed my response to the cluster director but sent a copy of this letter and a copy of her reprimand to each school board member, Colonel Davis, and the president of the Principals' Association.

I wrote a lengthy rebuttal refuting the charges against me, challenging the mandated School Facility Committee procedures, documenting the treatment that the school and I had continuously received from this lady, and demanding a public hearing to allow me to clear my name. I am including the entire letter because fewer words simply would not capture the significance of the moment.

May 20, 2002

_____ Ph. D.
Executive Director
Cluster C Elementary Schools
New Orleans Public Schools
3510 General DeGaulle Drive
New Orleans, LA 70114

RE: Correspondence dated May 10, 2002 regarding
      "Willful Neglect of Duty and Insubordination"

Dear Dr. _____:

I must say that I was not surprised to receive your memorandum dated May 10, 2002 which you titled "Willful Neglect of Duty and Insubordination". A copy of that memorandum is attached.

Please consider this letter a formal protest of the charge of "Willful Neglect of Duty and Insubordination."

Further please consider this a formal demand for a public hearing on your charges of insubordination and willful neglect of duty at a mutually agreed upon place, date and time and in accordance with established New Orleans Public Schools procedures.

Your memorandum relates that you arrived at the New Orleans Free School on May 9, 2002 for the Parent Forum. Your letter fails to point out that the purposes of that Parent Forum were for the New Orleans Free School community to receive the School Facility Committee's recommendations to keep the Free School open and for members of the Free School to have their say on this important issue which greatly affects their lives.

Your memorandum further states that you "directed" me to conduct the meeting. I would like the record to reflect that up to the time of the Parent Forum, which began at 4:30 p.m. on Thursday, May 9, 2002, I had received no orders or directives from you on how to conduct the forum other than being told the time and date of the forum. This made sense to me because I thought that your role at the forum was to make sure parents received the committee's recommendations concerning the issue of keeping the school open and to hear our voices concerning the Free School. We knew no board members would be at the forum because the School Board meeting was taking place at this same time. In fact, when the committee learned that the School Board meeting was set at the same time as the mandated Parent Forum, a committee member asked, "Well, who will be there to hear our side?" You replied, "I will."

236

Let the record also reflect that the meeting was in progress upon your arrival when you approached me. It was being conducted by me, as well as by the parents, students, teachers, and other community representatives. Remember, when you came and spoke to me you were practically talking into my ear because the forum was already in progress and the speakers spoke into an elaborate sound system so that all in the basement could hear. You asked me if I had an agenda. I said, "No, the teacher introducing the speakers had it." You told me that you needed to see the agenda. I got it from the teacher and gave it to you. You then told me that I needed to stop the meeting, which was already in progress, and introduce you, ⁻ ⁻⁻⁻ and Dr. ⁻ and that after this was finished, I needed to read the committee's recommendations to everyone. I stopped the meeting and introduced you three. You three then took over the forum and talked for about 15 minutes. After that you called me up to read the committee's recommendations. Kojo Livingston said to me as I got up that he was coming with me. I said to him, "Oh good! You can read the recommendations." After all, in the committee meeting, he volunteered to draft the recommendations, which he subsequently did. Remember, you were the chair of this committee and you agreed to let him write these recommendations.

Never for a second did I understand that I and only I was being **ordered** by you to read the recommendations. I just thought that one of the purposes of the forum was to share the recommendations of the committee with the parents. This is what we did. To my knowledge there is no policy or written directive instructing the principal to read the committee's recommendations at the Parent Forum. I sincerely thought that you were just making sure that the recommendations were being shared with the Free School community. Again, this is what I accomplished.

After Kojo read the recommendations and made his speech, he turned the microphone over to people in the audience so that they could speak if they chose to do so. About ten people spoke - all strongly in favor of keeping the Free School open - and the meeting ended at 6:00 p.m. with everyone joining hands in a very large circle expressing unity. At no time was the meeting out of control. At no time was the meeting leaderless.

In your May 10, 2002 memorandum, you state that the forum "strayed from its purpose". You did not identify the "purpose" that was "strayed from". What purpose did it stray from? The administration had its say at the meeting; the School Facility Committee's recommendations were shared with those present; and the Free School community had its say at the meeting. I must tell you that everyone with whom I have spoken was extremely pleased with how the forum went, though no one was pleased with having no School Board member present. We accomplished what the administration demanded of us and we accomplished it with dignity and a strong voice of unity. Again, what purpose did we stray from?

I was pleased to hear Dr. _____ ____ tell our community that the money for the renovations is still available and that the plans for the work on the Free School building are completed. He indicated that all he needs from the School Board is the nod to go. I was disappointed to learn that back in October this money was put on hold because of this reconfiguration issue. I was not told of the possible closing until March 27, 2002.

Your allegations that I engaged in willful neglect of duty and insubordination on May 9, 2002 are outrageous and cannot go unchallenged. To substantiate the ridiculousness and intimidating essence of your charges I would like to take this opportunity to publicly state my concerns about the administration's procedures with respect to the process for challenging the administration's recommendation to close the New Orleans Free School:

I am shocked and dismayed about how you and the administration have handled the proposed closing of the New Orleans Free School. You, in particular, have been mean-spirited and dictatorial since this process began. The system has made extreme efforts to control the entire process of community input and reaction, to say the least. Everything that has been done so far has been to try and prevent us from presenting our fervent belief that the New Orleans Free School should not be closed. This is a sad commentary for a public school system in a democratic society. The parents, students, and faculty at the New Orleans Free School are entitled to challenge the administration's recommendation that the New Orleans Free School be closed; they are entitled to make every effort to bring their concerns to the attention of the administration, the School Board, and the public, in any manner they see fit.

My appreciation of your actions in this process follow:

On the evening of April 10, 2002 at approximately 6:00 p.m., you called me on my cell phone to tell me that you had not been invited to a meeting that was held that evening. You were angry and fussing at me for not inviting you to that PTSO meeting which was held to allow the parents and faculty to discuss the recommendation to close the New Orleans Free School. Colonel Davis was invited to this meeting and you were upset that you were not. I informed you that I did not invite Colonel Davis to that meeting. He was invited by Mr. Kojo Livingston, head of the New Orleans Free School PTSO. You then ordered me over the phone not to attend any more meetings in our school building concerning this matter unless you were informed. I have complied with that request.

That was our first discussion of the recommendation that the New Orleans Free School be closed. From that moment on I have received only short, abrupt phone calls from you, each of which consisted of you issuing orders. You have never expressed any sensitivity to our community needs or concerns.

Shortly after the above phone call on April 10, 2002, you informed me by phone that you were the chair of our School Facility Committee and that you would set the date and time of our committee meeting and our school forum. You told me to schedule the committee meeting for Monday, May 6, 2002 up to 4:00 p.m. or Wednesday morning up to noon. I told you that I would do my best but that these committee members were important busy people and that we should try to accommodate their schedules. You told me that you were an important person and to schedule the meeting in the allotted time. I complied.

I scheduled the meeting for Monday, May 6, 2002 for 2:00 p.m. at the Royal Sonesta Hotel. All the committee members agreed to the time and the place. I informed Mr. Hans Wandfluh, President and General Manager of the Royal Sonesta, that you had suggested (I did not know it was an order) that we meet at the Free School. He said, "No, let's have it here. This is a more neutral site."

I received a call from you on April 23, 2002 saying that the meeting would be at the Free School not at the Royal Sonesta and it would be at 1:00 p.m. not 2:00 p.m. No explanation for the place change or time change was given. Why the committee meeting had to be at the Free School and not downtown where all of our business committee members work is beyond me. Nevertheless, I complied. In that same conversation, you also informed me that our forum was scheduled for Thursday, May 9, 2002 at 4:30 p.m. Again, I complied.

On or about May 2, 2002 I received another phone call from you stating that the committee meeting was changed from Monday, May 6, 2002 at 1:00 p.m. to Tuesday, May 7, 2002 at 8:00 a.m. and that I was to inform the committee members. Once again, you provided no explanation for the change of the date and time of the meeting. No courtesy was afforded our committee members or me in announcing your decision to change our meeting. You were very abrupt and dictatorial. Once again, I complied. Subsequently, I found out from Mr. Kojo Livingston that the change in the date and time of the meeting was made because our board member, Carolyn Green Ford, wanted to attend the meeting. Needless to say, we were elated at her decision to attend our meeting. We want board members to hear our case from us and not have it filtered in any way.

As stated above, you scheduled our Parent Forum for Thursday, May 9, 2002. It was not until May 6, 2002 that we learned that there was to be a School Board meeting scheduled for Thursday afternoon, May 9, 2002, running concurrently with our mandated Parent Forum date and time. We, of course, realized that once again we were being administratively blocked from presenting our case directly to the members of the School Board. Nevertheless, we complied and had the Parent Forum on the date and at the time you dictated. At the Parent Forum you specifically told the Free School community that only the School Board members had the authority to decide to close the Free School. But you set the meeting at the same time that the School Board was meeting.

However, I am getting ahead of myself. On Monday, May 6, 2002, after school hours while I was at my home, I received another one of your harsh phone calls demanding that I tabulate the results of the parent and faculty and staff surveys. When I informed you that this had been done, you asked if I had written out each question on our tabulated sheets rather than using numbers because the teacher survey form had incorrect numbers on it. I informed you that I did not know exactly how it was done, but that the results were very, very clearly stated. You said, "No! No! They must have the questions on them and that I must get to school early the next day and have my secretary put the questions on the tabulated form and have the form ready for the 8:00 a.m. meeting." You repeated this statement. For your information, this was the only time you gave me directions (I guess I should say orders) concerning these surveys and I would like you to know that my secretary had tabulated and typed up these results days earlier and that they were done correctly with the questions included.

I must tell you that I felt that you were harassing me. In fact, this whole process with you has been nothing but harassment. Let the record reflect that you did not request or demand to see the results of the parent and faculty surveys at our committee meeting on Tuesday, May 7, 2002. In fact, I believe that you left the committee meeting without seeing or receiving the results of the surveys. The results, of course, mirrored the committee's recommendation: Keep the Free School open and if at all possible keep us in our present building.

On Thursday, May 9, 2002, the day of the mandated Parent Forum, I received another phone call from you demanding to know what time I had told the parents to come to the forum. I simply replied that we had a rally scheduled for 4:00 p.m. and the forum for 4:30 p.m. You said, "OK." Not even in this phone call did you give me direction (orders) concerning the forum.

For me, the issue is about saving the Free School. I will do everything in my power to keep the Free School open. I feel that you have been domineering and unpleasant in this whole process. Your memorandum lacks any basis for the accusations you make. And you have failed to follow any procedures afforded New Orleans Public School employees for due process.

I wrote to Colonel Davis on April 29, 2002 expressing my feelings that I thought this School Facility Committee process was unfair and flawed. In essence, I feel that it is being used administratively to stifle community input and impact. Your letter of reprimand solidifies my belief.

I also need to note that you have not sent me, or anyone on our committee that I know of, your final recommendations to Colonel Davis. The fact that you not us are telling him what the New Orleans Free School wants bespeaks of this whole rotten process.

Our message is simple. It has not and will not change: "Keep the Free School open."

I request the opportunity to have a public hearing to address your charges of
willful neglect of duty and your charges of insubordination. Both are completely
unfounded and without merit. I want the opportunity to clear myself.

Sincerely,

Robert M. Ferris, Ed.D.
Principal
New Orleans Free School

cc: Board Members, Orleans Parish School Board
        School Facility Committee, New Orleans Free School
        Colonel Al Davis, CEO, New Orleans Public Schools
        Florida Woods, President PANOPSI

To my amazement, I never received a reply, not one word from Colonel Davis, any board member, or the head of the Principals' Association concerning this letter denouncing my cluster director's reprimand or my request for a public hearing.

However, just a few days after I sent out my letter refuting charges of insubordination, I received a memorandum from Colonel Davis requesting my attendance at the board meeting on May 28, 2002, for the vote on closure. He requested we have the following people lined up to speak at the meeting: the school principal, the PTO president, one committee member of our choice, and two individuals opposed to our committee's recommendation. The Colonel also included his recommendations concerning closing the schools. For the Free School, his recommendation read, "I concur with committee's recommendation #1 which read, 1.) Let the New Orleans Free School exist as it is with 300 students in the current building. Make the repairs that have been promised and budgeted for the school."

We were ecstatic; this is exactly what we wanted. However, while we were overjoyed in seeing this in writing, we knew we still needed board approval. We went to that meeting with a large crowd and, of course, happily made our presentations. No one spoke against our school as our committee recommendation was unanimous. No one in our group considered the cluster director to be part of our group, nor do I remember seeing her that night.

When it was time for each in our group to make our presentation, I went to the microphone carrying a large trash bag full of goodies. I presented letters documenting the soundness of the structure of our building; I quoted the head of the facilities department, Dr. John McCarty, who had publicly agreed to the soundness of our building but who was always behind closing our school because of our size and, ironically, the soundness of our building; I presented documentation that funding for the renovations of the Free School was in the bank waiting to be spent; and then I produced the massive drawings by the architects for the upgrading of our building. I believe I ended my presentation as I often did, with the quote I heard Bobby Kennedy give as he ended his rallies in California shortly before he was killed: Some people see things as they are and ask "Why?" I dream of things that never have been and ask "Why not?"

Colonel Davis spoke, stating that he was recommending that the board not close the Free School. He promised to study which option would be more economically feasible: to move the school or to do the renovations. This was a significant deviation from his written proposal stating to commence the work. Then, he actually praised the Free School program.

We won the vote of the board that evening! The Free School was to remain open, but we did not receive any guarantee that work was to begin on our building.

The event was recorded in the next day's *The Times-Picayune* by staff writer Brian Thevenot:

Principal Robert Ferris, backed at the meeting by more than 50 parents and teachers, told a tale of $1 million in renovations promised for a decade but never performed.

Free School educators offered to relocate in the past, he said, but stayed after being assured repeatedly that renovations would be completed shortly.

At the meeting Ferris sought a commitment from schools chief, Al Davis, that the work would be performed.

"I'm confused and to be honest, frustrated, and it is all over the building," said Ferris, who called the building at 3601 Camp Street "Possessed."

"We just need a little clarity on what the repairs will be," he said.

Davis only committed to study the matter further, however, saying he would have his staff determine whether moving was a less expensive option that fixing the school. "We are looking at whether to repair your existing, possessed building or whether to go to another site, but we are not closing you," he said.

Davis did assure Ferris that the Free School's unique academic program has the respect of his administration. (A-6)

Immediately after the meeting, Woody, our sixth-grade math teacher and band teacher, shook my hand and thanked me for demonstrating the proper way for students to make a project presentation for social studies and science classes. Woody's humor always kept us smiling. On our annual three-day May camping trips to Fountainebleau State Park, where we had a large air-conditioned kitchen, he would say to people outside, "If you can't stand the heat, go into the kitchen." We were happy, we were alive, but we had the issue of the building still hanging around our neck.

I only saw my cluster director one more time. Shortly after the school board meeting, Dr. Hatler held the final (and her final) cluster director's meeting for principals. As I have already recorded, I hated those meetings and particularly did not wish to attend this one. I could not skip it for fear of her vengeance. We both made saccharin look like pure cane sugar with our overly polite behavior. I hightailed out at the first available moment with a foul taste in my mouth, relieved to be out of her presence.

Very shortly thereafter, to my utter surprise, the lady resigned. I never knew what happened or why, nor did anyone ever give me an explanation. I only knew she was gone. I was certainly relieved, but not overjoyed. Bureaucracy brings out the wickedness of too many people. She was not the exception; unfortunately, she was the rule. I knew I would have to face more bureaucratic supervisors who, though maybe not as rude or evil as she was, would continue sending waves of attacks against our school.

You see, our little boat was still afloat but its captain was drowned. The administration had denied me all those years what I loved the most, to be an educator. I may have started my career as an activist but I loved the classroom and the school. I loved working on plays with students, teaching them dances, taking trips with them, helping them master math and English skills, reading novels together, engaging in social studies, performing science experiments, and living and growing together.

The administration diminished my ability to do all of these and other great activities with our students. They may have forced me to struggle for survival, but I longed for my political days to be behind me. I just wanted to be an excellent educator. I did not want to engage in another conflict with a school administrator or with an administration determined to squash us. After this last struggle I would go home each day and tell Sue, my wife, I did not want to go back to work, not because of the Free School—which I still loved dearly—but because of the administration, which I could no longer tolerate or fight.

I made Sue promise not to tell this to anyone because I felt obligated to put up the best front of energy, dedication, and determination I could muster for as long as possible. My soul was drowned and my spirit was atrophied. I was through and I knew it. I felt like the title character in *Cool Hand Luke*, when, at the end of the movie, after being captured once again, he tells his prison buddy, "They broke me." His prison buddy did not seem to understand or at least accept the message, but the audience did.

Orleans Parish school administrators may not have put a bullet through my head as the prison officials did to Luke, but they broke me. I knew I only had three years until I would retire, but I also knew I was going to hate every minute of it. I remember when I was younger and witnessed principals who were counting the years, months, and days until their retirement. I thought ill of them at the time because I did not understand that many of their spirits had been broken, too.

Not very long after the cluster director left, and again being taken by surprise, Colonel Davis resigned. Gone, both of them, just like that. Relief yes, celebration no. I now knew we would never go back to the days when I could call the superintendent's office only to be asked, "Are you sure you are part of the Orleans Parish School System?" We were now too entrenched as a public school to be unknown.

13

The Con Artist

The system hired Anthony Amato in the summer of 2002 to be the next Superintendent. He was not a Colonel and he did not have Doctor before his name, so he reverted back to being called Superintendent, the name that gave him the power. He exercised this power in the expected Superintendent way—all decisions came through him. But he had one very weird way of demonstrating his power. At every meeting that I saw him run or attend, he inevitably would end up standing very still along a wall staring intently at everyone in attendance. He was not a tall man and I always expected him to place his hand in his shirt to complete the Napoleonic pose. To my amazement he did this standing and staring even at school board meetings.

In one way he seemed like a breath of fresh air. He conducted his own in-service workshops and he talked education. Initially he impressed me, but after two years of struggling with his ideas, witnessing his Napoleonic mannerisms, and ending up believing he was a con artist at best, he disgusted me and I was elated to see him, also, abruptly leave. He was a master of shuffling the three cups with a pea supposedly under one of them. However, there was no pea—there was only harm under each one of them. Under cup number one you found our students treated as though they were dum-dums; under cup number two you found our teachers treated as lackeys only capable of following a script; and under cup number three you found our principals treated as leaderless prison wardens controlled by the scripted police.

Amato brought to the district the Success for All (SFA) and Direct Instruction (DI) reading programs, with Success for All obviously being his preference. I will give the man credit for his tenacity. He implemented and forced SFA and DI on the schools thoroughly and swiftly. In order to implement his two programs, he took all Title I monies from our schools and redefined how these monies were to be spent, which meant implementing either SFA or DI. His external SFA and DI consultants were ever present in our schools, to the point where we, and others, began calling them the SFA or DI police. He initially gave schools the choice of implementing either of the two programs or rejecting them both. Schools that rejected them both were required to increase test scores by ten points within one year or essentially lose the school. With very little knowledge and little choice in the matter, we chose SFA.

I, like most of our faculty, quickly soured on SFA for a number of reasons. Initial training proved to be more of a sales pitch for SFA than an education into the true workings of the method. Amato promised all teachers and principals all the necessary SFA materials by the start of the 2002 school year. Many materials, particularly for middle grades, never arrived for the entire 2002–2003 school year. The SFA police implied there was no middle school program, or a weak one at best, even though Amato had promised that there was. The entire program was quickly proving to be a sham and, truly, never materialized. The K-5 program was more intact but still very piecemeal and proved to be a very dumbed-down, scripted program. Flexibility for the teachers and a strong academic program for the students all had to surrender to the script and to the pronouncing of letter sounds, ad nauseam. Every teacher had to become a reading instructor regardless of background for at least a 90-minute reading block. It did not matter if the teacher was a math teacher, a coach, or an art teacher. Each one had to teach reading according to the SFA or DI prescription or else face the scorn and threatened punishment from the SFA or DI police. All hope of progressive quality education vanished.

My second objection to the SFA and DI centers on curriculum issues. These two programs were restrictive, narrowly focused, and prescriptive programs. Teachers were actually told what to say and when to say it. Curriculum for the different levels was limiting, tightly controlled with every student on the same page, the same sound, while constantly attempting to break learning down to its simplest form. These concepts defy what true education should be. Teachers should not be viewed as or treated as robots or assembly line workers. We must demand and expect our teachers to be professionals working in an environment where they function as professionals and not underlings in a powerful, top down, controlled system. We should focus our resources on teacher training in the latest best practices and not squander our funds on store-bought programs. Excellent teachers do not need a script. They need to operate in a system that unleashes their intellect and creativity. They need to be functioning members of a learning community, not factory workers in a dead institution. Curriculum must never be staid or static; it must always be rich and fluid. Curriculum in the broadest sense is anything studied. It should focus on discoveries, not just ends or simple right answers or narrow sounds.

We know that learning happens best when the learner has a need to know. Thus, any curriculum must be based on the needs of the learner and the ability to help the learner create new needs. The centerpieces behind the curriculum should be meaningfulness and connections that activate and engage the thinking process. We must move the school curriculum from a mind-numbing experience to an intellectually kaleidoscopic endeavor with emphasis on depth over coverage, development rather than sorting, activity instead of passivity, and creativity versus mechanics. We must provide the basics but also offer students an opportunity to use these basics in meaningful, challenging, and exciting ways.

Brain-based learning research teaches us that the brain thrives on complexity, meaningfulness, patterns, and connectedness. The mantra of brain-based learning is "high challenge, low threat." SFA seemed to emphasize knowledge acquisition on the lowest, most simplistic level possible, and the program demeaned the teachers by dogmatically forcing them to read a script instead of using their intellects. The mantra behind SFA and DI seemed to be "high threat, low challenge."

Another factor that caused me to lose faith in the program was that, according to the SFA police, students could not read during this "reading block" except at designated times. Teachers and students must follow the script. Our sixth-grade language arts teacher, Sandra Guichard, complained that her students went from reading many novels a year to reading just a few. Reading should be the focus of a reading program and not just the tail of scripted time.

My objections to these so-called reading programs were not just focused on reading, but also on the excessive amount of time spent on testing and data collection. I heard a leading SFA administrator, or consultant, state that through the many SFA mini-tests, careful breakdown of word sounds, and minute detailed attention to data, there should be no surprises when students receive their results on standardized test. This statement hurt me to my soul.

I do not believe that educational focus should be solely based on data, test scores, and more tests. I believe the focus must be on the child. As an educator, I believe that education is at its best when there are many surprises exhibited by the students along the learning journey—when students have that "aha" moment, when they cannot put down a book that they have fallen in love with, when they giggle with the love and joy of learning, when they have multiple serendipitous and spontaneous experiences, and, hopefully, when they get their test results. Education should not be about fragmented, broken-apart learning. Education should be wonderment, exploration, challenge, and joy. Being able to pinpoint a child's score on a standardized test means that we have so narrowed education that we have taken all meaningfulness and purpose out of education and have successfully made testing the education we are providing. I believe this to be miseducation and it is wrong, seriously wrong.

My final objection to SFA and DI was that the programs were not ethical. The unkindest cut of all came when we were directed to produce a "hot topic" list—a list of students just under the fiftieth percentile on the CTBS test. Improving the scores of these students to achieve 50 percent or better offered our school the best chance of improving our overall school performance score. Therefore, our school scores would look good and, of course, SFA and DI would look great.

The SFA leaders were quick to say that we must work to improve all student scores, but if we were successful with this target of "hot list students," then we would achieve the most bang for our buck on test scores. They demanded lesson plans that clearly documented a focus by teachers on these targeted students, and they wanted to witness classroom experiences depicting an emphasis on improving targeted students' scores. I personally found this practice to be immoral.

In essence, they were giving up on those students farthest behind and abandoning a most challenging program for students who scored highest on the standardized tests. Providing a challenging program is what is needed for all students—those at the bottom, the targeted "hot list" and those on the top. I feel SFA, DI, and similarly scripted programs should be discarded. We must embrace the concept that poor kids can learn; we must abandon the concept that we must wait for students to catch up before we offer high quality, high challenge education. We must offer all children, including children of the poor, a challenging, high quality educational experience from the very first day they enter the classroom.

Alas, Mr. Amato, like Dr. Holmes and Colonel Davis, put his tail between his legs and left New Orleans. He was only in town two years, but I would say he successfully destroyed what little meaningful education went on in public schools in New Orleans and bankrupted the Orleans Parish School System by spending millions on his two reading programs, particularly SFA. He was an excellent example of too much power being placed in the hands of one person, which always spells educational disaster.

It was during Amato's first few months that the issue of grades came up again. Immediately after his arrival, he brought in a lady to be his second in command. He presented her as the guru of education, particularly in math. I met with her shortly after her arrival to discuss our non-graded policy. In that conference without discussing it with Amato, she told me that Amato would not allow it. He wanted grades. Within days after that conference, she left the system, leaving me with no directive. During this same period, our staff voted to use grades. The movement was led by Jeanette who was tired of writing lengthy reports. This move was also supported by our other eigth grade teacher who argued that because we were giving grades, the written narratives were unnecessary. Eighth-grade teachers did have to give grades at the end of the year for students to enter high school. Other teachers had to give grades if a student exited the Free School and enrolled in another school.

One faculty member abstained from the grades vote and one voted against it. The rest wanted grades. The faculty granted my one request that they would write at least one narrative paragraph on each child's report to help individualize it. As I said before, the system had beaten me and I had no fight left in me. This meant that I did not want to or have to fight the administration over grades and this was fine with me. I should also note that grades no longer held the importance they once did. A child's educational worth became much more tied to passing or failing high-stakes tests than they ever did with just grades. I did use this opportunity to let the faculty know that I was going to retire in a couple of years.

Amato and his reading programs never proved to be the salvation he had promised. The experience under Amato clearly illustrated the need to unleash the passion, intellect, and creativity of those already in our school buildings. We need those closest to the education of our children in charge of running our schools. I was glad to see him leave, but expected no improvement from his successor, which unfortunately proved to be the case.

14

Moving the Free School

In the spring of 2005, Dr. Ora Watson replaced Anthony Amato. Sometime during Amato's administration, he had brought in Dr. Watson from Dallas, Texas, as his assistant superintendent and she took over as interim superintendent after he left. Her focus was not on SFA or DI, though she continued the programs; her focus was on physically reconfiguring the school system: closing schools, merging schools, moving schools, and changing grade configurations of some schools. I first became aware of this massive plan and the Free School's proposed role in it at an area superintendent's meeting.

I believe this new area superintendent, Jim Jones, (fictitious name) was brought in by Amato. He was a tall, slightly heavy set, soft spoken person, and he mumbled or spoke with a lisp. I always had trouble understanding what he was saying. Anyway, when he was describing the reconfiguration plan and came to the Free School, he quickly and clearly pointed out that they were not proposing to close the Free School. He emphasized that they were going to close the Jackson school and move the Free School to this new location.

This was the first I had heard of any such thing. As usual, no one had consulted us on this proposal. I was sure that this was the situation with most, if not all, of the other schools trapped in this plan. The higher-ups in bureaucracies like to pontificate; they do not like to share power or open up decision making to the masses. Bureaucracies have an insatiable appetite for control.

Our initial reaction to this news was to try to stay out of this fray. We knew that many people affected by these proposed movings and/or closings were going to be quite unhappy. Some of the meetings on these issues were going to be downright ugly. We desperately wanted no part of this negative scene but felt certain that we were in for a change.

We quickly let it be known that Jackson school was not an ideal location for the Free School. It was too big. The location and structure of the building met our needs, but the size frightened us. We also did not want to be pitted against any other school. If Jackson was to remain open, that was fine with us—we would prefer staying in our building anyway. Yet if the school system was truly going to close and vacate Jackson, then they could move us in that building.

During this time we found a close ally in our new school board member, Phyllis Landrieu. Mrs. Landrieu was a member of the political family that included former Mayor Moon Landrieu, U.S. Senator Mary Landrieu, and now New Orleans Mayor Mitch Landrieu. Mrs. Landrieu was a savvy politician, a senior citizen, kind and seemingly fair. She made it clear that she wanted to make happen whatever we wanted, but that she really liked the idea of moving us to Jackson because she thought that would put an end to school system administrators constantly trying to close us. She was very helpful and a pleasure to deal with.

Almost immediately after we began consulting with Mrs. Landrieu, my area superintendent, Jim Jones, quickly and firmly let me know that I should not go to her with our concerns. I should only go through the system. I told him "Yes sir" and went right on dealing with Mrs. Landrieu. She came to me as often as I turned to her, and she genuinely radiated concern about our program. This was refreshing.

Things had to move quickly because the start of the school year was rapidly approaching. On May 31, 2005, the board approved the 2005 School Closing Merger and Program Relocation Plan, which closed Jackson Elementary School, moved the Free School to the Jackson building, and allowed the Jackson parents to apply to the Free School or enroll their children in Laurel Elementary.

This presented a problem for us because we were a City-Wide Access School, CWAS, (a school of choice for parents that must offer a unique program for students). I was afraid we were going to have to battle to keep this standing. This would be an easy way to end our program, by eliminating choice and any need to offer a unique program. To my surprise, the administrator of the CWAS program publicly stated that the Free School was easiest of all CWAS schools to gain enrollment and he foresaw no problems with the merger. This allayed my fear and we began to enroll Jackson students.

Sometime in early June, I received the strangest of all strange calls. My area superintendent, Jim Jones, called me and actually asked me what I thought the board had approved concerning the Free School. I was caught off guard by this question, but I told him that I thought the board clearly voted to close the Jackson School, move the Free School to the Jackson building, and allow the Jackson parents to apply to the Free School or attend Laurel Elementary.

Area Superintendent Jim Jones told me that he also thought that this was what the board had decided to do, but he was hearing rumors that Jackson was not to be closed and was to share the building with the Free School. My heart stopped. He claimed that he did not know where the rumor was coming from.

I instantly knew that if this were true, it had to be coming from the interim superintendent, Ora Watson, herself. Who else could possibly ignore the board's decision? The rumor quickly proved true and the fight we wanted to avoid was on. This was the worst of all possible scenarios for the Free School, short of closure. We were being placed in a much larger building, almost twice the size of ours, with a very traditional, rigid school program and with people who thought the entire building was theirs (which in my opinion, it was).

While we were in a terrible position, I felt I needed to take quick action. Our little boat was forced to sail in the wrong direction. On June 23, 2005, I wrote a handwritten letter to the area superintendent restating the phone conversation we had just had on this matter. I carefully described the action we had taken to comply with the school board's May 31, 2005, decision to move the Free School to the Jackson building because the school there was being closed. In spite being told not to go to Phyllis Landrieu, I sent her a copy. Once again I knew that I could not leave this untenable situation in the hands of top administrators or we would lose for certain. I also sent a copy to Ora Watson—the very person who created this chilling situation.

There would be no board vote on this; the closing and moving of schools had already begun. It was now around the first of July with school starting on August 18. Rumors were plentiful with the worst being that they were closing the Free School and moving our students to the Jackson school. We quickly wrote a letter to all board members articulating our quandary and requesting that we remain in our building. We were desperately offering cooperation while seeking a reprieve from this dismal situation.

To: Torin Sanders, Orleans Parish School Board President
Lourdes Moran, Board Vice-President
Heidi Lovettt Daniels, Md.D., Board Member District 1
Cynthia Cade, Board Member District 2
Jimmy Fahrenholtz, Board Member District 3
Phyllis Landrieu, Board Member Dristric 5
Una B. Anderson

From: Robert M. Ferris, Ed.D.
Principal, New Orleans Free School
Jeanette St. Etienne
Ranking Teacher, NOFS
Shelia Jones
UTNO Building Representative, NOFS

Re: Moving the Free School

Date: 7/7/05

We are writing to you because of our concern about what is to happen to the New Orleans Free School. Our understanding of the board's decision (your decision) was that Andrew Jackson School was to be closed and the Free School was to move into that building. Parents at Jackson School had the option of sending their child(ren) to Laurel Elementary or they could apply to the Free School, a CWAS school.

This process was set into operation by Dr. ⁻ ⁻ ⁻ ⁻ , Area III Superintendent, and Dr. ⁻ ⁻ ⁻ ; compliance officer. Please see enclosed documentation concerning this matter and approved letter to Jackson parents.

After this process began we started hearing rumors that the Jackson School was not closing and that we, the Free School, were to share the Jackson building with the Jackson School. In fact, it is our understanding, that Jackson teachers have received a letter stating that they were not moving and the Free School would be on the 3rd floor. We do not know who authorized the letter; but, we, the faculty at the Free School, have received no such letter.

Also, please see the enclosed hand written letter by the principal of the Free School to Dr. ⁻ ⁻ and copied to Dr. Ora Watson and Phyllis Landrieu addressing this issue of placing the Free School in the same building as the Jackson School. Dr. ⁻ ⁻ ⁻ met with Ms. St. Etienne, ranking teacher of NOFS, on June 21, to discuss this matter. To his credit, according to Ms. St. Etienne, he too expressed reservations about placing the two schools in the same building. Again, according to Ms. St. Etienne, no definitive decision on this matter was stated.

While we sincerely attempted to stay out of conflicts surrounding the closing and moving of schools, we now find ourselves in a most uncomfortable position. We have never been opposed to moving as long as an appropriate and suitable building became available. We have never sought to move out of our present building. It is a fine old building right sized for the Free School. However, moving the Free School to the Jackson building with the Jackson School seems to place the Free School program in turmoil. For us it does not make educational sense to place two schools with significantly different philosophies and practices in the same building, not to mention all the issues centered around scheduling, space, turf wars among students, etc.

What we are requesting is that if Jackson School is to remain open and in that building, that the Free School be allowed to stay in our present building for at least another year. This would have the added advantage of involving the Free School community in any such move in the future.

If we are allowed to stay in our present building, we just need a commitment from the system to keep all window air-conditioned units properly working, to fix all lighting fixtures to maintain proper lighting, to patch all holes in walls, to place computers (room has already been wired) in "I Can Learn" lab, and to patch roof in the last needed roof repair area (most work has been completed).

Finally, we obviously need a decision on this matter as soon as possible.

We can be reached at the following cell phone numbers:
        Bob Ferris—
        Jeanette St. Etienne—
        Shelia Jones—

Thank you, in advance, for your consideration.

cc. Dr. Ora Watson, Interim Deputy Superintendent
    Dr   , Area III Superintendent

I knew this letter went over Interim Superintendent Watson's head, but this was July 7 just a few weeks before school would start. To go to the superintendent who had made this decision (possibly with little or no board consultation) would only solidify her power, waste precious time, and provide her with the opportunity to personally tell me to acquiesce and follow orders. I also knew that going over her head most definitely made her a formidable enemy whom I would be loath to deal with in the future. I had no choice. I also felt that the superintendent did not want it to get out that she had completely ignored a very public board decision about the closing and moving of schools.

Even though it caught me by surprise (I thought the system would simply leave us in our old building), seven days later the interim superintendent, on the recommendation of our area superintendent, agreed to move our school to the smaller Arthur Ashe building. This was much more to our liking as it better mirrored our present building on Camp Street. Mrs. Landrieu was afraid that it was too small for our needs; but with my assurance that with a little adjustment it would be perfect for our program, she readily agreed with the switch. The building was almost the same size as our building, very much in the same architectural style, with an additional building for our cafeteria and one useable portable where we could house our P.E. and part-time art teachers, along with our band.

Once it was confirmed that we were moving into the Arthur Ashe building we realized that we needed one room divider removed, one divider built, holes patched, some painting, minor plumbing and electrical work, and much furniture and junk to be removed. We also had to move all of our materials and furniture from our old school to this new school.

The school system did some minor plumbing and electrical work and did move all of our materials and furniture. However, Mrs. Landrieu came through like a champ. She brought over Sheriff Marlin Gusman and trade union officials to look at our building and assess our needs. They quickly agreed to fix and repair all that we needed, except for moving one of the portable trailers off the school grounds. This decision would have to wait until after school opened. Sheriff Gusman sent over trustees from our parish prison who were incredibly talented and hard working. The trade union people came in and did all the technical work needed.

The building was miraculously transformed by these men in five days. The school system moved all of the junk out of this new building and moved our desks and materials from the old building to our new old building on the weekend of August 13 and 14. They placed the desks in classrooms and materials in halls. Our teachers had exactly three days to sort everything out, set up their classrooms, and greet students on Thursday, August 18, the first day of school. One teacher, Ann White, broke her arm in the rush, but we were ready and opened for students on August 18. Mrs. Landrieu came to greet the students and parents and to cheer us on.
254

For the first seven days of school with students we had a beautiful, seven-day opening of school year 2005–2006, slightly short in numbers but enrolling students every day. Remember, a month and a half before, we did not know if or where we were going to open—enrolling kids had then come to a standstill.

During that seven-day period, the only acknowledgement I received on our putting the building in order to start school on opening day was a phone call from the interim superintendent. She did not call to thank me for making her look good by pulling off this amazing move/transformation in such a ridiculously short period of time; rather, she called to tell me to stop going to "that woman," (meaning Mrs. Landrieu), to get what I needed. She stated, "You know, this is not how we do business" and "I do not expect you to do it again." I did not argue with her; I simply kept saying, "Yes ma'am. Yes ma'am." While I had no fight left in me, I still knew that I was going to write her a letter with copies to board members criticizing her need for organizational power and her lack of insight to the beauty of community togetherness.

15

Katrina

I planned to write the letter during the weekend of August 27–28, 2005, but I never got the chance. I evacuated to Baton Rouge, Louisiana, on Sunday, August 28, escaping Hurricane Katrina. I went to bed on Monday, August 29, thinking the worst was over and that we would probably return on Wednesday at the earliest or the following Monday at the latest. On Tuesday morning, August 30, when I awoke and saw on TV the flood waters pouring into New Orleans, I instantly realized that I would probably never work for Orleans Parish School Administrators again as long as I lived. No letter to the acting Superintendent was needed.

Katrina had accomplished through her flood waters what the school system was never able to do: Katrina drowned the New Orleans Free School—not literally because the new Free School building did not flood and only suffered fixable damage, but figuratively because the Free School never reopened—it was shuttered forever. Ironically, Katrina did to the Orleans Parish School System what the Free School was never able to do: Katrina drowned the bureaucratic stranglehold the school system had over public schools. Katrina collapsed the battleship—literally. The only thing the school system salvaged out of Katrina was a dingy—four or five select-enrollment schools and oversight of some of the charter schools that were opening up. God forbid if the school system ever regains control over the rest of the schools in Orleans Parish, which are now primarily charter schools.

While I was truly saddened by the loss of the school, I was also overwhelmed by the destruction of our city. I desperately wanted to see the city myself and to view our house to assess the damage. I snuck back into New Orleans two days later. On Tuesday or Wednesday night, my friend Dr. Justin Lundgren informed me that he was hitching a ride with a first responder back into the city the next morning. I asked if I could go with him and he agreed, if the driver agreed. The next morning I asked the first responder if I could tag along and he said, I could if I had some kind of pass that would help us get through the roadblocks. I showed him my Orleans Parish School Board picture clip-on ID. He said, "Let's go." His van/truck had emergency lights and a siren that enabled him to drive quite fast on Interstate 10, although there was little to no traffic on the highway going to or from the city. His emergency vehicle allowed him passage through the roadblocks, giving him easy entrance to anywhere in the city, difficult though it was to drive around.

As we were approaching New Orleans, I remember seeing a lot of damage in Metairie, and then stopping on the interstate at I-10 and

Causeway Boulevard. It was a hot, sunny day and the area was immersed with destitute people waiting to be taken anywhere. Apparently this was a drop-off point for people made homeless by Katrina. Trash and clothes were spread all over the area. These were broken down, hot and thirsty people with their only salvageable clothes trashed around them as they sat or stood on the roadside on this otherwise beautiful day. It presented a futuristic, destructive scene frightening to witness and difficult to adequately describe. We were told to keep moving if we wanted to get into the city but had to change routes because the interstate was flooded further on and impassable.

We took Causeway Boulevard to Highway 90/Jefferson Avenue, another major artery through the City of New Orleans. Before we could reach the city line, we ran into more flooding, which blocked further entrance. We then went down to River Road to Magazine Street. Once we hit Magazine Street I was amazed at the amount of debris on the road and surrounding area, especially as we drove through Audubon Park. We literally zigzagged around fallen trees and limbs.

We took this direction because it followed the "sliver by the river"— the part of New Orleans that did not flood. This part followed the Mississippi River and included Uptown, Garden District, Lower Garden District, Warehouse District (which is where the Convention Center is located), most of downtown, the French Quarter and slightly below the French Quarter. Essentially, from about two blocks off St. Charles, including St. Charles, to the river, did not flood. The rest of the city, 80 percent of New Orleans, was under water, except for a very few houses that were built on ridges.

We drove by my house, which is only a couple of blocks off Magazine Street. Our driver was anxious to get downtown where all the action was, so we did not stop. I did get to see that my house was still standing, but I wanted to stay with Justin. He was going to be with his wife, Kiersta Kurtz-Burke, a physician and also a close friend who was working at Charity Hospital. I thought I could be of help at the hospital, where, according to news coverage, doctors, nurses, staff, and patients were in desperate situations. We drove by the home of Pam Kaster and Lee Mullikin, good friends of ours who stayed through the storm. They had kindly opened our refrigerator doors and cleaned out all the food that could spoil. They also had cut away all trees and branches blocking all four doors to our house. They paid themselves with some of the wine and liquor we had in the house— you know, when you are stranded in a city with no electricity, little food and water and almost no people, it is important that you commandeer the important survival stuff. Justin managed to speak a few words with Lee. I only got to wave, but it was sure good to see his smiling face.

Our trio proceeded to drive downtown and drove within a block or two of the Convention Center. We could see and feel the tension of thousands of stranded, destroyed people languishing at the Center, but we were advised by authorities not to go any closer. I remember feeling relieved that we were not advancing into that destitute crowd. We continued driving downtown, which was only a few blocks further. Every block or two, we stopped and talked to someone armed and on patrol. The conversation was always the same. "Be careful. They are shooting at us from everywhere. Keep your head down."

We got as far as we could in the car and then had to take small motorized boats to Charity Hospital. All boat pilots were armed to the teeth and kept repeating that people were shooting at them and to lie low. One of the boats we went on was filled with liquor that one of the boat pilots said he salvaged from his restaurant. The conversation about the shooters and the orders to keep our heads down was incessant. When we finally reached the hospital, Justin and Kiersta were overjoyed to be reunited. This ordeal was obviously traumatic for Kiersta and everyone trapped at that hospital. Relief radiated in her crying eyes.

I quickly learned that the worst was over for those at Charity Hospital. Most patients were already evacuated from the hospital and many doctors and staff people were just waiting until they could leave. I was not needed. I found it eerie walking alone in the hospital especially down the darkened staircase, but I found the location where the boat pilots were taking anyone who wanted to leave from the hospital to the Superdome. I stood around as they filled the small, canoe-like boats until I heard one guy loudly proclaim that he had room for one more. When no one came forward, I volunteered and was taken to the Superdome. Again, we were warned to stay down because of the shooting.

When I got to the Superdome, I was in for a shock. It was like I landed in the land of the living dead. I only stayed on the ramp; I did not go into the Superdome itself. I was afraid to—outside was more than scary enough. The hundreds, if not thousands of people on the ramp, appeared to be in a daze, listlessly walking around, if moving at all. They appeared sun-dried, shriveled, and sickened. Many had been out there now for three days with little or no water, food, or a place to sleep. At this moment of the day, around noon, there was only concrete and sun—lots and lots of hot, relentless sun. One of the ironies of a hurricane is the sun and calm that usually follows, and Katrina proved the rule. One of the blessings of the sun was that it did not rain in New Orleans, except for once or twice, for almost eight or nine months after Katrina, and only lightly for a few months after that. This gave many people a chance to patch and/or replace their roofs and get on with the business of rebuilding our homes and businesses. Insurance companies and government were not always so accommodating, but you should see our city now. It is testimony to a people hell-bent on returning home and rebuilding their city. Not all have been able to return; but, thankfully, most have.

No rebuilding happened that day. Compared to the people at the Superdome, I had the advantage of being well fed, rested, and not thirsty. I was determined not to become a refugee in need of emergency help, nor did I want to become a burden on anyone for any reason. I could offer these people nothing because I had nothing—no water, no food, no transportation—nothing. I decided to leave, not knowing how I was to get home. I only knew that I had to get off the Superdome ramp, to dry land, and then to my home. Entrance into my flooded city had proven easy thanks to hitching a ride with that first responder. Leaving the city would prove more challenging. I did not want to stay overnight in a city that had no electricity or running water and I certainly did not want to be trapped with the destitute and abandoned citizens on that ramp. My exit plan for that day was to ride my daughter's bike out of New Orleans, if I could only get to my house.

I then heard someone on the ramp say, "Those with Group B come with me to the bus." I saw a small group of people start following him. I did not know where this man was taking them or if it would provide me with an escape route, but I joined the small group this man was leading down some stairs. When we got towards the bottom of these stairs, there was nothing but water and a few of these people walked aimlessly around in it. I had lost the man leading the group and there certainly was no bus waiting for anyone. But, I was on the ground with almost no one—I guess they went back up. The water was hip deep. I took my chances and started heading toward St. Charles Avenue, which I knew was on dry land.

Very quickly I was all alone with the water getting shallower with almost every step. I stayed on side streets to avoid police or soldiers who might arrest me, claiming that I had no right to be where I was. Although I had been repeatedly told that people were shooting at anybody, particularly first responders I had yet heard any shots. I began to think of it more as urban myth and less as reality. To this day I am convinced that the shootings were not nearly as bad as they were presented to us that day.

I finally reached St. Charles and very quickly hitched a ride on a Kentwood water truck that may well have been one of the three water trucks I later heard had been stolen. Regardless, this was fortunate because there were a lot of troops and a few strange-looking people on St. Charles Avenue. I may never have made it to my house without this ride. The truck driver let me off at St. Charles and Napoleon where a group of people were gathered across the street. They called me to come over there, but not knowing who they were or knowing what they wanted, I avoided them and quickly got on side streets that were almost totally abandoned. I then walked about ten blocks to get to my house.

I had been one of the lucky ones. As I said before, my house was in the 20 percent area beside the river that did not flood. Entering my empty house was eerie but exhilarating. Because Pam and Lee had cut back all of the branches blocking our four doorways, it was easy to enter. Debris was everywhere but the path was clear. As I checked our house upstairs and down, I found that there was no internal damage. I found no damage outside. Our above-ground pool was still intact though full of yucky, debris-filled water. Somehow our hot tub remained undamaged. Our rear, shaded cover area also seemed unharmed. We were lucky and blessed. Later, once we were legally allowed to return to our homes, Sue and I filled what seemed to be one hundred trash bags of debris and even though our house was free of internal damage, ours, like the rest of New Orleans residences, had to get a new roof. We did have one interesting problem. A large tree that at first glance looked like a huge limb of a tree, hung dangling over our pool. Lee, playing superman, got up on the falling tree via a long extension ladder and cut the tree off piece by piece until it could not damage the pool if it fell. We were blessed to have a friend like Lee. He was and is one of our heroes.

On my risky and possibly illegal visit to New Orleans, I knew that I did not want to stay in our house overnight without electricity, food, or drinking water. I had planned my escape the night before assuming that I would not stay in Charity Hospital overnight and that I could reach our house. I had intended to ride my daughter's bicycle from my house to LaPlace, some 30 miles away. Sue was going to pick me up there. LaPlace was as close to the city as you could get legally if you weren't a first responder or possessed a pass authorizing your entrance.

I left the house on my bike sometime around 2:30 or 3:00 p.m. and, again, stayed on the side streets. I went past the new Free School building, which we had just moved into. It was intact, though with a few blown out windows and debris everywhere in the yard, but I did not venture in. I saved that moment for another time. While the houses I passed on my way to the Audubon Park to the Mississippi levee were still standing with little apparent damage, the grounds and roads were totally filled with endless debris from the storm. There was no doubt that something ferocious had come through here. On this strange fifteen-block ride and through the park, I saw not one person, only desertion. I then entered onto the bike path that led to the top of the Mississippi levee, which took me most of the way to LaPlace, and to Sue.

I was greatly relieved to be on the path, but painfully aware that I was on the longest bike ride of my life. Now, almost seven years after Katrina and at the age of sixty-eight, I often ride forty miles. I recently rode in an Ironman race for fifty-six miles. But, back on that day just after Katrina, I was not prepared to ride such a long distance. With adrenaline flowing and determination to succeed in this task, I peddled on. I never considered the possibility of having to sleep on the levee or encountering a pack of abandoned dogs. I only knew that I wanted to get to LaPlace, and to Sue.

As I rode along the levee in what seemed an endless physical endeavor, I remember four events. At one point I was accosted by two or three levee police vehicles. As they came out of nowhere, driving extremely fast, I was sure I was going to be stopped and arrested. However, they quickly started screaming at me, "Did you hear those shots over there? Did you hear those shots?" and pointed to an area about 200 yards behind me. I told them no and they zoomed on past me. They did not even ask me what I was doing on the levee all alone in the middle of this crisis.

If shots had been fired, I would have heard them. On this levee there was absolutely no sound—no people, no cars or trucks, no airplanes, no lawnmowers, no birds, no dogs, nothing. If shots had been fired, I would have been scared to death. Now I am not saying that people were not shooting at one another, or at first responders. The only thing I knew for sure was that the sum of the conversation from all the first responders that I talked to or overheard concerned people shooting at them and others. I never heard a shot. I am convinced that in this strange time if one or two first responders were shot at, embellishment and paranoia could easily have taken over.

Anyway, I simply continued on my solitary exodus.

The next thing I remember about the ride was the incredible emptiness with all the destruction. There was just silence and stillness everywhere. Along with this terribly lifeless feeling I experienced was the endless destruction, vividly illustrated by the broken telephone poles. River Road follows the levee for most of the journey and telephone poles follow the road. One pole after another as far as the eye could see, and the legs could pedal, was snapped in half, one after another, after another, after another, after another. The third thing I remember about this journey was a little more personal. When I had arrived at my house, I had only one thought in mind. It was getting late—I must get on the bike and head out of town. I had failed to get out of my damp clothes from walking in the Katina waters as I left the Superdome. As I rode on the levee, my damp underwear started irritating my skin. The more I pedaled and the father I went, the more the pain increased. But, as the old saying goes, "No pain, no gain." I kept on pedaling.

The final thing I remember after having been on the levee for at least three hours was that I saw a couple in a pickup truck pull into a grocery store. I do not remember if the store was open but it was sure good to see people. I rode my bike down to them and asked them how much further it was to the spillway. I knew I had to cross the spillway to get to LaPlace. They told me just to keep following the road and eventually I would get there. It was not many miles further. I continued on my journey. About forty-five minutes later, the same truck passed me and then stopped. The couple got out of the truck and waved for me to come over to them.

They asked me if I wanted a lift. They were not going across the spillway, but they would gladly take me. By now it was starting to get dark and I was starting to get scared. I was so relieved and quickly accepted their beautiful offer.

By the time we reached the spillway it was dark. The spillway turned out to be a winding, pothole-dotted dirt road with no lights. With tears in my eyes, I realized I never would have made it if were it not for these two kind people. I failed to get their names so I was never able to properly thank them. I feel bad about this to this day but will always appreciate them.

One of the ironies of this situation was that top school system administrators had given all principals a BlackBerry many months before Katrina. We were daily pressured to just use our BlackBerry as our sole phone communication with all administrative employees, especially our area superintendents. For me this was just a burden of learning another phone number and I viewed it as one more control tool imposed by the administration to keep track of our every move. We already had to let the area office know every time we left the building even to grab a quick lunch. Now, I was elated that they had given me one. Regular cell phones in the New Orleans area worked poorly if at all because of their overuse in this time of crisis. On this sole, lonely journey, the BlackBerry provided me the opportunity to call Sue.

Sue and Teresa were waiting for me in LaPlace. Teresa and Sam Staub are dear friends with whom we stayed during and immediately after the storm at their home in Baton Rouge. There were about ten people and eight dogs staying in Sam and Teresa's house during this trying time. Sue and Teresa brought some cold beer in an ice chest, which I greedily consumed. Since breakfast, which now seemed like so long ago, I had had nothing to eat or drink. As I drank the beer, I realized that I had escaped my underwater city but that I wanted to go back and be part of its rebirth. I was saddened by all that I saw but my love for our city only strengthened my resolve to return and to help rebuild.

A week and a half later, I returned to New Orleans with Sam, Sue, and my daughter Iyana. We drove straight into New Orleans encountering no road blocks, even though no permission had been granted for anyone to return to their homes. First, we went to our house to examine it and to get some clothes. When we left New Orleans for the hurricane, we, like almost everyone else, thought we were only going to be gone for a couple of days at most, thus would need only a few clothes. It proved to be six weeks before we could officially return to our homes, so we badly needed some clothing. We next went to my daughter's house, which she had been renting out at the time of Katrina. Her house did not flood although it was right on the flood line. From her house all the way to Lake Pontchartrain, houses flooded. From her house to the Mississippi River, houses did not flood. However, many roof shingles and her roof air vent had blown off during the hurricane, letting the rain saturate her house. Her sheetrock walls and ceilings were mold mosaics, beautiful in a weird way. Rugs, books, appliances, couches, beds, and other items were waterlogged and ruined. It was a mass mess of destruction.

This began our day's job of cleaning out refrigerators. We cleaned out seven refrigerators before the day was over; two at my daughter's house, two at a friend's house, and three at a house on Magazine Street where rental property that Sue and I own is located. My daughter's was the only house that was completely inundated with water, but each of the other structures had major roof damage, some water damage and of course, no electricity. All of the refrigerators had now been off for at least nine days and as we opened each one, we were greeted with the foulest, most putrid odor, a flood (pardon the pun) of rotten food and millions of maggots crawling everywhere. It was a disgusting job causing Sam to throw up when he grabbed a banana that quickly disintegrated and sent rotten dust fumes to his nose.

My friend Sam is a contractor. He told Iyana that he would fix and rebuild her house for whatever insurance money she received. This was a good example of people working together to rebuild New Orleans. Unfortunately the insurance company was not so cooperative. My wife is an attorney and had to fight the insurance company for many months to secure proper payment for my daughter's house. This was just one illustration of how the insurance companies made it difficult, if not impossible, to achieve proper settlements. Katrina taught us all that insurance companies had lost their mission—to cover losses. It became painfully apparent that insurance companies were no longer risk management companies; they were now primarily money making endeavors. However, Sam's company, Sam Staub, Enterprises, did a marvelous job, and Iyana's home has been beautifully restored while preserving the old charm it already had.

Two or three weeks later I got a job with Cajun Contractors in Baton Rouge, and for the next eleven days I went into the eastern part of New Orleans and helped with a crew pumping water out of the city. Often, I would look over a flood wall and see rows of houses under water. One house particularly caught my attention. Not only was it under water, but three cars in the driveway were underwater. The city was literally a sea of destruction.

Every few days while on this job I could see that the waterline on the houses had gone down a couple of inches, creating a new lower flood line not as deeply colored as the previous line. The water pumping went on twenty-four hours a day. Our crew would get there after leaving Baton Rouge around 3:30 a.m. and returning around 2 p.m. I did this for eleven days nonstop. I should note that when I got this job I bought two pairs of blue jeans, the first I had worn since high school. No one recognized me, though everyone made fun of me. When Sue and I heard that Mayor Ray Nagin had officially opened the parts of the city that were dry and had electricity, we went back home immediately.

It was at this time that I was finally able to enter the Free School building that we had just moved into. There was some damage, though nothing major. All I could see was just a couple of blown-out windows in only one or two classrooms. There, of course, was glass on the floor, papers blown everywhere, and some minor water damage.

In my office, the window air conditioning unit was literally blown onto my desk and papers were everywhere. I managed to salvage all important papers and take home my personal belongings, which were mostly books and a few important papers I needed to complete the history of the school. I knew that this was the end of the Free School, which most definitely caused me to have mixed emotions. On the one hand, I had gotten my wish: I no longer had to work with bureaucrats who were generally more concerned about their power, position, compliance, and keeping the ship ramming their opposition than they were with providing challenging, caring, and creative education. I say generally because there were many good people in the bureaucracy who were attempting to do the best job they could under the circumstances. On the other hand, I knew I would painfully miss the Free School which, after all these years and even after all the brutal battles, I still loved. I was joyful over never having to attend another meaningless principals' meeting, but heartsick over never being able to go to the school in the morning and greet the faculty and students ready to continue our journey through life. I still loved the school and would miss it. I still do.

In one last effort, I did try to reach my superiors by BlackBerry, but neither would respond. I left messages on their voice mails letting them know that the Free School could be up and running within a few weeks with just minor repairs, but I knew that this message would fall on deaf ears. They wanted nothing to do with me and this was their opportunity to be rid of me forever. I am not sure that the area superintendent even returned after the storm. The acting superintendent did return at the helm of the school system (what was left of it) but she only stayed about a year and then departed. The storm destroyed many public school buildings and eliminated the school system as we had experienced it. The system seemed immobile and incapable of attempting any education in any form. They had no school up and running until almost a year after Katrina. This brought renewed criticism of them but, in the void, a massive charter school movement emerged.

I quickly learned that I could probably have converted the Free School to a charter school, but I truly had no more fight in me. The struggle with Colonel Davis followed by the fight with Ora Watson had been the nails in the coffin. I wanted out and this horrendous situation enabled me to throw up my hands and say, "I quit." Now the school system, what was left of it, fired everybody, including me. With what authority and how they did this, I do not know. So here I was, caught in the proverbial, "You can't fire me—I quit!" conundrum. Anyway, it seemed like the natural time to let go. I was now sixty-one years old with my teachers scattered all over the Southern states, most having no home to return to. Almost all our students were gone. Even if we had started a charter school, it would not have been the same. I decided to leave the creation of charter schools to the young who so desperately wanted to be part of and to lead the transformation of New Orleans. It was an exciting and challenging time for our city with so many young people coming here to do what we had done thirty-five years ago, start a school trying to make a difference in the lives of children, especially children of the poor. It was definitely the right time to let go and let others take over.

16

Charter Schools: The Present Wave of the Future

The charter school concept is what I wanted for the Free School: freedom from bureaucratic control, city wide enrollment, more resources, a better facility, more control over the hiring and firing of staff, freedom to develop our own curriculum including teaching methods, and small student enrollment. I wanted to keep enrollment at the Free School as low as possible, but still in the public school arena. I am also enamored with the passion, love, determination, intelligence, energy, and creativity that many charter school people bring to the educational table. They have a strong vision, coupled with a desire to educate and transform the lives of those students whom they touch. Our schools need this new-found and renewed passion for education. For far too long school systems, especially urban school systems, have monopolized schooling into a lobotomized state, particularly for the poor and minorities. The New Orleans Public School System lost its power on August 29, 2005, and charter schools quickly started filling the void, bringing new and hopefully lasting life to our public schools.

One of the most critical issues charter schools will face is power. Right now charter schools are able to operate with an amazing amount of autonomy. This is as it should be. Presently, New Orleans charter schools are under a number of umbrella organizations including the Louisiana State Education Board, the state Recovery School District (RSD), the Orleans Parish School Board (OPSB), the Algiers Charter Schools Association, and more. There is a move to return most, if not all, charter schools and the twelve traditional schools presently managed by the RSD to the Orleans Parish School Board. If this board becomes the sole overseer of most if not all public schools in New Orleans, I fear total disaster. First, this board will whittle away at charter school autonomy by making one policy decision after another that slowly, ever so slowly, will chip away at the autonomy currently held by charter schools. The New Orleans Free School testifies to this reality. They will use race, economies of scale, building conditions, shifting populations, student enrollment, fads, test scores, power conflicts, neighborhood attendance, curriculum issues, budgets, complaints, staffing, whatever it takes, to justify the erosion of charter school autonomy and the march to uniformity. Then one day the fight will no longer be against interference by the school board: the fight will have been lost and the charter schools will have become standardized with little or no freedom to deviate or innovate. The ugly monster, the Orleans Parish School Board, which pre-Katrina managed to suck the lifeblood out of all progressive education and provide some of the worst schools imaginable, especially for children of the poor, will be back in business. It is unacceptable to let the lone board approach with tight bureaucratic control which was responsible for running our public schools into the ground oversee rights to a network of independent and community schools that are promising and demonstrating hope for lasting educational excellence.

Another issue of power confronting charter schools is high-stakes testing. As long as testing is used as a bludgeon to determine schools, smash schools, flunk students, evaluate teachers, and determine paychecks, many, if not all, charter schools will succumb to the absolute necessity of teaching the tests. Human development, exposing students to new books, new art forms, the power of geography, the love of music, and the excitement of learning will be swept away to make room for the tests.

Proponents of charter schools must also deal with the issue of who has the power to issue charters. After all, achieving charter status means lots of money for the school. If one agency maintains this determining power, we are dangerously close to reinventing the one shoe fits all concept. There must be a variety of avenues for schools to achieve charter status and we must make sure that community input is part of the process. This will further guarantee democratic schools and better foster variety in school options.

An absolute concern about charter schools is the move to privatize public education; that is, taking schools out of the public arena and placing them in private/corporate hands with little or no accountability to the public. Is New Orleans after Katrina not the perfect Naomi Klein's "Shock Doctrine" scenario? Is it not true that after Katrina we witnessed what Klein described as "selling off pieces of the state to private players [i.e., charter schools] while citizens were still reeling from the shock, then quickly making the 'reforms' permanent" (7). In proposing to close large school boards and crumble bureaucratic education, am I not falling prey to the privatization movement? Consider what is happening in Louisiana. In *The Times Picayune* May 12, 2011, edition, the following was reported:

> The business lobby smoked the education establishment Tuesday, winning a lopsided House Education Committee vote in favor of allowing new partnerships between corporations and charter schools. House Bill 421 by Rep. Steve Carter, R-Baton Rouge, would allow corporations to secure spots on charter governing boards and reserve student enrollment slots for children of employees. To qualify, a corporation would have to donate the parcel on which the school is built, donate an existing building for the school's use or pay for major renovations to an existing building. The corporation could lay claim to up to half of the enrollment spaces in the school and control up to 50 percent of the seats on the governing board. (A-2)

Wow! Talking about giving away the store! This bill clearly illustrated public schools being taken out of the hands of the public and placing them in the hands of corporations. In no way do I endorse or support privatizing public education. I may want to change public education by making it more democratic and by providing a much better education for all of our children, but I do not want to harm it and I certainly do not want to place public schools in the hands of corporations. I have never considered myself to be a revolutionary. During the civil rights and anti-Vietnam War years, I never advocated the overthrow of our government. I believed that civil disobedience was an acceptable practice but I never suggested, considered, or encouraged bombing buildings or shooting police. In fact, I was never in the company of those who even suggested such action. What many thought of as a radical approach to change, I simply viewed as the right thing to do. Registering black people to vote and supporting demonstrations to end segregation seemed more a moral imperative than a revolutionary act. Participating in anti-Vietnam War demonstrations was a democratic act, not an act of violence. I felt and feel the same way about education. For me, the Free School was never an attempt to destroy public education; rather, it was to demonstrate that we could and should do public education differently than the bureaucratic, urban model of education which squelched deviation from the norm and inflicted a very inferior education on the poor. I never wanted to destroy the public school: I wanted to change it and make it work for all students. Charter schools now face the dilemma of privatization: providing school for the chosen, or true public access, providing school for all.

At the same time let me proffer that larger urban public education is not democratic education, either. It amazes me that the horrendous state of urban education was not the shock factor that caused the walls of urban bureaucracy to come tumbling down. Ghastly though it was, Katrina sunk a battleship of horrific education. But Katrina did not end democratic education—it may have returned public schools to the people. The pitiful education provided by the Orleans Parish School Board through its administrators was not democratic education as we all have been led to believe. I believe that we have lost true democratic public education in the United States. Since our country is so consumed by numbers these days, let me quote a few figures to make my point. Deborah Meier in her chapter titled, "NCLB and Democracy" in the book, *Many Children Left Behind*, wrote:

> In 1930 there were 200,000 school boards in the United States. Today with twice as many citizens and three times as many students in our public schools, we have only 15,000. Once one of every 500 citizens sat on a school board; today it's one out of nearly 20,000. Once most of us knew a school board member personally; today it's rare to know one. (66)

268

In 1930 we had approximately 262,000 public schools serving students in grades one through twelve. By 2001 we had only about 93,000. As schools became larger and school boards became smaller, power shifted from the parents and local communities to large centralized bureaucracies, with decision making coming from the top instead of from school sites. We lost our public schools.

However, I do not see this as an either/or conundrum. Either we privatize our schools and abandoned the public school concept, or we return all schools to one school board with the deleterious probability that standardization will rule. There is another solution—a solution that better complements the charter school concept of self-determination. What I propose is the dissolution of the Orleans Parish School Board. End it. Get rid of it. Katrina crushed it; now, bury it. In its place I recommend a city with just charter schools, with each charter school or small cluster of charter schools establishing their own school boards by appointment, election, or a simple voluntary system. The charters would determine how each board would be formed and what the duties of that board would be. First, this approach would help solidify school-site autonomy by eliminating the monolithic board that has traditionally determined practices and policies for all schools to implement and follow. Secondly, it would significantly increase community participation in the operation of our public schools. Participation is democracy at its best. Finally, it would afford every parent, including the poorest, choice in where their children attend school, something that is presently reserved for the wealthier parents of our society. This reform would transform our schools from a school system to a system of schools.

This move towards multiple community schools also presents the greatest opportunity for transforming our schools from large tightly controlled institutions to much smaller, more manageable and focused schools. In essence, we would be returning to many more local school boards overseeing one to a few schools while greatly increasing community participation. For years we have given lip service to community involvement while we have steadily removed our public schools from the democratic process. Do not end the public school concept—revitalize it by returning schools to the people. Give the schools back to the people! If only the Free School could have had that option. We would have spent thirty-four years hellbent on education instead of struggling for survival and skirting compliance in every manner possible.

I realize that not all charter schools will work best for students. Some will be the mirror image of our already rotten, large urban public schools; some will be no more than testing factories and/or soft prisons; others will be modeled after the very corporations that have raped our country; some will be too soft; and some will be too harsh. I believe that implementing measuring devices other than high-stakes testing, along with parental choice, will help schools that are having difficulty make corrections, get needed help to restructure, or be eliminated. While I just listed some of the horrors that might come out of charter schools, let me be perfectly clear that I hope most charter schools will be focused on visionary, innovative, challenging and enlightening education—schools that engage and challenge students rather than just impose information on them and keep them standing in line and seated in desks, all the while forcing them to take more and more tests.

In addition to the issues mentioned above, I realize that charter schools face a number of hurdles and roadblocks they must overcome if they are to survive as major players in the educational framework of our country. Local and national-level obstacles raise the following questions. Will charter schools play a role in the elimination of the achievement gap between rich and poor students, or is this just another strategy to perpetuate this gap? Are marketplace, competition, and high-stakes testing improving education, or are these weapons of mass educational destruction? Why are we not providing quality education for children of the poor, including our three- and four-year olds (and maybe our two-year olds)? Why is education serving the poor always dumbed-down education and never high-quality schooling?

17

The Achievement Gap and Selective Enrollment

The achievement gap between white and black, rich and poor students persists in U.S. schools. Libby Quaid, AP education writer, in *The Times-Picayune* on June 15, 2009, noted the U.S. Education Department's findings that "despite unprecedented efforts to improve minority achievement in the past decade, the gap between black and white students remains frustratingly wide" (A-3).

Barton and Coley, in *The Black-White Achievement Gap, When Progress Stopped* (Educational Testing Service, June 2010), also documented this persistent and bothersome educational disparity:

> In summary, most of the progress in closing the achievement gap in reading and mathematics occurred during the 1970s and 1980s. Since then, overall progress in closing the gaps has slowed. With the exception of the 2008 gap in reading for 9-year-olds, the size of the gaps seen in the late 1980s has never been smaller. (7)

The authors also contend that there is not yet a definitive reason for this lack of growth in diminishing this achievement gap during the last twenty years: "Anyone looking for a smoking gun as to why progress halted, establishing dead certainty, will not find it in this report" (3). For me this last statement is disappointing. I wish their study would have considered the implementation and meteoric rise of high-stakes testing during the past twenty years. In my opinion, the intensified testing during these last twenty years has led to the demise of public education, while especially harming our poor and minorities.

Charter schools must participate in the elimination of the achievement gap between our poor and our wealthier students or they too, like our large bureaucratically structured schools, will fail. Charter schools must be non-discriminatory and non-religious, both in written philosophy and practice. In almost every case, they should be open-access schools. How these schools assimilate the haves and the have-nots is crucial to the elimination of the achievement gap that persistently exists. I prefer community-based schools, which successfully mix the incomes and races in their school populations, over the ones that serve only the poor, though these schools may be necessary first steps.

The Morris Jeff Community School in New Orleans best exemplifies what I am talking about. In addition to having open enrollment, one of the major stated missions of this school is to offer an integrated school community. Presently it has 60 percent black, 30 percent white and 10 percent mostly Asian and Spanish students categorized as "other." These numbers mirror the New Orleans population. This school is a grassroots, community school which should be the norm and not the exception. I do not endorse corporate charter schools because I fear their motive to be more profit-oriented than educationally motivated and selective, and unavailable to too many, meaning mostly children of the poor. I also worry that they would be accountable to no one but the corporate office and they would erode the public school concept while removing education from the public domain and placing it in the hands of corporate America.

I believe the only hope for the achievement of equity in education and quality education for all our students must and will come from a great public school education, though this goal has certainly proven elusive. In sum, I strongly oppose privatization of public schools. I want schools that greatly increase public involvement, not decrease it.

However, this transformation to charter schools is not without critics. They argue that charter schools are set up to draw all of the best students, even from the poorest neighborhoods, leaving only the worst students and special education students—who are most in need—to enroll or be placed in the traditional public schools. The critics of the charter schools in New Orleans also make the charge that the charter schools here are siphoning off the best of the poor and leaving the rest suffering in the larger, more traditionally run schools. Some critics also argue that charter schools fare no better than traditionally run public schools.

Diane Ravitch, in her book, *The Death and Life of the Great American School System*, described the selectivity exercised by charter schools and pointed out that research on charter schools versus traditional schools demonstrate mixed results, with no clear cut findings. She noted that one study (led by Margaret E. Raymond with researchers at Stanford University), showed charter schools fairing no better than traditionally run schools in closing this achievement gap. This 2009 study concluded that 80 percent of the charter schools in the study performed either "the same as or worse than the local public schools" (142). However, Ms. Ravitch included another study conducted by Caroline Hoxby and her colleagues which "determined that disadvantaged students who attended charter schools for nine consecutive years, from kindergarten to eighth grade, closed most of the 'Scarsdale-Harlem' achievement gap" (142).

While results have been mixed, there is no clear cut evidence for or against charter schools. Those few charters that are excelling with the poor are suspect because of their selection process, their ability to get rid of students who do not fit in with their standards and procedures, and their huge money flow. In New Orleans, at least one charter school is paying the principal at or over $200,000/year. This is not a school that serves children of the poor; this is a school with a very selective enrollment. I fail to see how making some charter schools more like private schools while enrolling the better performing public school students enhances public education. It doesn't. This practice continues and widens the gap between the have and the have-nots as it erodes the public school concept. Paying principals/administrators ridiculous salaries could prove to be the death knell of the genuine charter school movement if not kept under check because there is no way the larger charter school movement can sustain such expenditure.

The highly acclaimed KIPP charter schools have recently come under scrutiny by a study conducted by researchers at Western Michigan University, titled, "What Makes KIPP Work? A Study of Student Characteristics, Attrition, and School Finance," led by Gary Miron. The study reported the following on school finance: "Combining public and private sources of revenue, KIPP received, on average, $18,491 per pupil in 2007-2008. This is $6,500 more per pupil than what the local school districts received in revenues" (ii). Wow! At $6,500 times 300 students, the Free School would have received an additional $1,950,000 per year. We could have bought or built the building we wanted, sent our kids on camping trips in jet airplanes, and I could have been a rich man. On student attrition, the study reported the following:

> KIPP schools have substantially higher levels of attrition than do their local school districts. Our analysis revealed that on, average, approximately 15% of the students disappear from the KIPP grade cohorts each year.
>
> Between grades 6 and 8, the size of the KIPP grade cohorts drop by 30%.
>
> When these figures are further broken out by race and gender, we can see that a full 40% of the African American male students leave KIPP schools between grades 6 and 8. (ii)

To be fair to KIPP, I should note that a *Washington Post* article by Nick Anderson reprinted in *The Times-Picayune*, March 31, 2011, reported that "KIPP officials said that the study was riddled with errors because of flaws in the data" (A-7). While this KIPP dispute may intensify the debate as to whether charter schools will successfully wipe out this pernicious achievement gap dividing our country, it also gives weight to the need for a very close examination of charter schools, especially in New Orleans.

The Times-Picayune staff writer Andrew Vanacore pointed out in his August 7, 2011, article, "Schools in N. O. closing the gaps," that "Local black students make gains in statewide achievement tests" (A-1). Quoting

Louisiana Department of Education data, he noted that "in 1999 only 18 percent of blacks scored at grade level on statewide tests while in 2011, 53 percent scored at grade level" (A-10). I would urge this close examination of charter schools in New Orleans to continue because of their large numbers, because many of these open enrollment schools do serve a large number of our most needy students, because of the rising tests scores in New Orleans, and because our city may become the first urban city with an almost exclusive charter school approach.

In Orleans Parish some seven years after Katrina, there has been a rise in the number of charter schools, while there has been a steady decline in traditionally run state schools. Charters actually outnumber traditionally run schools with forty-seven charter schools to twenty-three traditional schools for school year 2010–2011, though this number may be off by one or two schools either way.

The success rate of these open enrollment charter schools has amazed everyone and these schools deserve close study. Are New Orleans tests score gains, seen in charter as well as traditional schools, a result of the charter school initiative which is growing in school numbers each year or is it because more money has been spent on schools in New Orleans? Is it because of a changed student population in New Orleans since Katrina or is it a better gaming of the test? Or, as school administrators claim is this the result of better overall education in New Orleans? I should note that on the recently released National Assessment of Educational Progress (NAEP) scores, Louisiana did not fare so well. Our results kept us very close to the bottom of the nation and demonstrated little to nothing about closing the achievement gap. The Sunday *Times-Picayune*'s lead editorial on November 6, 2011, described these results:

> Overall, Louisiana scores still rank near the bottom of the nation.
>
> Just as worrisome, Louisiana's results were mixed in closing the achievement gaps among student populations based on race and income.
>
> The state narrowed the gap in math scores between white and black students, compared to results in 1992. But the gap in math results remained essentially the same between low-income students and those of middle class families. In reading, the achievement gap was 'not significantly different' than it was in 1998 in both race and income. (B-6)

The NAEP test is considered a more genuine gauge of student

achievement than state and federal tests mandates because the NAEP test does not have high-stakes consequences tied to it. There is far less pressure to teach what is on it than the LEAP test.

As more charter schools come to New Orleans, the siphoning argument may disappear, and we will once and for all witness whether or not charter schools can successfully and permanently eliminate the achievement gap between white and black, rich and poor. I also urge the elimination of high-stakes testing. Without the specter of these damning tests and the suffocating bureaucracy, and with a renewed commitment to provide quality public education to each and every child regardless of neighborhood or plight in life, this persistent educational gap between the rich and the poor, whether by intent or unfortunate events, can and will be eliminated.

Because economic gaps shade the educational system today, the language of the marketplace dominates the conversation. The buzz words are data, tests scores, merit pay, value added, market, choice, performance-based assessment, competition, profit, and so forth. No longer in education do we hear about development, excitement, challenge, quality education, joy, transformation, discovery, creativity, puzzlement, engagement, and the like. In fact, in this high-stakes testing era all talk and all practice is reduced to test scores and data-driven curricula.

The beauty of charter schools is that they offer choice to parents, that they are competitive, and they survive because they attract and maintain a student clientele. When I talk about charter school competition, I am not talking about business competition. Public schools are not in the business of making money or turning a profit. They should be run as sound business entities but their business is to educate children. Thus, schools should be well-run from a business point of view, but competition should be focused on the quality education that the school provides. I am not impressed with a corporate school that turns a profit or a charter school that excels by cherry-picking students. I am inspired by an open access charter school that excites and ignites students about learning. It is not competition, per se, that I speak against; it is reducing learning to a test score and/or the passing of the test that I oppose.

At the Free School competition was alive and strong on the basketball, four square and volleyball courts. As an illustration, Jeanette and Jim's volleyball contests became legendary. For years I could dominate the four square court until the sixth, seventh, and eighth graders stayed the same age year after year while I managed to get a year older every year. We even had a flag football team that played other junior high school teams. Whenever we put on a play or had an elocution evening, excellence was the goal. We forever encouraged our students to improve on their projects and we were proud beyond words when our school won the citywide chess tournament. But when it comes to learning, I do not feel that competition has a major place in the classroom or the pursuit of knowledge, especially through the use of grades and test scores. In the classroom we need to facilitate learners, not pit students against one another. In schools we need to seek quality education, not higher tests scores.

18

High Stakes Testing

High-stakes testing, like bureaucratic control, locks the public school into a very narrow position of thought and practice, while it continues to destroy children of the poor. I have opposed high-stakes testing from its inception some twenty years ago and, though retired from being a principal, I would like to continue my battle to end such an ill-advised educational practice that has consumed our nation's public schools while destroying children of the poor by the thousands.

When Louisiana first implemented its high-stakes testing program titled Louisiana Educational Assessment Program, LEAP, *The Times-Pica-yune* had an editorial cartoon that went something like this: Two educational administrators are having the following conversation. One asks the other what he will do if many of our fourth and eighth graders fail the LEAP tests? The other answers as he is looking out the window: LEAP!

The tragedy of this situation is not administrators leaping out of the window; the true horror of this story is the thousands of students, primarily children of the poor, whom we are throwing out the window by flunking them for failing to pass the high-stakes test. High-stakes testing means just that. The stakes are incredibly high for students, teachers, principals, administrators, and whole school systems. In Louisiana the high-stakes testing program is the state law; in federal law it is the bill known as No Child Left Behind (NCLB). In Louisiana, failure by a student in either math or English in grades four, eight and twelve on the LEAP test usually means the student fails the grade or does not graduate. Thus, thousands of our fourth and eighth graders have been held back each year, and many of our students have been blocked from graduation. The results for poor and minority students have been horrific.

Unfortunately, the Free School was not immune to the high-stakes testing frenzy as we were increasingly forced to focus our curriculum on the test, while abandoning a more creative and insightful approach to learning. Most of the time we were able to hold our own on these tests but the mere fact that one test determined whether the student passed or failed and put a number label on our school forced us to narrow the curriculum and let many creative activities disappear. I battled a number of our younger-grade teachers to offer art on a daily basis and I struggled with our older-grade teachers to maintain our sign-up program, the final period of each day that offered creative classes in dance, music, art, and fun. The pressure was so great that I had a fourth-grade Teach For America teacher actually shout at me that if I wanted excellent LEAP scores from her students, she did not have time to teach science and social studies. She clearly and forcefully said, "If this is what I am going to be judged on, this is what I am going to teach!" I had no rebuttal. Her students did very well on the LEAP test that year but they experienced little or no science or social studies. When administering high-stakes tests to our students, our school too became like a lock-down prison with the movement and voice of every student and teacher under close scrutiny.

It is not standardized testing that I oppose; it is the overuse and misuse of standardized testing that I struggle to end. Stephen Jay Gould in his book, *The Measure of Man*, quoted Charles Darwin as follows: "If the misery of the poor be caused not by the laws of nature, but by our institutions, great is our sin" (19). The abuse of testing is one of our sins.

High-stakes testing so permeates public school education that no one is doing much independent thinking. I have heard many educational bureaucrats, politicians, lay people, and friends advise that since it is here to stay, we should just concentrate on how to raise tests scores. I have heard many people claim that we need some way to evaluate how well students are doing and some way to compare schools. I have encountered the arguments that put high-stakes critics, though few in number but now growing, on the defensive: Surely you are not suggesting that black students can't compete with white students or poor people are less capable to learn than others! *The Times-Picayune* editorial on November 20, 2002, captured these arguments succinctly:

> It would be a shame for anyone to use these performance scores (The disparity between scores of white students and black students in Louisiana) to try to prove the backwards notion that black students can't compete with white ones or that being poor limits one's ability to learn. It would also be unfortunate if the students' results were used to attack the validity of the standardized tests. While such tests are not perfect, they do a fairly good job of measuring how much students have learned.
>
> Besides, such tests are here to stay, so it's important that all state's public school students be sufficiently prepared to take them. (B-4)

Here it is in black and white: the tests are valid, they adequately measure learning, they are here to stay, and one would be a racist to imply that they are not fair and just for black and/or poor students.

The arguments go on and on. Business argues that high school graduates will no longer be able to graduate, knowing so little. Lay people claim that high-stakes testing will end social promotion. Everyone celebrates that students will now have to pass a test to move to the next grade or to graduate. Some educators proclaim that the benchmarks are so low that no school should exist with such high failure rates. Politicians declare that these tests will force competition on our schools and will put an end to the inertia of bureaucratically controlled schools. I, of course, want to end bureaucratic control of schools but I find high-stakes testing even a stronger choke hold on schools than bureaucratic control.

How can anyone argue against such American-pie arguments and, outwardly, such sound educational decisions? On the surface the arguments sound great: The poor can and should compete, we will now be able to label our schools, high school graduates will achieve degrees knowing the material, social promotion will be ended once and for all, and our bureaucratically run schools will come tumbling down.

I once read that "you have nothing to fear if you don't ask the right questions." What if this massive testing is flawed? What if the purpose of testing is not for the development of the child or the enrichment of the school? What if the purpose is to perpetuate oppression, thereby harming the child, or for controlling public education, thereby harming the school? What if society could devise educational tests to be taken by all—tests that the middle and upper students would almost never have trouble with but which the poor and less fortunate would stumble over almost every time? What if the tests are scored in such a way that even minor advances do not move one out of the bottom quartile? What if your school shows significant gains on these all-powerful tests but your school receives a letter grade that does not take into consideration these amazing test scores gains.

This is what is happening in Louisiana and other states in the union. Your school may well get a D or F despite your school's gains. How many more ways can we denigrate schools serving the poor? Thus even minor advances can be labeled failure and we can perpetuate the cycle of poverty and ignorance in the name of intelligence and fairness instead of in the name of prejudice and hatred. Remember, George W. Bush pushed his testing agenda with his famous line attacking the deplorable condition of many of our public schools and those opposed to reforming these schools through testing as engaging in a "soft bigotry of low expectations." He was correct in attacking the despicable conditions and results of many public schools, but his solution of more and more massive and stringent testing with such heavy punitive measures has proven to be not an end to bigotry but a harsh weapon of mass destruction continuing and heightening the oppression of the poor. Is this by design?

As an educator, these high-stakes testing laws made me feel like one of Hitler's soldiers, following state and federal orders but, nonetheless, leading children and a race of people to mass destruction and destroying public education in the process. Now, I realize that this statement is a little heavy so let me add humor to this issue, which also points out the wrongness of high-stakes testing. I have mentioned before the humor that Woody, our sixth-grade teacher, often brought to issues. I recently received the following text message from him:

> Here's my new classroom consequences:
> 1. warning
> 2. detention
> 3. conference
> 4. suspension
> 5. standardized test
> 6. expulsion

My first concern over high-stakes testing is the deleterious effect it is having on the public school concept. The main purpose of high-stakes, standardized testing is supposedly to provide an objective gauge of the effectiveness of the teaching/learning process. However, as we have placed more emphasis on testing, we have increasingly experienced the need to narrow the curriculum and to teach the test.

Remember the words of my fourth-grade teacher, "If this is what I am going to be judged on, this is what I am going to teach!" Now that we have sanctified testing to the point of failing a child if he or she does not pass the test, tying teacher salaries and evaluations to tests results, and labeling schools almost exclusively on their test results, we have successfully altered the purpose of public education. With high-stakes testing we have reversed the purpose of public education. Instead of testing genuine education, we have made testing the actual education. We are now using education to see if we can teach testing. Instead of viewing education as the transformation of lives and the road to discovery and enlightenment, we have narrowed public education to the purpose, discussion, and implementation of raising test scores and passing the tests.

This flip-flop on educational purpose and practice has foisted inflated and oftentimes erroneous test scores on the populous. In educational circles, gaming is a term I first saw used by Diane Ravitch in *The Death and Life of the Great American School System* (154). Gaming the tests means cheating, grade retention, pushing out, counseling out, kicking out, dropping out, rejecting out the neediest students. Cheating is not an issue to be ignored. I have already shared with you the quick exit of Morris Holmes seemingly over the cheating issue as exposed in the 1997 *Times-Picayune* series, "Too Good To Be True." Even the Free School was not immune to the horror of cheating on these tests. One year, the day we received the students' LEAP test results as we were all celebrating our high rate of passage especially by our eighth graders, one eighth-grade girl told her teacher that one of her classmates had looked at her paper to get answers. Both students had passed the LEAP tests. She stated that she did not let him look at her answers but he kept looking toward her answer sheet. The male student emphatically denied that he cheated. No other student could or would corroborate the girl student's account of what happened. The eighth-grade teacher did not see any attempt by any student to cheat. It was getting late in the afternoon, so I had to send the two students home, informing them that I would get in writing the next day their version of what had happened. At this point I only had a "he said, she said" situation and was unsure how to proceed.

The next morning solved this situation for me, quickly and firmly driving home how these high-stake tests seriously impact students, their families and their lives. The girl returned the next morning with her mother. The girl's mother was upset but under control. She stated that her daughter did not know of any cheating. The daughter thought the boy might have been looking at her paper but was not really sure. The mother went on to say that her daughter would not put this in writing because there was no accusation of cheating and because this might somehow end up getting her child's test score invalidated. That result would force her daughter into meaningless summer school and would eliminate the possibility of her getting into one of the better high schools.

She firmly stated that she wanted the issue dropped and this matter closed. I had been in consultation with my area superintendent, who told me that I had to let it go because I had no proof of cheating, and now everyone denied that cheating had occurred. He also informed me that I should have gotten the charge in writing the day it was made. This would have made it more difficult for the girl to change her story. I informed both parties that since I had no proof of any wrong doing, I had to drop the matter. This incident clearly showed me that no school, even our precious Free School, was immune to the possibility of cheating. The stakes are simply too high. The massive cheating scandal presently being investigated in Atlanta, Georgia, bespeaks of this horrendous issue.

Getting rid of our poorest performing students and keeping them out of our schools is also a strong tactic to raise test scores. As we discard our lowest performing students, we celebrate our rising test scores. Everyone knows that the best way to get better test scores is to get better students. This is a caution raised about the charter schools in New Orleans. Yes, tests scores in New Orleans are rising but only about 60 percent of students from pre-Katrina New Orleans have returned, with the most impoverished dominating the 40 percent who did not return. More study is needed to determine whether charter schools in New Orleans are really improving tests scores or if these scores are rising because of a significantly changed student population?

Other nefarious practices harming our public schools as a result of high-stakes testing include narrowing the curriculum, teaching the test, offering prep test classes that replace educational classes, pushing students into special education, receiving special education 504 classification just to receive test accommodations, avoiding diversity to avoid subgroups that can greatly lower a school's score, legislating lower passing scores enabling school test scores to rise, granting waivers to students who did not pass, and so on.

The effects of this high-stakes mania are mind boggling. This list is only the beginning. Even our middle and upper income schools are suffering a numbness of practice while schools struggle every year to show annual progress to keep from falling into an unacceptable category. Out goes recess, theater, arts, music, dance, sports, thought, depth, and engagement in subject matter; in comes test prep classes, a narrowed curriculum focused on just what is tested, more drill and surface coverage, craftier selection processes, and tougher discipline policies. Field trips are postponed until after the tests have been taken and they become fewer in number as ever more time is needed during the school schedule for future tests preparations. Everything parents and educators thought made for a good school, challenging curriculum, depth of study, strong enrichment program, and engagement in learning, are being pushed aside so that tests scores can rise.

And for the less fortunate students who were supposedly going to be helped by high-stakes testing, the greatest harm seems to fall on them. These students, mostly the poor and minority, are being trapped into the traditional public schools, which cannot play the games that many other schools can play. These schools serving the poor must take the rejected, the discarded, the pushed out, the flunked out, the transferred out, the special education student, the homeless, and the abandoned. The schools these children attend typically have much less money spent on them and are in deplorable condition. They are overcrowded, have fewer qualified teachers, diminished resources, and offer only a stultified curriculum. These schools are forced to implement the most dumbed-down curriculum imaginable.

The scripted programs treat our teachers and principals as imbeciles and our students as too dumb to teach and/or handle meaningful and thoughtful educational materials. We require these students to read nonsense books while discouraging if not eliminating their opportunity to read real books because the students as well as the teachers must follow the script or face the wrath of the script police. Our children are forced to digest hogwash and we dare to call it education. It is little wonder that nobody with means would dare send their child to a school servicing the poor. These schools with such meager resources and poor education become more of a gateway to prison and/or violent death than a road to opportunity.

While this narrowing of educational purpose and curricula offering is disheartening, a look at educational research clearly shows that these high-stakes testing laws are based on bad educational principles (and I should add that they also annihilate too many innovative and creative principals and teachers). One of the most exciting fields of educational research is on what is being termed brain-based learning. This research is on how the brain works, how we learn, and what affects learning. A major area of study focuses on how threats and stress "downshifts" learning. A leading expert in this field, Eric Jensen captured the poignancy of this issue in his book *Teaching with the Brain in Mind*:

> A part of the Hippocratic Oath says that the first rule in medicine is to do patients no harm. That may well apply to educators, too. Excess stress and threat in the school environment may be the single greatest contributor to impaired academic learning. (52)

Jensen went on to say "Learners with lower stress can put together relationships, understand broad underlying theories, and integrate a range of material" (57). On this salient issue Renata and Geoffrey Cane in their book, *Making Connections-Teaching and the Human Brain*, wrote that schools and classrooms must be places of "High challenge, low threat" (78). There is nothing low threat about this high-stakes testing agenda.

The Times-Picayune editorial staff again missed the point in their December 29, 1999, editorial "The LEAP Monster" about an elementary school's fourth graders chanting, "No more LEAP" when it concluded the editorial with the following lines: "And there's certainly no use in making them feel panicky. They need to be confident when they take the LEAP in mid-March, not terrified" (B-6).

While middle- to upper-income kids may have less to be panicky about because of the LEAP tests, children from lower income brackets have much to be terrified about because of these tests—thousands of poor children fail the test each year, which then subjects them to an never ending dumbed-down, isolated skill, teach-the-test-year-long curriculum since they must now also attend summer school because of failing the test. Let me give you one example of just how frightening these tests can be for children of the poor. I remember this big gruff, tough-looking black male eighth grader, the kind of person you cross the street to avoid, coming into our office the day students were told their LEAP results. He came in bawling like a baby. Everyone in the office, me included, was too embarrassed to say anything until finally someone managed to say, "I'm sorry that you did not pass." He replied between sobs and trying to catch his breath, "No! No! I passed." There was not a dry eye in the office. Even though this student passed the test, we should not subject our children to this stress. They are not responsible for the educational opportunity we offer them. We are. We should take this unfair, unwise, and unnecessary pressure off our students and we should stop this massive flunking of fourth and eighth graders now.

This leads to my second concern about the total disregard for educational research by our ever present high-stakes testing laws. The proponents of these laws proudly proclaim that these tests prevent promotion to any child who fails, which will finally end social promotion. While this may sound great to lay people and the politicians who pass these laws, educational research shows that retention is not a solution to our educational ills and does more harm than good. Remember the Hippocratic Oath? Just like doctors, educators should do no harm.

Gerald Bracey, one of the leading experts on standardized testing, in his book, *Put to the Test*, wrote: "About retention in grade, this much can be said: it doesn't work. Study after study has found the consequences to be negative. One study ranked forty-nine educational innovations in terms of their impact on achievement. Retention in grade ranked forty-ninth. It was among the few innovations that clearly produced negative results" (11). Linda Darling-Hammond in her NCREST (The National Center for Restructuring Education, School and Teaching) essay also pointed out the ills of retention: "A related finding is that the practice of retaining students in grade, often on the basis of standardized test scores, harms achievement and significantly increases dropout rates" (23).

Tucker and Codding mentioned this issue in their book, *Standards for Our Schools,* which I recall was one of the books given to principals by Colonel Davis when he took over the leadership of the Orleans Parish Public Schools. The authors clearly stated that the choice between retaining a student, or passing a student is a false choice. "The forced choice between making students repeat a grade and passing them on when they have not mastered the material is an artificial choice. The best option is to monitor student progress constantly and, at the first sign that a youngster is falling behind, to put that student into afternoon, Saturday, and summer programs that will help the child stay even with others" (145).

Regarding retention in grade based on LEAP scores, James Anderson, former director Department of Accountability/Assessment New Orleans public schools, made the following eloquent point in his published letter to the editor of *The Times-Picayune* dated November 30, 1999 "Branding innocent students and making them feel like they're some kind of academically inferior beings is not the way to begin any reform" (B-4). Simply stated, it is cruel and unjust to base reform on the backs of children, especially knowing that you are going to break so many of those backs. I guess educators are fortunate that we do not have to take an oath to do no harm.

I believe that the people in the Louisiana Department of Education and the U.S. Department of Education were aware of research on brain-based education and on the deleterious effects of retention. The school's written improvement plan demands that in every public school practices must be based on educational research. Thus for educators and state legislators to foist upon the public laws and programs that are clearly antithetical to research-based educational practices, one should ask whether the purposes of these laws are educational or of malevolent intent.

When I have presented this argument to friends, they look at me as though I am crazy and ask their rhetorical questions, "Surely you are not suggesting that power people sat in some back room and consciously devised a plan to destroy black and poor children? Surely you are not suggesting the makers of these laws are racist?" I keep my mouth shut but I cannot help thinking, "It has happened before." Educational policy that primarily harms the poor and ruins public education is wrong and harmful, no matter what the motive. The effects are disastrous, regardless. We are creating a two-tier system memorable to our segregation days which relegated our poorest and neediest students to the worse education imaginable or, in too many cases, no education at all. These kids do not need more tests—they need quality education. We are leading them from the classrooms not to the halls of higher education but to the streets and a life of crime, joblessness, health problems, shelter issues, the judicial system, early death and/or lifetime imprisonment.

This leads to my next criticism of high-stakes testing. You see if truth be told high-stakes testing is not just bad legislation and bad education: it is evil legislation, evil education. On May 28, 2009, on the CBS News series, "Where America Stands," reporter Bill Whitaker said, "of the 4 million students who enter high school every year, one million of them will drop out before graduation. That's 7,000 every school day—one dropout every 26 seconds." Louisiana has even worse scores on student dropouts even though its LEAP scores keep edging up and educators and politicians keep bragging about our improved educational system as a result of the LEAP high-stakes testing program. Writer Bill Barrow of the Louisiana Capital Bureau for *The Times-Picayune* recorded the following on June 9, 2009:

> Louisiana's high school dropout rate is worse than the one third rate typically reported by the state Department of Education, according to leading lawmakers pushing a revision of the state's high school curriculum.

> Following the national standard, the state measures dropouts by tracking students beginning in the ninth grade... But following students from the seventh grade, the number

ranges from 42 percent to 48 percent in a new analysis completed at the request of Sen. Robert Kostelka, R-Monroe, and Rep. Jim Fannin, D-Jonesboro.

The difference is due to students who leave school before reaching ninth grade. That population is significant in Louisiana because of the state's requirement that a student pass the Leap test to qualify for promotion to the ninth grade. (A-3)

This means that in Louisiana at least four out of every ten students are dropping out of school before completion in twelfth grade. Is it any surprise that Louisiana expels students at five times the national rate, as was reported in *The Times-Picayune* in "Report: Louisiana soars in expelling student," (A-1) by Sarah Carr, April 21, 2010? Should we not be horrified that Louisiana has the world's leading incarceration rate as reported by *The Times-Picayune* Capital Bureau writer Jan Moller in her front page June 6, 2011, article, "Bills aim to reduce lockup rate"? Ms. Moller reported the following: "Nowhere in the world is the rate as high as in Louisiana, where one in 55 residents is locked up" (A-1 & A-6). In other words, Louisiana has the highest rate of incarceration of any state in our nation and any nation of the world. Are our slightly increased LEAP test scores, which are of questionable educational value, worth the destruction of so many young lives? How many children does Louisiana have to fail before we can claim victory?

At the same time, Louisiana is not the only troubled state. Our nation is becoming a prison state. Linda Darling-Hammond in her book, *The Flat World and Education*, made the following eye-opening statement: "Representing only 5% of the world's population, America has 25% of the world's inmates" (24). Ms. Darling-Hammond, in her chapter in the book, *Many Children Left Behind*, raised the horrific issue that we are entrapping too many of our low-income and minority students on the wrong side of the law. She stated the following: "These students join what is increasingly known as a 'school-to-prison pipeline' carrying an increasing number of uneducated youth almost directly into the criminal justice system" (23). Instead of educating our students of the poor and of color, we are criminalizing them, costing way more in the process due to court, incarceration, and crime costs. Ms. Darling-Hammond continued: "California and Massachusetts had the dubious distinction this year of paying as much for prisons as for higher education" (24).

As our nation pushes out, kicks out, flunks out, locks up and buries a significant number of our students, mostly children of the poor and/or minorities, we must grapple whether we should do more of the same or do we reconsider how we educate our children, especially children of the poor. Presently, the single most important solution that our government implements to eliminate this educational calamity is high-stake testing, which results in the eradication of almost 50 percent of our poor students from our schools, but not from our streets and our prisons and our graveyards.

In summary, it is not standardized testing that I oppose, it is the misuse and abuse of standardized testing that I abhor. Standardized testing should serve as an indicator and as a diagnostic tool for education; it should never dictate the education we offer in our schools. Standardized testing should be a compass, not a battering ram. Standardized testing should never be the education.

19

Poverty

I once saw a *Pontius' Puddle* cartoon where two characters were having a conversation something like this. One asks, "Why does God allow hunger, poverty and injustice to continue in the world when he could do something about it?" The other character responds, "Why don't you ask him?" The first character replies, "I'm afraid that he might ask me the same thing!"

The "P" word "poverty" is never to be used in educational circles. Poverty is no longer viewed as a major obstacle to be overcome by children of the poor in order to find any semblance of success. Poverty has now been reconfigured to be an unacceptable excuse for poor performance. But poverty is real and it is crushing. While it is not an excuse for poor performance, it is an incredibly powerful life factor greatly affecting learning.

Proponents of the agenda for testing want to box critics like me into a corner by asking the rhetorical question, "Surely you are not suggesting that the poor or blacks or minorities are not as capable as whites?" No, I am not suggesting that blacks or poor students are not as capable as white students. But ignoring critical factors of poverty, which have considerable effects on educational achievement, is evilness inflicted and racism disguised. Just consider the severity of the problem. The Children's Defense Fund's (CDF) document, *The State of America's Children 2011*, began the overview with the opening chilling statement:

> CDF's *State of America's Children*, 2011 paints a devastating portrait of childhood across the country. With unemployment, housing foreclosures and hunger still at historically high levels, children's well-being is in great jeopardy. Children today are our poorest age group. Child poverty increased by almost 10 percent between 2008 and 2009, which was the largest increase since data were first collected. As the country struggles to climb out of the recession, our children are falling further behind...
>
> Black children are facing the worse crisis since slavery, and in many areas, Hispanic and American Indian children are not far behind. (ix)

Poverty is not a simple low-income issue, though low income is a critical issue. In the powerful document, *The Measure of America, American Human Development Report 2008–2009*, it is reported: "The average income

288

in the top fifth of U.S. households in 2006 was $168,170. This is almost fifteen times the average income of the lowest fifth, with an average income of $11,352 per year" (6).

If the above disparity in income does not shake you out of complacency, let me suggest some other numbers that might make you start asking different questions. Again quoting from *The Measure of America*:

> The United States ranks second in the world in per capita income (behind Luxembourg), but thirty-fourth in survival of infants to age one. (12)

> African American babies are two and a half times more likely to die before age one than white babies. (12)

> We (the United States) rank forty-second in global life expectancy and first among the world's twenty-five richest countries in the percentage of children living in poverty – exerting a drag on the prospects and futures of roughly one in six American girls and boys. (12)

> Nearly one in five American children lives in poverty (with more than one in thirteen living in extreme poverty), one in six lives in a family whose head didn't graduate high school, one in eight lives in overcrowded housing, one in ten is born to a teen mother, and one in twenty lives in a household where no adult is working. Two-thirds of all poor children have had at least one experience of prolonged food insufficiency in the past year. (84)

The Annie E. Casey Foundation report, *Kids Count*, 2011, stated that the number of children living in poverty in the United States by the end of 2009 was 20 percent. If my math is correct, this means one in every five children in our country lives in poverty. Not only do we have an alarming number of our population living in poverty, but the effects of living in poverty only add to the horror story and to the diminished academic achievement on the part of these entrapped children. A document published in 1999 by the Council for a Better Louisiana (CBL) titled, *Fighting Poverty, Building Community,* recorded the ill effects of poverty. The document began with the ominous statement, "Poverty in Louisiana is pervasive and directly threatens the future of all Louisiana" (i). It continued, "Louisiana has a greater proportion of children living in poverty than any other state in the nation" (v). Remember: Louisiana has over a 40 percent dropout rate, an expulsion rate five times the national average, the world's leading incarceration rate, and one of the strongest high-stakes testing programs approved by NCLB in the country.

The CBL report listed one compounding aspect of poverty after another: "The limited choices that are associated with poverty have devastating consequences that are passed on from parent to child in a continuing cycle of poverty" (v):

Health – "Poverty too often means poor health." (vi)

"Infants born to teenagers and to low income women of all ages are more likely to be of low birth weight, which has been linked to numerous health and developmental problems." (7)

"The health risks that infants from poor families face do not diminish as they grow. Poor children are significantly more likely to have vision and hearing deficiencies, dental problems, speech defects, anemia, sickle cell disease, elevated blood lead levels and behavior problems such as hyperactivity...Moreover, when poor children do become sick, they are more likely to suffer more serious consequences than non-poor children...Low-income children suffering from asthma are more likely to be hospitalized." (7)

Education – compounded by poor funding"Louisiana was 45th in the nation in per pupil spending in 1997–1998 school year." (vi)

Violence – those in poverty are "...more likely to engage in criminal activity...those living in poverty are also more likely to be victims of crime." (vi)

Housing – Safe and secure housing "elude the poor." (vi)

Hunger – "Those in poverty face a constant threat of hunger. Malnutrition among the poor is increasing, and it is children who suffer the most from inadequate diets. Very young children are the most affected—their cognitive development can be substantially impeded." (vi)

Suffering – "Children are among those who suffer the most due to inadequate food...These children are more likely to be tired, have headaches, catch colds and develop anemia due to iron deficiencies. Iron deficiency anemia can have serious effects. It often leads to developmental and behavior problems that can affect a child's ability to read or understand mathematics." (12) (These are the two subjects which are pass/fail on LEAP and which dominate the high-stakes testing policies– my words.)

Race – "While Louisiana of all races are disproportionately poor, race and poverty remain closely connected in Louisiana…Any consideration of poverty must take into account the disabling distinctions imposed by years of discrimination." (3)

LEAP and other high-stakes testing programs ignore these critical factors of race and poverty. In determining a school's performance score or the passing of tests by students, the conditions of neighborhood, family educational background, school conditions, spending on their schools (or lack thereof), and racism are not considered and have no weight in calculating scores. The proponents of this high-stakes testing strategy proudly argue that all schools and all students should be held to the same high standards. What about the standards of being well fed, having a decent roof over our heads, securing health care, being employed, living in a safe environment, and attending properly financed and high quality schools?

All children can learn, but as Gerald Bracey, a leading testing expert has repeatedly stated, "poverty and discrimination are not excuses." They are critical conditions which affect every aspect of life and certainly learning. The literature is replete with information documenting the connection between poverty and low test scores. Bracey, in his book *Put to the Test*, has taken notice: "We have noted elsewhere that test scores are highly subject to the influence of family and community variables. We know well in advance of any test that affluent communities will outperform poor communities. It could be that a poor district is doing more with the available resources than an affluent community which could be 'coasting' on the knowledge that its students are likely to do well in any event" (71).

Even Louisiana's first round with LEAP showed a high correlation between poverty and low performance. Quoting again from *Fighting Poverty, Building Community*, "Of the 57 schools that placed in the 'academically unacceptable' category, nearly all had high percentages of students in poverty" (8).

Research tells us, the experts tell us, and high-stakes testing demonstrate the correlation between poverty and low test scores. Nevertheless, our states and our nation create ever more tests, making our poor students the victims of this strategy and our schools that serve the poor the scapegoats for this catastrophe. Poverty should not so easily be dismissed! This book is obviously not about how to end poverty in America. It needs to end, but I leave that to others. I strongly recommend an end to this great financial disparity we presently spend on the education of our wealthier students at the expense of our impoverished students.

20

Equal and Equitable Funding

I will not spend much time discussing the disparity between funding of our poorest schools and school districts compared to the wealthier schools and school districts. Jonathan Kozol's *Savage Inequalities* presents a brilliant exposé of this disparity by quoting figures after figures. Thus, I will just offer you a few numbers to drive home this unfair disparity. These numbers come from the book, *Moving Every Child Ahead: From NCLB Hype to Meaningful Educational Opportunity*, by Michael A Rebell and Jessica R. Wolff:

> …on average, spending on children in high-poverty school districts is $825 less per student than spending on students in low-poverty districts, or $20,000 per year for each class of 25 students. In certain states, the situation is even worse: in New York, the funding gap between students in rich and low-income districts is $2,319; in Illinois, it is $1,924; and in Minnesota, it is $1,349. (96-97)

In the Free School with our population of 300 students, this $825 average would have come to $247,500 additional yearly funding—not as much as KIPP funding but almost enough to bring one out of retirement. Louisiana is on the bottom of this average so we would probably have been eligible for a lot more if we had had equal educational funding for every child in the United States no matter what the child's zip code or the condition of the house or the income of the family. With proper funding given directly to the school, the Free School could have had a structurally sound air-conditioned building with humane bathrooms. I would no longer have had to greet parents on opening day wringing wet from the humid heat and our students and teachers would no longer have had to engage in learning in saunas that looked like classrooms. Our classes could have had a much lower teacher/pupil ratio and our teachers could have been better trained and better paid. Increased funding would have helped tremendously and certainly made a difference.

Another despicable reality caused by this inequitable funding between our wealthier and poorest students is the fact that the poorer students depend more on the school than the wealthier students do. Lisa Dubois in her *Peabody Reflector* magazine Summer 2010 article, "The Achievement Gap: Is it too wide to bridge?" made this point and supported it by quoting Joseph Murphy from his book, *The Educator's Handbook for Understanding and Closing Achievement Gaps*:

Minority and low-income children are markedly 'school dependent,' meaning that it's difficult for them to access resources and opportunities outside of school to help them overcome their deficiencies in their education. "If you're a poor kid and you're in a bad school, you're in a world of hurt," Murphy says, "because you don't have a lot of other support systems that are going to make up for it." (14-15)

The report *The Black-White Achievement Gap, When Progress Stopped*, described this "world of hurt" as a "triple whammy":

Children in these neighborhoods, on average, are impaired in their development, lack of family capital, and face hostile neighborhood environments. They are also likely to attend lower-quality schools staffed by lower-quality teachers. In school, they face greater violence, disruption, and fear. Children growing up in these places are hit with a triple whammy in the home, neighborhood, and the school. (33)

Now, I know a lot of critics of education like to make the argument that we are not going to fix our educational problems by just throwing money at it. However, I doubt that many of these critics have their children in one of our poorly funded schools with a dilapidated school building, sick and hungry children, dire teacher needs, paltry resources, a meaningless and stultifying curriculum, and students who start school two and three years behind their peers. The solution lies in equal per-pupil expenditure and, when appropriate, equitable spending. I am definitely not suggesting that we give large educational bureaucracies or the testing industry more money. I want to end the bureaucracies along with the testing mania and put all of the this spending into schools with only a modicum spent on any type of central office, no matter what the cluster size of schools involved. At the same time, throwing money at the right people like KIPP (a concept I got from my good friend, Mary Garton, a Teach for America alumna) just might make the difference.

This issue of unequal funding is not an isolated educational issue; it is interfaced with the gap in educational scores, poverty, the need for early childhood education, the absolute lack of quality education offered to the poor, dropout issues, and so on. *The Times-Picayune* July 15, 2009 article titled "Racial gap persists in U.S. schools," by Libby Quiad poignantly described this frustrating educational malady permeating our country:

The divide between minority and white students is considered one of the most pressing challenges in education. Experts say it stems from entrenched factors that hinder education.

More black children live in poverty; which is linked to an array of problems: low birth rate weight, exposure to lead poisoning, hunger, too much TV watching, too little talking and reading at home, less involvement and frequent school-changing.

The gap exists even before kids start school. But schools don't mitigate the problem, said Kati Haycock, president of Education Trust, a children's advocacy group. "African-American students are less likely than their white counterparts to be taught by teachers who know their subject matter," Haycock said. They are less likely to be exposed to a rich and challenging curriculum," she said, "And the schools that educate them typically receive less state and local funding than the ones serving mainly white students.

The implications of the disparity reach beyond school walls. Minority students are also much more likely to drop out of high school—half of minorities drop out, compared to about 30 percent of students overall. (A-5)

In other words, the educational life disparities between black and white, rich and poor students continues, while we simultaneously continue to spend less on poor kids' education.

To emphasize how important fair and equitable spending is for all our children, I would like to again quote Linda Darling-Hammond in her chapter, "From 'Separate but Equal' to 'No Child Left Behind': The Collision of New Standards and Old Inequalities" from the book *Many Children Left Behind*:

The first problem—one that NCLB does not acknowledge or effectively address—is the enormous inequality in the provision of education offered in the United States. Unlike most countries that fund schools centrally and equally, the wealthiest U.S. public schools spend at least ten times more than the poorest ones—ranging from over $30,000 per pupil at the wealthy schools to only $3,000 at the poorest.

…schools serving large numbers of low-income students and students of color have larger class sizes, fewer teachers and counselors, fewer and lower-quality academic courses, extracurricular activities, books, materials, supplies, and computers, libraries and special services. (6-7)

It does not take a rocket scientist to put this information together to realize that high-stakes testing, suspensions, expulsions, incarceration, and unequal and unfair spending on education are not the answers to our societal problems. To state this in the most simplistic manner possible: Jailed people costs society money; educated people contribute to society. A major solution to some of the United States' social ills lies in providing quality education for all our children, including our three- and four-year olds, and possibly for the first time, our children of the poor.

When we put together this disparity of funding, our high-test frenzy, the crumbling school buildings housing the poor with some of the least qualified teacher, and our low level curriculum provided to the poor we find not only a deepened two-tier educational system, but also one that has segregated, once again, our public schools. Again quoting from *The Measure of America*:

And the last twenty years have not seen greater integration but rather growing racial isolation in the public schools. African American and Latino children tend to be concentrated in struggling, high-poverty schools; while white students have surprisingly little interaction, on the whole, with minority students.

The *de facto* result of this sorting-by-income-and-race is that America has two educational systems. The one serving predominantly white, suburban children is working—though there is still considerable room for improvement. The other, serving low-income, almost entirely minority children in urban areas and poor rural areas, is in crisis. The two systems diverge on every measure of educational quality: the skills and qualifications of the teachers; the physical state of the facilities; the breadth and rigor or the curriculums; funding and resources; the likelihood of instruction in art, music, and physical education; and the levels of student achievement, graduation rates, and college attendance. (85)

If poverty is not damning enough, we also spend less, provide the least qualified teachers, offer a most limited curriculum, provide minimum resources, and house students in schools in mostly dilapidated buildings for our children of the poor. Poverty and the conditions of schooling should not be ignored, nor should we spend our educational monies so unfairly for children of the poor, once again forcing them to the bottom. Now, this is a score that we should pay attention to and eliminate.

21

Early Childhood Education

This situation of spending more of our educational dollars on wealthier students and less on poorer students is unjust on so many levels. There are two remaining issues which I feel are imperative if we are to transform education for the poor. The first is early childhood education for the poor and the second is the need to provide a rich and engaging curriculum for all students including the children of the poor.

Study after study shows that children of the poor start school two to three years behind and rarely catch up, oftentimes falling further behind. I have two granddaughters, ages four and five, who attend day school. The cost for this wonderful experience runs about $1000 per month for each girl. Both girls have amazing vocabularies, have had travel experiences, speak in complete sentences, love life, and thoroughly enjoy every experience that these schools and we, their parents, provide for them. They will start kindergarten knowing how to read or be on the crest of reading, knowing how to swim, and how to discuss books and movies. They will be more than two years ahead of our poor children who start kindergarten not always knowing their colors, how to count even the simplest numbers and recognizing the alphabet. George Will, in an editorial printed in *The Times-Picayune* on August 31, 2010, titled, "Failure by the numbers" made the following statement:

> By age 4, the average child in a professional family hears about 20 million more words than the average child in a working-class family and about 35 million more than the average child in a welfare family—a child often alone with a mother who is a high school dropout. (B-5)

As a society, we must close this gap where it starts with universal quality preschool for every child in the United States regardless of the child's status in life. To buttress this issue, let me again quote from that most powerful document, *The Measure of America*:

> Significant investment in early childhood education is money well spent. Sizeable gaps in both cognitive and behavioral capabilities exist between poor and nonpoor children before their first day of kindergarten. The greatest documented social and economic returns on investment in education come not from programs for school-aged children but from high-

quality interventions for at-risk infants, toddlers, preschoolers, and their parents.

However, quality programs require the resources to be able to afford college-educated teachers with early childhood expertise, low teacher-to-child ratios, developmentally appropriate materials, and enrichment activities. Early childhood intervention on the cheap—mediocre custodial care dressed up with flashcards and drills–does nothing to help poor children close the gaps with middle-class peers. (83)

Thus, the more our country spends on quality early childhood education the more we increase the return on the dollar. A sliding fee scale can be imposed for those children not trapped in poverty but who live with families whose incomes fall far short of our wealthier citizens. This will increase our need for quality teachers and help close the achievement gap so persistently harming our poorest children.

Just how effective is quality early childhood education? Apparently very effective according to the ongoing study by Arthur J. Reynolds, researcher at University of Minnesota, titled *The Chicago Longitudinal Study: A Study of Children in Chicago Public Schools*. In summarizing this study Lindsey Tanner, reported in *The Times-Picayune* June 10, 2011, in an article aptly titled, "Preschool pays off for life":

Better jobs, less drug abuse and fewer arrest are among advantages found in the study that tracked more than 1,000 low income, mostly black Chicago kids for up to 25 years.

The average cost per child for 18 months of preschool in 2011 is $9000, but Reynolds cost-benefit analysis suggests that leads up to at least $90,000 in benefits per child in terms of increased earnings, tax revenue, less criminal behavior, reduced mental health costs and other measures, he said. (A-10)

In advocating for universal early childhood education, I am suggesting that we offer children a myriad of experiences filled with language, books, music, art, the opportunity of social interaction, hands-on activities, manipulative materials, and so on. I want field trips to everywhere, drama experiences, abundant play, discovery toys, and naps. When I taught Head Start every child in my class took a nap and fell asleep because they knew I too would take a nap and fall asleep. They were wonderful—they did not want to disturb me. Let's put fun, challenge and excitement back in education and keep it there.

However, at this point let me be perfectly clear that I am not suggesting that equalizing educational funding or any of the other suggestions I make in this book will solve all of our nation's problems. I am not claiming that they will wipe out hunger, eliminate prisons, end war, or bring world peace. I am asserting that if we equalize educational funding, end abuse and overuse of testing, dismantle bureaucratic education, return schools to the people, insist on high quality low threat schools for all of our children, including children of the poor and our three- and four-year olds, we will most definitely change our educational landscape and move our country towards vibrant and amazing public schools for all children. To put all of this in plain simple English, we can educate or we can incarcerate. Or, as former Louisiana State Supreme Court Justice Pascal Calogero reportedly said, "Do we invest in the playpen or the state pen?" You see, the right question might lead you to a sensible solution.

But let not my words be the last considerations on the educational possibilities that I have espoused. For more than twenty years, Finland has moved away from standardized tests, abandoned a centralized bureaucratic approach and put an end to disparity in funding. LynNel Hancock's September, 2011, *Smithsonian* magazine article "Why Are Finland's Schools Successful?" documented the Finland story:

> There are no mandated standardized tests in Finland, apart from one exam at the end of students' senior year in high school. There are no rankings, no comparisons or competition between students, schools or regions...The difference between the weakest and strongest students are the smallest in the world, according to the most recent survey by the Organization for Economic Co-operation and Development (OECD).
>
> Ninety-three percent of Finns graduate from academic or vocational high schools, 17.5 percentage points higher than the United States.
>
> In the 2009 PISA (Programme for International Student Assessment) scores released last year the nation (Finland) came in second in science, third in reading, and sixth in math among nearly half a million students worldwide. (96)

Linda Darling-Hammond in her book, *The Flat World and Education*, also has documented the Finish educational success story. She wrote about Finland's small schools, teacher training, an end to bureaucratic education and equitable teaching practices:

Finish Schools are generally small (fewer than 300 pupils with relatively small class sizes in the 20s) and are uniformly well equipped. The notion of caring for students educationally and personally is a central principle in the schools. Policymakers decided that if they invested in very skilled teachers, they could allow local schools more autonomy to make decisions about what and how to teach—a reaction against the oppressive, centralized system they sought to overhaul. (168-69)

The egalitarian Finns reasoned that if teachers learn to help students who struggle, they will be able to teach all students more effectively and, indeed, leave no child behind. (171)

Ms. Darling-Hammond also wrote about the assessment of children in Finish schools: "Indeed, there are no external standardized tests used to rank students or schools in Finland, and most teacher feedback to students is in narrative form, emphasizing descriptions of their learning progress and areas for growth" (169). Wow! It appears that we at the Free School were correct in fighting for our non-graded policy back in the eighties. Too bad that I did not have enough fight left in me to struggle for this practice to continue in the early twenty-first century.

Ms. Darling-Hammond also articulated Finland's success on international test scores based on OECD (2007) and she also pointed out that almost all of Finland's schools finance is public financed and almost none is by private sources:

Once poorly ranked educationally, with a turgid bureaucratic system that produced low-quality education and large inequalities, it now ranks first among all the OECD nations on the PISA assessments in mathematics, science, and reading. The country also boast a highly equitable distribution of achievement. (165)

Ninety-eight percent of the costs of education at all levels are covered by government, rather than by private sources. (165)

We, in the United States, need to get rid of our "turgid" bureaucratic approach to education. We also need to end our reliance on high-stakes testing and we must spend our money in an equitable and just manner so that every child in our land receives a quality education and so that we, too, can educate leaving no child behind.

22

Quality Education:
A Robust and Rich Curriculum for All

This leads to the final educational issue I wish to discuss. For far too long we have foisted on our poorest students and racial minorities not only the poorest funded education in our country, but also the worst, most retrograde education imaginable. It is one thing to offer rote learning to children; it is quite another to make that rote learning the sole education that the children receive. Yet this is exactly what has happened with the education we have offered to the poor and to the minorities. One of the tragedies, or design, of high-stakes testing is that it began at a time in our history when we were beginning to offer high quality education to all. It was when the educational gap was closing. Lauren B. Resnick, who wrote the National Research Council's 1987 report, *Education and Learning to Think*, had a lot to say on this subject and I am going to share with you some of her writings:

> If we examine the educational institutions aimed at the elite in the population, today's higher order goals are nothing new.
>
> Historically, it must be stressed, the academics did not treat education of the full population of young people as within their purview. School for the masses arose from different roots and a much more recent phenomenon in the history of education. Mass education derives from a "low literacy" tradition…aimed at producing minimal levels of competencies in the general population.
>
> As cities began to grow, massive urban school systems grew as well. Only racial minorities were systematically excluded or separated within the schools…Routinized performance was, from its inception, concerned with inculcating routine abilities, simple computation, reading predictable texts, reciting religious or civil codes. It did not take as goals for students the ability to interpret texts, create materials others would want and need to read, construct convincing arguments, develop original solutions to technical or social problems.

Although it is not new to include thinking, problem solving, and reasoning in someone's school curriculum, it is new to take seriously the aspiration of making thinking and problem solving a regular part of a school program for all the population, even minorities, even non-English speakers, even the poor. It is a new educational challenge to develop educational programs that assume that all individuals, not just the elite, can become competent thinkers. (3-7)

I included Rasnick's comments at length because if we do not know this history we can never appreciate the lost opportunity for true quality education for all. Premature and overuse of testing to a denied and unprepared group of people only perpetuates oppression, maintains the educational gap between poor students and the elite, and forces an incredibly weak curriculum on the poor, killing all hope for advancement. Poor children, all children, deserve an education that affords them discovery, complexity, meaningfulness, engagement, and human interaction; it should never be reduced to mindless seat work, excessive drill practices, repetitive nonsense, and tests and more tests.

The advent of the overuse and misuse of testing not only halted meaningful education for the poor but also has contributed to the belief by even the poor and the minorities that poor children are somehow inferior to the rest of the population. Cherry Banks, Associate Professor of Education, University of Washington, Bothell, in her article titled, "The Challenges of National Standards in a Multicultural Society," wrote:

The lack of recognition and response to the connection between assessment and performance, perhaps more than any other aspect of the standards movement, raises historic and troubling concerns related to fairness, justice, and educational equality. Even though we know that unequal resources can affect quality of teachers, availability of advanced resources, the safety of the school environment, and other factors that can contribute to what students know and can do, performance assessments do not account for these factors. Without information on the factors that contribute to high and low performance, students from low-income families as well as many students of color may fall victim to historic beliefs about their genetic inferiority that are accepted by many educators.... (130-131)

In this country, too many people hold to the belief that blacks, other minorities, and the poor in general are less capable than the rest of the population. As a result of this belief, we have casually spent less on their education, causing the poor to be educated in the worst buildings, with the least qualified teachers, with few resources, and with a low-level curriculum.

Now with high-stakes testing we are purporting that we are fairly judging the children of the poor without factoring any of life's realities that directly affect performance. Then, as the poor and minorities perform poorly, we not only reinforce this feeling of inferiority, but also exacerbate the problem by flunking more and more of these children. We label their schools as academically unacceptable and reduce their curriculum to gibberish. We hold to the erroneous belief that because the poor are so far behind educationally we must wait for them to catch up before we offer them meaningful and challenging curricula. Nothing could be further from the truth.

As we have learned from brain-based research, the brain has an insatiable desire for complexity, puzzlement, meaningfulness, and so on. To wait for people who are behind to catch up before we offer quality education does no good and certainly does harm by perpetuating the achievement gap and relegating our poorest children to a substandard education. What we must do to put an end to this unfair disparity is provide equal and equitable educational spending for every child in America while offering each child a robust, engaging curriculum from the day she or he enters our schools, hopefully at least by age three.

The solution to education of the poor is not to continue our mind numbing approach, but to change how and when we educate them. The challenge to charter schools, which has eluded the traditional public school, is how to offer a rigorous, exciting, and mind expanding educational experience for all children including children of the poor. The challenge for us as a country is how to offer fair and equitable educational spending for every child in the United States including three- and four-year olds, regardless of the child's circumstances. The educational urgency for our country is to eliminate the nooses around education, to dismantle, that is, abolish bureaucratic control, and end high-stakes testing. We may need a yardstick to guide us on life's journey: but, remember, it is not just the length of the journey that matters. The quality of the journey must also be our focus.

Conclusion

I have come to the end of my tale. During the years before Katrina, we struggled year after year to keep the New Orleans Free School afloat while we experienced administration after administration whittling away our program and perpetually attempting to close us. We learned that bureaucracies were like giant battleships ramming and destroying our schools. Schools that serve mostly the poor have deflated curriculum, minimal resources, and prove to be more a gateway to prison than to the land of opportunity. Trapped in the jaws of bureaucracy which operate under the rule of the chain of command, compliance dominates. Creativity, independence, and innovation have been treated as dreaded diseases which must be destroyed at all costs.

Bureaucracies have created some quality schools but ones that almost always have had a more elite clientele than the traditional public school serving mostly the poor. These schools serving the poor have always had less spent on them, have always been more controlled and have always offered the poorest curriculum. Then we standardize-test these children to death as we constantly document their supposed inferiority. Routine, seat work, and docile behavior have become the marks of what a good school looks like; conversation, movement, active engagement, a robust curriculum, and excitement over learning have not only been frowned upon but have been systematically denied.

Then in the nineties came along the mother of all monsters, the mega flood of high-stakes testing which took over public schools like a shark in a small lake. The tests became education's be all and end all. We lost the true purposes of education: the transformation of life, the elevation of the human being, and the expansion of knowledge. We singularly made testing the aim of education and now, erroneously, teach our students that the purpose of education is to pass the test. The effects on public education, especially though not exclusively the education of the poor, have been devastating.

We have narrowed the curriculum to guttural sounds, forced our teachers to be script-following fools, and relegated our principals to function solely as compliance officers. We have made teaching "teaching the test," and have forced teachers, principals, schools, and school systems into gaming the tests—cheating, kicking out, pushing out, counseling out, retaining students, placing students unnecessarily in special education to receive 504 test accommodations, and, all the while, preventing entrance into our schools for students who will most likely fail the tests and bring school scores down. Our dropout rates are abominable. Stultifying the curriculum has become the norm as educators are required more and more to teach what is on the tests. Meanwhile we offer even more tests, the very engine that is deadening the education that we are offering all of our children and pushing so many of our students out.

We have imperiled the public school concept while we are constantly and consistently ignoring critical factors that affect learning such as health, housing, income, hunger, neighborhood, school conditions, and school finances. The achievement gap has only fluttered during the last twenty years, neither gaining nor losing ground. We continue to spend more on our wealthier students and less on our poorer students while proclaiming that testing is fair. We have ignored the youngest children of the poor who start kindergarten two to three years behind the rest of the students. We are doing so much harm and we are doing it in the name of education. For too many people, especially children of the poor, education in our country has been reduced to the crushing reality, "Spend less on 'em, test 'em, flunk 'em, fire 'em, close 'em, incarcerate 'em, bury 'em, get rid of 'em." Shame on us!

The New Orleans Free School has closed its doors but I hope it played a part in convincing our city and our country to do public education differently. Here in New Orleans we have changed our approach by becoming almost an entirely charter school system. My dream is to end the school systems as we know them and transform our educational management into systems of schools.

Provide quality education to our three- and four-year olds who are trapped in the cycle of poverty. Do the right thing.

Provide equal, equitable and quality education for every child in the United States of America. "My country: when it's wrong, make it right!"

Create high challenge, low threat schools. "My country: when it is right, keep it right!"

Bury the bureaucracy. Return education to the schools.

Kill high-stakes testing. Return education to education.

Thank you for reading this book. I sincerely hope that you have enjoyed it and in some meaningful way found it inspiring.

And thanks to all: family, faculty, students, parents, friends and supporters of the New Orleans Free School who made all those phone calls, wrote all those letters, signed all those petitions and attended all those nail biting meetings. You're the best!

Bob (Dr. Bob) and now "Baba"—the name given to me by my four-year-old granddaughter, Teagan (and it's sticking). Go figure!

bsmi4@cox.net

References

A Blueprint for Success. National Foundation for the Improvement of
Education, 1986.

Aburdine and Naisbitt, P & J. *Reinventing the Corporation*. Warner, 1985.

Ashton-Warner, Sylvia. *Teacher*. Touchstone, 1986.

Banks, Cherry A. "The Challenge of National Standards in a
Multicultural Society." *Educational Horizions*, Spring 1977.

Barton & Coley. *The Black-White Achievement Gap*. Educational Testing Ser
vices, 2010.

Bracey, Gerald. *Put to the Test*. Phi Delta Kappa International, 1998.

Burd-Sharps, Lewis and Martins. *The Measure of America*. Columbia
University Press, 2008.

Caine, Geoffrey and Renate. *Teaching and the Human Brain*. ASCD, 1991.

Codding and Tucker. *Standards For Our Schools*. Jossey-Bass, 1998.

Darling-Hammond, Linda, et al. *Many Children Left Behind*. Becon Press,
2004.

Darling-Hammond, Linda. *Standards of Practice for Learner-Centered Schools*.
NCREST, July 1992.

Dubois, Lisa. "The Achievement Gap: Is it too wide to bridge?" *Peabody
Reflector Magazine*, Summer 2010.

Ferguson, Marilyn. *The Aquarian Conspiracy*. J.P. Tarcher, 1980.

Fighting Poverty, Building Community. Members of the Council for a Better
Louisiana Futures Institute, December 1999.

Goodlad, John. *A Place Called School*. New York: McGraw Hill, 1984.

Gould, Stephen Jay. *The Measure of Man*. W. W. Norton & Company, 1996.

Hancock, LynNell. "Why Are Finland's Schools Successful?" *Smithsonian* Magazine, September 2011.

Jensen, Eric. *Teaching With the Brain In Mind*. ASCD, 1998.

Kearns, David and Doyle, Denis. *Winning the Brian Race*. Institue for Contempory Studies, 1988.

Kids Count. Annie E. Casey Foundation, 2007

Kline, Naomi. *Shock Doctrine*. Picador, 2007.

Kozol, Jonathan. *Savage Inequalities*. Crown Publishers, 1998.

Meier, Deborah, et al. *Many Children Left Behind*. Beacon Press. Boston, 2004, Part two, Chapter 4, "NCLB and Democracy."

Miron, Gary. *What Makes School Work? A Study of Student Characteristics, Attrition & School Finance*. Western Michigan University, 2011.

Maxwell, John. *Developing the Leader Within You*. Nelson Brothers, 1993.

Nathan, Joe. *Free To Teach*. New York Pilgrim Press. 1983.

Ravitch, Diane. *The Death and Life of the Great American School System*. Basic Books, 2010.

Resnick, Lauren. *Education and Learning to Think*. National Research Council's 1987 Report.

Reynolds, Arthur. *The Chicago Longitudinal Study: A Study of Children in Chicago Public Schools*. University of Minnesota, 2011.

Seder, Deno. *Wild About Harry*. Edition Dedeaux, 2001.

The State of America's Children. Children's Defense Fund, 2011.

Who Will Teach Our Children? California Commission on the Teaching Profession. Dorman L. Commons, Chair, November, 1985.

Films:

Why Do These Kids Love School? Dorothy Fadiman.

The Free School. Mika Ferris.

www.ingramcontent.com/pod-product-compliance
Lightning Source LLC
Chambersburg PA
CBHW070020100426
42740CB00013B/2563